An Introduction to English Grammar

AN INTRODUCTION TO
ENGLISH GRAMMAR

SIDNEY GREENBAUM

LONGMAN

Longman Group UK Limited,
Longman House, Burnt Mill, Harlow,
Essex CM20 2JE, England
and Associated Companies throughout the world.

First published 1991
Fourth impression 1993

British Library Cataloguing in Publication Data
Greenbaum, Sidney
   An introduction to English grammar.
   1. English language. Grammar
   I. Title
   428.2

   ISBN 0-582-03957-6

Set in 10½/13 pt Ehrhardt

Printed in Malaysia by VVP

Contents

Part I: The Grammar

Part II   The Applications

Preface

This book introduces students to basic grammatical concepts and categories that are common to the competing theoretical schools of linguistics. It begins with an introductory chapter on the nature of grammar and on varieties of English. Part I provides an outline description of English grammar beginning in Chapter 2 with an overview of sentence types, which are examined in greater detail in Chapter 6. Part II applies the grammatical information from Part I, giving students guidance on punctuation, on solving problems of usage, on improving their writing style, and on ways to analyse the language of literature. The Appendix on spelling includes spelling rules for inflections, such as the plurals of nouns. The Glossary briefly explains the many terms that are needed for a study of grammar.

At the end of the book appear a large number of exercises. Most of these are intended to help students understand the text and give them practice in applying the grammar, but some introduce topics that are not included in the text. I have drawn freely on the exercises compiled by Professor Charles F. Meyer (University of Massachusetts-Boston) for the parallel American version.

The American version is called *A College Grammar of English* (Longman Inc., 1989), a textbook that I wrote for college students in the USA and Canada. I have adapted it to the needs of British students, incorporating changes that take account of differences in language and in cultural settings. I have also taken the opportunity to introduce some revisions.

I am grateful to Marie Gibney for her careful typing of the manuscript.

SIDNEY GREENBAUM

Acknowledgements

We are grateful to the following for permission to reproduce copyright material:

Cambridge University Press, the Crown's patentee, for an extract from the *Authorised Version of the Bible* (*the King James Bible*), rights vested in the Crown; Faber & Faber Ltd for an extract from the poem 'Four Quartets', extracts from the poem 'The Waste Land' & an extract from the poem 'Whispers of Immortality' from *Collected Poems 1909–1962* by T S Eliot; Grafton Books, a division of the Harper Collins Publishing Group, for the poem 'ygUDuh' by E E Cummings from *Complete Poems*; the author's agent for the poem 'This Bread I Break' by Dylan Thomas from *The Poems* (pub J M Dent & Sons Ltd), copyright The Trustees of the Dylan Thomas Estate; Yale University Press for an adapted extract from *The Book of God: A Response to the Bible* by Gabriel Josipovici.

To Sholem and Wendy
Jonathan, David, and Sima
with affection

1

Rules and Variation

1.1   What is grammar

I will be using the word **grammar** in this book to refer to the set of rules
that allow us to combine words in our language into larger units. Another
term for **grammar** in this sense is **syntax**.

Some combinations of words are possible in English and others are not.
As a speaker of English, you can judge that *Home computers are now much
cheaper* is a possible English sentence whereas *Home computers now much
are cheaper* is not, because you know that *much* is wrongly positioned in
the second example. Your ability to recognize such distinctions is evidence
that in some sense you know the rules of grammar even if you have never
studied any grammar. Similarly, you operate the rules whenever you speak
or write (you can put words in the right order) and whenever you interpret what others say (you know that *Susan likes Tom* means something
different from *Tom likes Susan*). But knowing the rules in evaluative and
operational senses does not mean that you can say what the rules are.

You acquire a working knowledge of your native language simply
through being exposed to it from early childhood: nobody taught you, for
example, where to position *much*. You study grammar, however, if you
want to be able to analyse your language. The analytic grammar makes
explicit the knowledge of the rules with which you operate when you use
the language. There is a clear difference between the operational grammar
and the analytic grammar. After all, many languages have never been
analysed and some have been analysed only relatively recently. People
were speaking and writing English long before the first English grammars
appeared at the end of the sixteenth century.

1.2   Grammar and other aspects of language

Linguistic communications are channelled mainly through our senses of
sound and sight. Grammar is the central component of language. It

mediates between the system of sounds or of written symbols, on the one hand, and the system of meaning, on the other. **Phonology** is the usual term for the sound system in the language: the distinctive sound units and the ways which they may be combined. **Orthography** parallels phonology in that it deals with the writing system in the language: the distinctive written symbols and their possible combinations. **Semantics** is concerned with the system of meanings in the language: the meanings of words and the combinatory meanings of larger units.

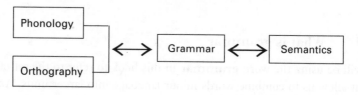

Three other aspects of language description are often distinguished: phonetics, morphology and pragmatics. **Phonetics** deals with the physical characteristics of the sounds in the language and how the sounds are produced. Sounds and letters combine to form words or parts of words. **Morphology** refers to the set of rules that describe the structure of words. The word *computer*, for example, consists of two parts: the base *compute* (used separately as a verb) and the suffix *-er* (found in other nouns derived from verbs, e.g. *blender*). **Pragmatics** is concerned with the use of particular utterances within particular situations. For example, *Will you join our group?* is a question that, depending on the speaker's intention, is a request for information or a request for action.

For descriptive purposes, it is convenient to deal with the components of language separately, but because of the central place of grammar in the language system, it is sometimes necessary to refer to the other components when we discuss the grammar.

1.3   Grammars of English

There are many grammars of English, that is to say books describing English grammar. They differ in how much of the grammar they cover and in how they set out the rules. There are also some differences in the categorization and terminology they use. Nevertheless, most categories and terms are widely shared, deriving from a tradition of grammatical description.

The grammatical analysis in this book follows the approach found in *A*

Comprehensive Grammar of the English Language by Randolph Quirk, Sidney Greenbaum, Geoffrey Leech, and Jan Svartvik. First published in 1985, that is a reference work on contemporary English grammar that contains nearly 1800 pages. Future reference works of this scope are likely to be even longer. Despite the immense amount of research on contemporary English in the last few decades, many grammatical phenomena have yet to be discovered and described.

1.4   National varieties

English is the first language of over 300 million people. Most of them live in the United States of America, which has about 216 million native speakers of English, and the United Kingdom, with about 53 million. Other countries with large numbers of English native speakers that also constitute the majority of the population are Canada (about 16 million), Australia (about 14 million), the Irish Republic (about 3.4 million), and New Zealand (about 3 million). Some countries have concentrations of English native speakers, though they do not constitute the majority of the population; for example, South Africa has about 1.6 million native English speakers apart from about 8.5 million bilingual speakers of English. While recognizing that these people all speak English, we can distinguish the national varieties they use as American English, British English, Canadian English, and so on.

English is a second language for over 300 million people who speak another language as their native tongue but also use English in communicating with their compatriots. For example, the first language for about 30 per cent of Canadians is French and for millions of Americans it is Spanish. English is also the second language in countries where only a small minority speak it as their tongue but where it is the official language or joint official language for government business. Among these countries is India, where it is estimated that about 21 million people speak English fluently as their second language (though these constitute only about 3 per cent of India's vast population). Other countries where English is the official or joint official language include Gambia, Ghana, Nigeria, the Philippines, Puerto Rico (where about 1.3 million inhabitants are bilingual in Spanish and English), Tanzania, Uganda, Zambia, and Zimbabwe. Since the English in each of these countries has certain distinctive features, it is reasonable to refer to such national varieties as, for example, Indian English or Nigerian English.

Finally, English is studied as the primary foreign language in most other countries. One estimate is that over 150 million children are currently studying English as a foreign language in primary or secondary schools. Its popularity lies in its value as an international language. A knowledge of English is perceived in most parts of the world as essential for international communication in commerce and tourism, in economic and military aid, and in scientific and technological literature.

1.5   Standard and non-standard English

In addition to differences between national varieties of English, there are differences within each national variety. Each has a number of dialects. In countries where the majority speak English as their first language one dialect is used nationally for official purposes. It is called **Standard English**.

Standard English is the national dialect that generally appears in print. It is taught in schools, and students are expected to use it in their essays. It is the norm for dictionaries and grammars. We expect to find it in official typed communications, such as letters from government officials, solicitors, and accountants. We expect to hear it in national news broadcasts and documentary programmes on radio or television.

Within each national variety the standard dialect is relatively homogeneous in grammar, vocabulary, spelling, and punctuation. Pronunciation is a different matter, since there is no equivalent standard accent (type of pronunciation). For each national variety there are regional accents, related to a geographical area, and social accents, related to the educational, socio-economic, and ethnic backgrounds of the speakers. In British English, Received Pronunciation (RP) is a non-regional social accent associated with public school education but it is not regarded as a standard accent to be learned in schools throughout the country. It is spoken by about 3 per cent of the population in Britain.

Standard English has prestige because people connect it with education and with higher-income groups. It is not intrinsically better than other dialects, though many believe it is. One of its major advantages is that it has developed a range of styles to suit different kinds of uses of the language, particularly in writing.

Non-standard dialects tend to be restricted to people from a particular region or from a particular social group or to social groups within a region. Many people speak more than one dialect, perhaps using different dialects at home and at work.

1.6   Variation according to use

Besides the variation that depends on the regional or social affiliations of users, some variation reflects the uses to which speakers put their language. Certain types of activity have clearly recognized language features; examples include scientific papers, legal documents, sermons, news broadcasts, and fiction. Newspapers have a distinctive layout, headlines are often highly compressed (*Banks warned on student loans*), cookery books tend to use many imperatives (*Mix the ingredients*), labels omit words understood from the object to which they are attached (*Shake well*).

Some variation depends on the medium, the channel of communication. The major distinction is between spoken and written language. Conversation, the most common type of speech, involves immediate interchange between the participants, who convey their reactions either in words or through facial expressions and bodily movements. There is more spontaneity in conversation than in writing; self-correction occurs in the flow of conversation, whereas it is eliminated through editing in writing. Writing needs to be more explicit, since obscurities and misunderstandings cannot be removed immediately. People feel more committed to what they write because of the potential permanence of the written communication. The differences in the nature of the media is reflected in the greater concision that is possible in writing and in the greater care that writers take over their choice of words.

Language also varies according to the attitude of the speaker or writer towards the listener or reader, towards the topic, and towards the purpose of communication. We can select from features that range from the most formal to the most informal. *Comprehend* and *strive* are more formal than their respective equivalents, *understand* and *try*. Similarly, *This is the student to whom I gave the message* is more formal than *This is the student I gave the message to*. We can end a letter with the casual and friendly *Yours ever*, the neutral *Yours sincerely*, or the distant *Yours faithfully*.

1.7   Descriptive and prescriptive rules

At the beginning of this chapter I said that the rules of grammar state which combinations of words are possible in the language and which are not. My example of an impossible sentence in English was *Home computers now much are cheaper*. The rule that disallows that sentence is a **descriptive** rule, a rule that describes how people use their language. The validity of this descriptive rule depends on whether it is true that *Home computers are now much cheaper* is a possible English sentence and *Home* *computers now much are cheaper* is an impossible English sentence. The evidence to validate this rule is drawn from the knowledge that speakers of English have of their language as well as from samples of their actual use of the language. Of course the descriptive rule must be accurately formulated to make the valid distinctions.

Sometimes people speaking the same dialect disagree in their evaluation of particular sentences. For example, some speakers of standard British English find acceptable *I demand that she gives her reasons*; others prefer or require a different form of the verb in the *that*-clause, either *give* or *should give*.

A number of differences in the use of standard British English have acquired social importance. Some speakers of the standard dialect consider that certain usages mark their user as uneducated. Rules that specify which usages to adopt or avoid are called **prescriptive** rules. Examples of prescriptive rules are:

> Don't use *like* as a conjunction, as in *He speaks like his father does*.
> Don't use *between you and I*.
> You may use *and* at the beginning of a sentence.
> Avoid splitting an infinitive.
> *Whose* may be used of things as well as people.

Speakers of the standard dialect tend to pay greater attention to prescriptive rules when they are on their best behaviour, in particular when they are writing in a formal style.

1.8 Why study grammar?

The study of language is a part of general knowledge. We study the complex working of the human body to understand ourselves; the same reason should attract us to studying the marvellous complexity of human language.

Everybody has attitudes towards the English language and its varieties, and has opinions on specific features. These attitudes and opinions affect relationships with other people. If you understand the nature of language, you will realize the grounds for your linguistic prejudices and perhaps moderate them; you will also more clearly assess linguistic issues of public concern, such as worries about the state of the language or what to do about the teaching of immigrants. Studying the English language has a more obvious practical application: it can help you to use the language more effectively.

In the study of language, grammar occupies a central position. But there is also a practical reason to emphasize the study of grammar. It is easy to learn to use dictionaries by yourself to find the pronunciation, spelling, or meanings of words, but it is difficult to consult grammar books without a considerable knowledge of grammar.

There are several applications of grammatical study: (1) A recognition of grammatical structures is often essential for punctuation; (2) A study of one's native grammar is helpful when one studies the grammar of a foreign language; (3) A knowledge of grammar is a help in the interpretation of literary and nonliterary texts, since the interpretation of a passage sometimes depends crucially on grammatical analysis; (4) A study of the grammatical resources of English is useful in composition: in particular, it can help you to evaluate the choices available to you when you come to revise an earlier written draft.

This book provides a survey of the grammar of standard British English. It also includes applications to punctuation, usage problems, writing style, and the analysis of literary language. It ends with an appendix on spelling, a glossary of terms used in the book, and sets of exercises.

Part I

The Grammar

2

The Sentence

2.1 What is a sentence?

Grammar deals with the rules for combining words into larger units. The largest unit that is described in grammar is normally the **sentence**. You may therefore think that grammarians should be embarrassed at not being able to offer a simple definition of the term 'sentence'.

It is sometimes said that a sentence expresses a complete thought. This is a **notional** definition: it defines a term by the notion or idea it conveys. The difficulty with this definition lies in fixing what is meant by a 'complete thought'. There are notices, for example, that seem to be complete in themselves but are not generally regarded as sentences: Exit, Danger, 50 mph limit.

On the other hand, there are sentences that clearly consist of more than one thought. Here is one relatively simple example:

> This week marks the 300th anniversary of the publication of Sir Isaac Newton's *Philosophiae Naturalis Principia Mathematica*, a fundamental work for the whole of modern science and a key influence on the philosophy of the European Enlightenment.

How many 'complete thoughts' are there in this sentence? We should at least recognize that the part after the comma introduces two additional points about Newton's book: (1) that it is a fundamental work for the whole of modern science, and (2) that it was a key influence on the philosophy of the European Enlightenment. Yet this example would be acknowledged by all as a single sentence, and it is written as a single sentence.

We can try another approach by defining a sentence as a string of words beginning with a capital letter and ending with a full stop. This is a **formal** definition: it defines a term by the form or shape of what the term refers to. We can at once see that as it stands this definition is inadequate,

11

since (1) many sentences end with a question mark or an exclamation mark, and (2) capital letters are used for names, and full stops are used for abbreviations. Even if we amend the definition to take account of these objections, we still find strings of words in newspaper headlines, titles, and notices that everyone would recognize as sentences even though they do not end with a full stop, a question mark, or an exclamation mark:

> Trees May Be a Source of Pollution
> An Irish Airman Foresees his Death (title of poem)
> Do not enter

But the most serious objection is that the definition is directed only towards **orthographic** sentences; that is, sentences that appear in the written language. Spoken sentences, of course, do not have capital letters and periods.

It is in fact far more difficult to determine the limits of sentences in natural conversation, to say where sentences begin and end. That is so partly because people may change direction as they speak and partly because they tend to make heavy use of connectors such as *and, but, so,* and *then.* Here is a typical example of a speaker who strings sentences together with *and.* (The full stop marks a short pause and the dash a longer pause. The vertical line marks the end of a rhythmic unit in the intonation.)

> A: I'd been working away this week| trying to clear up| . the backlog of mail| caused by me being three weeks away| . and I thought I was doing marvellously| . and at about| . six o'clock last night|. I was sorting through . stuff on the desk| and I discovered . a fat pile of stuff| – all carefully opened| and documented by Sally| that I hadn't even seen|.

How many orthographic sentences correspond to A's story? There is no one correct answer. In writing it we have a choice: we could punctuate it as one sentence or we could split it into two or more sentences, each of the later sentences beginning with *and.*

Grammarians are not worried about the difficulties in defining the sentence. Their approach to the question is formal because they are in-terested in grammatical form. Like many people who are not grammar-ians, they are generally confident of recognizing sentences, and they specify the possible patterns for the sentences. Combinations of words that conform to those patterns are then **grammatical** sentences.

2.2   Irregular sentences and non-sentences

Sentences that conform to the major patterns (cf. 3.13) are **regular** sentences, and they are the type that will generally concern us in this book. Sentences that do not conform to the major patterns are **irregular** sentences.

If I ask you to write down the first sentences that come into your mind, you are likely to produce regular sentences. Here are some regular sentences in various major patterns:

> David and Doris have three sons.
> The liquid smelled spicy to Justin.
> Some people give their children a daily dose of vitamins.
> About a million visitors come to our city every summer.

Most irregular sentences are **fragmentary** sentences. These leave out words that we easily supply, usually from the preceding verbal context. Here is a typical example in an exchange between two speakers:

> A: Where did you put the letter?
> B: In the top drawer.

We interpret B's reply as *I put the letter in the top drawer*, and that reconstructed sentence would be regular. Similarly, the headline *Same gun used in IRA attacks* corresponds to the regular *The same gun was used in the IRA attacks*. Fragmentary sentences can therefore be viewed as directly derivable in their interpretation from regular sentences.

Finally, we often say or write things that are not grammatical sentences. These non-sentences may simply be mistakes. But they may also be perfectly normal, although they cannot be analysed grammatically as sentences. Normal non-sentences include such common expression as *Hello!; Yes; No; So long!; Thanks!; Cheers!;* and they include many headlines, headings, titles, labels and notices:

> Jail Riot (headline)
> On the Nature of the Model (section heading in book)
> The Captain and the Enemy (title of book)
> Naming of Parts (title of poem)
> Pure Lemon Juice
> No Smoking

In the next chapter we will be looking at the patterns of regular sentences, but first I have a few more general things to say about sentences.

2.3   Simple and multiple sentences

Here are two sentences placed next to each other:

[1]   The inquiry left in its wake a number of casualties. I was one of them.

I can combine the two sentences in [1] merely by putting *and* between them:

[2]   The inquiry left in its wake a number of casualties, *and* I was one of them.

I can also combine them by putting a connecting word in front of the first sentence:

[3]   *When* the inquiry left in its wake a number of casualties, I was one of them.

I can make a small change in the second sentence:

[4]   The inquiry left in its wake a number of casualties, I *being* one of them.

A sentence or a sentence-like construction contained within a sentence is called a **clause**. Constructions like *I being one of them* in [4] resemble sentences in that they can be analysed to a large extent in similar ways (cf. 6.8). The sentences in [2], [3], and [4] therefore all consist of two clauses. (Strictly speaking, the separate sentences in [1] are also clauses, but since they have only one clause each, it is convenient to refer to them just as sentences.)

A sentence that does not contain another clause within it is a **simple sentence**. If it contains one or more clauses, it is a **multiple sentence**.

Here are some more examples of multiple sentences with connecting words:

You can't insist *that* your children love each other.

The building was emptied *before* the bomb-disposal squad was
called.

When we returned three hours later, no wolves were in sight.

My father always hoped *that* I would become a doctor *and* that
must have been *why* he took me along *when* he visited his
patients.

We will be looking more closely at multiple sentences in Chapter 6.
Meanwhile, I will be using simple sentences to illustrate general matters
about sentences.

2.4   Sentence types

There are four major types of sentences:

1. **Declaratives** (or **declarative sentences**)
   She was attracted to an open-air job.
   The new proposals have galvanised the normally disparate community
   into a potent fighting force.
2. **Interrogatives** (or **interrogative sentences**)
   Do you have your own personal computer?
   Where will you be going for your holiday?
3. **Imperatives** (or **imperative sentences**)
   Open the door for me.
   Take a seat.
4. **Exclamatives** (or **exclamative sentences**)
   How well you look!
   What a large piece you've given me!

These four sentence types differ in their form (cf. 6.2–4). They correspond in general to four major uses:

1. **Statements** are used chiefly to convey information.
2. **Questions** are used chiefly to request information.
3. **Directives** are used chiefly to request action.
4. **Exclamations** are used chiefly to express strong feeling.

It is usual to refer to interrogatives more simply as questions.

We will be discussing these sentence types and their uses in a later
chapter (cf. 6.1–5). Declaratives are the basic type and I will therefore
generally be using them for illustrative purposes.

2.5   Positive and negative sentences

Sentences are either **positive** or **negative**. If an auxiliary ('helping') verb is present, we can usually change a positive sentence into a negative sentence by inserting *not* or *n't* after the auxiliary. In the following examples, the auxiliaries are *has*, *is*, and *can*:

Positive: Nancy *has* been working here for over a year.
Negative: Nancy *has not* been working here for over a year.

Positive: Dan *is* paying for the meal.
Negative: Dan *isn't* paying for the meal.

Positive: I *can* tell the difference.
Negative: I *can't* tell the difference.

The rules for inserting *not* and *n't* are somewhat complicated. I will be referring to them later (cf. 3.3f).

A sentence may be negative because of some other negative word:

She *never* had a secretary.
Nobody talked to us.
This is *no* ordinary painting.

Most sentences are positive, and I will therefore generally be using positive sentences for my examples.

2.6   Active and passive sentences

Sentences are either **active** or **passive**. We can often choose whether to make a sentence active or passive (cf. 4.15). The choice involves differences in position and differences in the form of the verb:

Active: Charles Dickens wrote many novels.
Passive: Many novels were written by Charles Dickens.

Charles Dickens and *many novels* are at opposite ends of the two sentences, in the passive sentence *by* comes before *Charles Dickens*, and the active *wrote* corresponds to the longer *were written*.

Here are two further examples of pairs of active and passive sentences:

Active: Many Members of Parliament read the Prime

Minister's warning as a retreat from her earlier commitment.

Passive: The Prime Minister's warning was read by many Members of Parliament as a retreat from her earlier commitment.

Active: The Rambert Dance Company won the country's largest arts prize, the Prudential Award.

Passive: The country's largest arts prize, the Prudential Award, was won by the Rambert Dance Company.

Actives are far more numerous than passives. Their relative frequency varies with the type of language. For example, passives tend to be heavily used in formal scientific writing.

The example sentences in the chapters that follow will generally be active rather than passive.

3

The Parts of the Simple Sentence

3.1   Structure, form, function

Consider this sentence:

[1]   A heavy snowfall has blocked the mountain passes.

There are various ways of analysing this. One way is to say that the sentence contains three units:

> A heavy snowfall
> has blocked
> the mountain passes

We cannot simply arrange the units in any way that we like. For example, [1a] below is not an English sentence:

[1a]   Has blocked the mountain passes a heavy snowfall.

Sentence [1] has a **structure** in that there are rules that decide the units that can co-occur in the sentence and the order in which they can occur.

The three units in [1] are **phrases**. Phrases also have a structure. We cannot rearrange the internal order of the three phrases in [1]. These are not English phrases: *heavy snowfall a; blocked has; the passes mountain.*

A heavy snowfall and *the mountain passes* are noun phrases (cf. 4.2) and *has blocked* is a verb phrase (cf. 4.11). We characterize them as these types of phrases because of their structure: in the noun phrases a noun is the main word, while in the verb phrase a verb is the main word. That kind of characterization describes the type of structure for each of the three units.

We can also look at the three units from a different point of view; their **function**, or how they are used in a particular sentence. For example, in [1] *A heavy snowfall* is the **subject** of the sentence and *the mountain passes* is the **direct object** of the sentence (cf. 3.5–7):

[1]   *A heavy snowfall* has blocked the *mountain passes*.

However, in [2] below *a heavy snowfall* is the direct object and in [3] *the mountain passes* is the subject:

[2]   They encountered *a heavy snowfall*.
[3]   *The mountain passes* are now open.

We therefore see that identical phrases may have different functions in different sentences.

Turning back to [1], we can combine the descriptions by structure and function. *A heavy snowfall* is a noun phrase functioning as subject, and *the mountain passes* is a noun phrase functioning as direct object. In this chapter we will be examining the function of the phrases, not their structure. In the next section, we will take a preliminary look at the functions of the parts of a sentence.

3.2   Subject, predicate, verb

It is traditional to divide the sentence into two main **constituents**: the **subject** and the **predicate**. The predicate consists of the verb and any other elements of the sentence apart from the subject:

subject	predicate
I	learned all this much later.
The chef	is a young man with a broad experience of the world.
The fate of the land	parallels the fate of the culture.

The most important constituent of the predicate is the verb. Indeed, it is the most important constituent in the sentence, since regular sentences may consist of only a verb: imperatives such as *Help!* and *Look!* The verb of the sentence may consist of more than one word: *could have been imagining*. The **main verb** in this verb phrase comes last: *imagining*. The verbs that come before the main verb are **auxiliary verbs** ('helping verbs'), or simply **auxiliaries**: *could have been*.

I have been following traditional practice in using the word *verb* in two senses:

1. Like the subject, the verb is a constituent of sentence structure. In [1] the verb of the sentence is *stroked* and in [2] it is *has been working*:

   [1] Marty *stroked* his beard.
   [2] Ellen *has been working* all day.

2. A verb is a word, just as a noun is a word. In this sense, [2] contains three verbs: the auxiliaries *has* and *been* and the main verb *working*. The three verbs in [2] form a unit, the unit being a verb phrase (cf. 4.11).

3.3   Operator

In section 3.2 I divided the sentence into two parts: the subject and the predicate. I then pointed to the verb as the most important constituent of the predicate.

We can now identify an element in the verb that has important functions in the sentence: the **operator**. Another way of analysing the sentence is to say that it consists of three constituents: the subject, the operator, and the rest of the predicate.

As a first approximation, I will say that the operator is the first or only auxiliary in the verb of the sentence. In [1] the verb is *could have been imagining*:

[1]   You *could have been imagining* it.

The operator is *could*, the first auxiliary. In [2] the verb is *can get*:

[2]   Karen *can get* to the heart of a problem.

The operator is *can*, the only auxiliary.

The operator plays an essential role in the formation of certain sentence structures:

1. We form most types of questions by interchanging the positions of the subject and the operator:

   [1]   You *could* have been imagining it.
   [1a]   *Could* you have been imagining it?

   This is known as **subject–operator inversion**.

2. We form negative sentences by putting *not* after the operator. In informal style, *not* is often contracted to *n't*, and in writing *n't* is

attached to the operator; some operators have very different positive and negative forms (e.g. *will* in [4] and *won't* in [4a]):

[3]   Barbara and Charles *are* getting married in April.

[3a]   Barbara and Charles $\left\{ \begin{matrix} are\ not \\ aren't \end{matrix} \right\}$ getting married in April.

[4]   Nancy *will* be staying with us.

[4a]   Nancy $\left\{ \begin{matrix} will\ not \\ won't \end{matrix} \right\}$ be staying with us.

3. Operators can carry the stress in speech to convey certain kinds of emphasis:

[5]   A: Finish your homework.
       B: I HAVE finished it.
[6]   A: I am afraid to tell my parents.
       B: You MUST tell them.

4. Operators are used in various kinds of reduced clauses to substitute for the predicate:

[7]   A: Are you leaving?
       B: Yes, I *am*.
[8]   Karen and Tom haven't seen the video, but Jill *has*.
[9]   I'll take one if you *will*.

3.4   *Do, Be, Have*

In 3.3 I identified the operator as the first or only auxiliary. But many sentences have no auxiliary, as in [1]:

[1]   Terry *works* for a public authority.

Here there is only the main verb *works*. If we want to form the structures specified in 3.3, we have to introduce the **dummy operator** *do* with the appropriate endings (*do, does, did*):

[1a]   *Does* Terry work for a public authority?
[1b]   Terry *doesn't* work for a public authority.
[1c]   Terry *does* work for a public authority, and her sister *does* too.

The auxiliary *do* in these sentences is a dummy operator because it is introduced to perform the functions of an operator in the absence of 'true' operators such as *can* and *will*.

There are two operators that are not auxiliaries. The verb *be* is used as an operator even when it is the main verb, provided that it is the only verb:

[2]   It *was* an awful system.
[2a]   *Was* it an awful system?

Under the same condition, the main verb *have* is optionally used as an operator:

[3]   Nora *has* just one daughter.
[3a]   *Has* Nora just one daughter?

But with *have* there is a choice. We can introduce the dummy operator as with other verbs (*Does Nora have just one daughter?*) or substitute *get* as the main verb (*Has Nora got just one daughter?*).

3.5   Subject and verb

Regular sentences consist of a subject and a predicate, and the predicate contains at least a verb (cf. 3.2). Here are some sentences consisting of just the subject and the verb:

subject	verb
A door	opened.
The sun	is setting.
The baby	was crying.
You	must leave.
Many of us	have protested.
They	have been drinking.

Sentences usually contain more than just the subject and the verb. Here are several examples, with the subject (S) and the verb (V) italicized and labelled:

His black boots (S) *had* (V) pointed toes and fancy stitching.
It (S) *rained* (V) every day of our vacation.
Every kind of medical equipment (S) *was* (V) in short supply.

The subject need not come first in the sentence:

> Eventually the *managing director* (S) *intervened* (V) in the dispute.
> Over the years *she* (S) *had collected* (V) numerous prizes for academic achievement.

Sometimes, a word or phrase comes between the subject and the verb:

> *They* (S) often *stay* (V) with us for their vacations.

Or there is an interruption between parts of the verb:

> *We* (S) *can* (V) never *thank* (V) this country enough.

The easiest way to identify the subject in a declarative sentence is to turn this sentence into a *yes–no* question (one expecting the answer *yes* or *no*). The operator (op) and the subject change places:

[1]   *The baby* (S) *has* (op) been crying.
[1a]   *Has* (op) *the baby* (S) been crying?
[2]   *Every kind of medical equipment* (S) *was* (op) in short supply.
[2a]   *Was* (op) *every kind of medical equipment* (S) in short supply?
[3]   Eventually *the managing director* (S) intervened in the dispute.
[3a]   *Did* (op) *the managing director* (S) eventually intervene in the dispute?

It may be necessary to turn other types of sentences into declarative sentences to identify the subject for this test and the next test. For example, the subject in [1a] is that part of the sentence that changes place with the operator when the question is turned into a declarative sentence.

Another way of identifying the subject of a declarative sentence is by asking a question introduced by *who* or *what* followed by the verb (without subject–operator inversion). The subject is the constituent that *who* or *what* questions:

[4]   *The World Bank president* (S) *predicted* (V) another world recession in the near future.
[4a]   *Who* (S) *predicted* (V) another world recession in the near future? *The World Bank President.*
[5]   *Tourism* (S) *has become* (V) *the fastest growing industry in our country*.

[5a] *What* (S) *has become* (V) *the fastest growing industry in our country?*
      Tourism.

We can identify the verb of the sentence because it changes its form or contains auxiliaries to express differences in time (for example, past and present) or attitude (for example, possibility, permission, and obligation). Here are some examples with the verb *predict*:

> predicts   was predicting   might predict
> predicted   may predict   could have predicted
> is predicting   will predict   should have been predicting

We could use any of these forms of *predict* as the verb in this sentence:

> He *predicted* (V) another world recession.

3.6 Subject

Many grammatical rules refer to the subject. Here are some examples, including several that I have mentioned earlier:

1. There are rules for the position of the subject. The subject normally comes before the verb in declaratives, but in questions it comes after the operator:

    [1]   *They* (S) *accepted* (V) full responsibility.
    [1a] *Did* (op) *they* (S) *accept* (V) full responsibility?

    The subject comes before the verb even in questions if *who* or *what* or an interrogative phrase such as *which person* is the subject:

    [1b] *Who* (S) *accepted* (V) full responsibility?

2. The subject is normally absent in imperatives:

    > *Help* (V) me with the luggage.

3. Most verbs in the present have a distinctive form ending in *-s* when the subject is singular and refers to something or someone other than the speaker or the person or persons being addressed:

    > *The older child* (singular S) *feeds* (singular V) the younger ones.
    > *The older children* (plural S) *feed* (plural V) the younger ones.

The senator (singular S) *has* (singular V) a clear moral position on racial equality.

The senators (plural S) *have* (plural V) a clear moral position on racial equality.

4. Some **pronouns** (words like *I, you, she, he, they*) have a distinctive form when they function as subject of the sentence or of clauses in the sentence:

    She (S) knows *me* well.

    I (S) know *her* well, and *they* (S) know *her* well too.

5. The subject decides the form of **reflexive pronouns** (those ending in *-self*, such as *herself, ourselves, themselves*) that appear in the same clause:

    I (S) hurt *myself* badly.

    The child cried when *he* (S) hurt *himself* badly.

    You (S) can look at *yourself* in the mirror.

    She (S) can look at *herself* in the mirror.

6. When we turn an active sentence into a passive sentence (cf. 2.6) we change the subjects:

    Active: *The police* (S) called *the bomb-disposal squad*.

    Passive: *The bomb-disposal squad* (S) was called by *the police*.

We can also omit the subject of the active sentence when we form the passive sentence, and indeed we generally do so:

    Passive: *The bomb-disposal squad* was called.

3.7   Transitive verbs and direct object

If a main verb requires a **direct object** to complete the sentence, it is a **transitive** verb. The term 'transitive' comes from the notion that a person (represented by the subject of the sentence) performs an action that affects some person or thing: there is a 'transition' of the action from the one to the other. Indeed, the direct object (DO) typically refers to a person or thing directly affected by the action described in the sentence:

    Polly snatched *my letter* (DO).

    Ronald stroked *his beard* (DO).

They have eaten *all the strawberries* (DO).
I dusted *the bookshelves in my bedroom* (DO).

One way of identifying the direct object in a declarative sentence is by asking a question introduced by *who* or *what* followed by the operator and the subject. The object is the constituent that *who* or *what* questions:

[1]   Carter has been photographing light bulbs lately.
[1a]   *What* (DO) *has* (op) *Carter* (S) been photographing lately? *Light bulbs.*

[2]   Sandra recorded the adverse effects of the changes.
[2a]   *What* (DO) *did* (op) *Sandra* (S) record? *The adverse effects of the changes.*

[3]   Don is phoning his mother.
[3a]   *Who* (DO) *is* (op) *Don* (S) phoning? *His mother.*

Some grammatical rules refer to the direct object.

1. The direct object normally comes after the verb (but cf. 3.11).

   Carter *has been photographing* (V) *light bulbs* (DO) lately.

2. Some pronouns have a distinctive form when they function as direct object (cf. 3.6 (4)):

   She phoned *us* (DO) earlier this evening.
   We phoned *her* (DO) earlier this evening.

3. If the subject and direct object refer to the same person or thing, the direct object is a reflexive pronoun (cf. 3.6(5)):

   The children hid *themselves.*

4. When we turn an active sentence into a passive sentence, the direct object of the active sentence becomes the subject of the passive sentence:

   Active: Radio telescopes have detected *cosmic radiation* (DO).
   Passive   *Cosmic radiation* (S) has been detected by radio telescopes.

In this section I have discussed one basic sentence structure:

   SVO: subject + (transitive) verb + (direct) object

3.8   Linking verbs and subject complement

If a verb requires a **subject complement** (SC) to complete the sentence, the verb is a **linking verb**. The subject complement (underlined in the examples that follow) typically identifies or characterizes the person or thing denoted by the subject:

[1]   Sandra is <u>my mother's name</u>.
[2]   Your room must be <u>the one next to mine</u>.
[3]   The upstairs tenant seemed <u>a reliable person</u>.
[4]   A university is <u>a community of scholars</u>.
[5]   The receptionist seemed <u>very tired</u>.
[6]   You should he <u>more careful</u>.
[7]   The distinction became <u>quite clear</u>.
[8]   The corridor is <u>too narrow</u>.

The most common linking verb is *be*. Other common linking verbs (with examples of subject complements in parentheses) include *appear* (*the best plan*), *become* (*my neighbour*), *seem* (*the wrong person*), *feel* (*a fool*), *get* (*ready*), *look* (*cheerful*), *sound* (*foolish*). Subject complements are typically noun phrases (cf. 4.2), as in [1]–[4] above, or adjective phrases (cf. 4.21), as in [5]–[8] above.

We have now looked at two basic structures:

(3.7)   SVO: subject + (transitive) verb + (direct) object
(3.8)   SVC: subject + (linking) verb + (subject) complement

3.9   Intransitive verbs and adverbials

If a main verb does not require another element to complete it, the verb is **intransitive**:

[1]   *The strikers* (S) *were demonstrating* (V).
[2]   *I* (S) *agree* (V).
[3]   *No cure* (S) *exists* (V).
[4]   *They* (S) *are lying* (V).

We have now seen three basic sentence structures:

(3.7)   SVO: subject + (transitive) verb + (direct) object

(3.8)   SVC: subject + (linking) verb + (subject) complement
(3.9)   SV: subject + (intransitive) verb

The structures are basic because we can always add optional elements to them. These optional elements are **adverbials**. We should be careful to distinguish adverbials from adverbs (cf. 5.15). The adverbial, like the subject, is a sentence constituent; the adverb, like the noun, is a word.

Adverbials (A) convey a range of information about the situation depicted in the basic structure (cf. 3.14). In [1a] below, the adverbial *noisily* depicts the manner of the action, and the adverbial *outside the White House* indicates the place of the action:

[1a]   The strikers were demonstrating *noisily* (A) *outside the main office* (A).

In [2a] *entirely* is an intensifier of *agree*, conveying the intensity of the agreeing:

[2a]   I *entirely* (A) agree.

In [3a] *unfortunately* supplies the writer's comment:

[3a]   *Unfortunately* (A), no cure exists.

Therefore in [4a] points to a logical connection between the two sentences. The evidence stated in the first sentence is the reason for the assertion in the second sentence.

[4a]   A reliable witness has testified that they were in Melbourne on the day they claimed to be in Sydney. They are *therefore* (A) lying.

The sentences [1a]–[4a] with adverbials have the basic structure SV, which we also see in the parallel sentences [1]–[4] without adverbials. In [5] the basic structure is SVO and in [6] it is SVC:

[5]   *For all its weaknesses* (A) the labyrinthine committee structure provides a useful function in disseminating information.
[6]   Jade is plentiful *in this area* (A).

In [5] the adverbial has concessive force ('despite all its weaknesses') and in [6] it indicates place.

As [1a] indicates, a sentence may have more than one adverbial.

3.10   Adverbial complement

I explained in section 3.9 that adverbials are optional elements in sentence structure. However, some elements that convey the same information as adverbials are obligatory because the main verb is not complete without them. Such obligatory elements are **adverbial complements** (AC).

Contrast [1] with [1a]:

[1]   The strikers were demonstrating *outside the main office* (A).
[1a]   The strikers were *outside the main office* (AC).

In [1] the sentence is complete without the adverbial, but in [1a] the sentence is not complete without the adverbial complement.

Typically, adverbial complements refer to space – location or direction:

The city lies *225 miles north of Guatemala City* (AC).
The nearest inhabitants are *a five-day mule trip away* (AC).
George is getting *into his wife's car* (AC).
This road goes *to Madison* (AC).

Adverbials may convey other meanings:

Their work is *in the early stages* (AC).
The show will last *for three hours* (AC).
The children were *with their mother* (AC).
These letters are *for Cindy* (AC).

We can now add a fourth basic sentence structure to our set:

(3.7)   SVO: subject + (transitive) verb + (direct) object
(3.8)   SVC: subject + (linking) verb + (subject) complement
(3.9)   SV: subject + (intransitive) verb
(3.10) SVA: subject + verb + adverbial (complement)

I have not named the set of verbs that require an adverbial complement because there is no traditional name for it. The most common verb in the SVA structure is *be*.

3.11   Direct and indirect object

We have seen that a transitive verb requires a direct object to complete the sentence (cf. 3.7). Some transitive verbs can have two objects: an **indirect object** followed by a direct object. The indirect object (IO) refers to a person indirectly affected by the action described in the sentence. The person generally receives something or benefits from something:

[1]   Ruth gave *my son* (IO) *a birthday present* (DO).
[2]   I can show *you* (IO) *my diploma* (DO).
[3]   My friends will save *her* (IO) *a seat* (DO).
[4]   You may ask *the speaker* (IO) *another question* (DO).

The indirect object is usually equivalent to a phrase introduced by *to* or *for*, but that phrase normally comes after the direct object. Sentences [1a]–[4a] parallel [1]–[4]:

[1a]   Ruth gave a birthday present *to my son*.
[2a]   I can show my diploma *to you*.
[3a]   My friends will save a seat *for her*.
[4a]   You may ask another question *of the speaker*.

The structures in [1]–[4] and those in [1a]–[4a] differ somewhat in their use, since there is a general tendency for the more important information to come at the end (cf. 9.2). For example, if the son has already been mentioned, but not the birthday present, we would expect [1] to be used rather than [1a], though in speech we can indicate the focus of information by giving it prominence in our intonation.

We can question the indirect object in a way similar to the questioning of the direct object:

[1b]   *Who* (IO) did Ruth give a birthday present?

The grammatical rules that refer to the direct object (cf. 3.7) also refer to the indirect object:

1. The indirect object comes after the verb:

Ruth gave *my son* (IO) *a birthday present* (DO).

Notice that the indirect object comes before the direct object.

2. Some pronouns have a distinctive form when they function as indirect object:

> *I* paid *her* (IO) the full amount.
> *She* paid *me* (IO) the full amount.

3. If the subject and indirect object refer to the same person, the indirect object is generally a reflexive pronoun (cf. 3.6(5)):

> The managing director of the company paid *herself* (IO) a huge salary.

4. When we turn an active sentence into a passive sentence, the indirect object of the active sentence can become the subject of the passive sentence:

> The principal granted *Tony* (IO) an interview.
> *Tony* (S) was granted an interview.

The direct object can also become the subject, but in that case the indirect object (if retained) is generally represented by a phrase introduced by *to* or *for*:

> An interview was granted *to Tony*.

We can now add a fifth basic sentence structure:

(3.7) SVO: subject + (transitive) verb + (direct) object
(3.8) SVC: subject + (linking) verb + (subject) complement
(3.9) SV: subject + (intransitive) verb
(3.10) SVA: subject + verb + adverbial (complement)
(3.11) SVOO: subject + (transitive) verb + (indirect) object + (direct) object

3.12   Direct object and complement

In 3.11 we have seen examples of transitive verbs that require two constituents: indirect object and direct object. In this section I introduce the two remaining structures, each of which consists of a subject, a transitive verb, a direct object, and a complement. In both structures the complement is related to the direct object.

In the first structure, the direct object is followed by an **object complement** (OC):

[1]   His jokes made *the audience* (DO) *uneasy* (OC).
[2]   I declared *the meeting* (DO) *open* (OC).
[3]   The heat has turned *the milk* (DO) *sour* (OC).
[4]   They elected *her* (DO) *their leader* (OC).

This SVOC structure parallels the SVC structure (cf. 3.8), but in the first structure the complement is related to the direct object and in the second it is related to the subject. Compare [1]–[4] with [1a]–[4a]:

[1a]   *The audience* (S) is *uneasy* (SC).
[2a]   *The meeting* (S) is *open* (SC).
[3a]   *The milk* (S) is *sour* (SC).
[4a]   *She* (S) is *their leader* (SC).

Finally, the direct object may be followed by an adverbial complement (AC) (cf. 3.10):

[5]   You should *put* (V) *the chicken* (DO) in the *microwave* (AC).
[6]   I *keep* (V) *my car* (DO) *outside the house* (AC).
[7]   He *stuck* (V) *his hands* (DO) *in his pockets* (AC).

Just as the SVOC structure parallels the SVC structure, so this SVOA structure parallels the SVA structure.

[5a]   *The chicken* (S) is *in the microwave* (AC).
[6a]   *My car* (S) is *outside the house* (AC).
[7a]   *His hands* (S) are *in his pockets* (AC).

We have now looked at four basic structures with transitive verbs and direct objects:

(3.7)   SVO: subject + (transitive) verb + (direct) object
(3.11)   SVOO: subject + (transitive) verb + (indirect) object + (direct) object
(3.12)   SVOC: subject + (transitive) verb + (direct) object + (object) complement
(3.12)   SVOA: subject + (transitive) verb + direct (object) + adverbial (complement)

3.13   The basic sentence structures

I will now summarise what has been described so far in this chapter. The following elements (major sentence constituents) function in the basic sentence structures:

subject	S
verb	V
object	O – direct object DO
	O – indirect object IO
complement	C – subject complement SC
	C – object complement OC
	A – adverbial complement AC

These elements enter into the seven basic sentence structures:

1. SV: subject + intransitive verb (cf. 3.9)
       Someone (S) *is talking* (V).

2. SVA: subject + verb + adverbial complement (cf. 3.10)
       My parents (S) *are living* (V) *in Chicago* (AC).

3. SVC: subject + linking verb + subject complement (cf. 3.8)
       I (S) *feel* (V) *tired* (SC).

4. SVO: subject + transitive verb + direct object (cf. 3.7)
       We (S) *have finished* (V) *our work* (DO).

5. SVOO: subject + transitive verb + indirect object + direct object (cf. 3.11)
       She (S) *has given* (V) *me* (IO) *the letter* (DO).

6. SVOA: subject + transitive verb + direct object + adverbial complement (cf. 3.12)
       You (S) *can put* (V) *your coat* (DO) *in my bedroom* (AC).

7. SVOC: subject + transitive verb + direct object + object complement (cf. 3.12)
       You (S) *have made* (V) *me* (DO) *very happy* (OC).

The structures depend on the choice of the main verbs, regardless of the auxiliaries. The same verb (sometimes in somewhat different senses) may enter into different structures. Here are some examples:

SV:	I have *eaten.*
SVO.	I have *eaten* lunch.

SV: It *smells*.
SVC: It *smells* sweet.

SVC: He *felt* a fool.
SVO: He *felt* the material.

SVO: I *made* some sandwiches.
SVOO: I *made* them some sandwiches.

SVO: I have *named* my representative.
SVOC: I have *named* her my representative.

SV: The children are *growing*.
SVO: The children are *growing* carrots.
SVC: The children are *growing* hungry.

SVO: She *caught* me.
SVOO: She *caught* me a fish.
SVOA: She *caught* me off my guard.

3.14   The meanings of the sentence elements

The sentence elements are grammatical, not semantic, categories. However, they are associated with certain meanings. In this section I will illustrate some typical meanings.

Subject

1. **agentive**

   In sentences with a transitive or intransitive verb, the subject typically has an agentive role: the person that performs the action:

   > *Martha* has switched on the television.
   > *Caroline* is calling.

2. **identified**

   The identified role is typical of structures with a linking verb:

   > *Jeremy* was my best friend.
   > *Doris* is my sister-in-law.

3. **characterized**

   The characterized role is also typical of structures with a linking verb:

   > *This brand of coffee* tastes better.
   > *Paul* is an excellent student.

4. **affected**

With intransitive verbs the subject frequently has the affected role: the person or thing directly affected by the action, but not intentionally performing the action:

> *They* are drowning.
> *The water* has boiled.

5. **'it'**

Sometimes there is no participant. The subject function is then taken by *it*, which is there merely to fill the place of the subject:

> *It*'s raining.   *It*'s already eleven o'clock.
> *It*'s too hot.   *It*'s a long way to Miami.

Verb

The major distinction in meaning is between verbs that are *stative* and verbs that are *dynamic*.

Stative verbs introduce a quality attributed to the subject or a state of affairs:

> I *am* a French citizen.
> Their children *are* noisy.
> She *has* two brothers.
> I *heard* your alarm this morning.

Dynamic verbs introduce events. They refer to something that happens:

> Her books *sell* well.
> We *talked* about you last night.
> Your ball has *broken* my window.
> I *listened* to her respectfully.

Dynamic verbs, but not stative verbs, occur quite normally with the *ing* form (cf. 4.12, 4.14):

> Her books are *selling* well.
> We were *talking* about you last night.
> They have been *playing* in the yard.
> She is *looking* at us.

When stative verbs are used with the *-ing* form, they have been transformed into dynamic verbs:

> Their children are *being* noisy. ('behaving noisily')
> I am *having* a party next Sunday evening.

Direct object

1. **affected**

   This is the typical role of the direct object. See **subject** (4) above.

   > I threw *the note* on the floor.
   > She shook *her head*.

2. **resultant**

   The direct object may refer to something that comes into existence as a result of the action:

   > He's written *a paper on his hobbies*.
   > I'm knitting *a sweater* for myself.

3. **eventive**

   The direct object may refer to an event. The eventive object generally contains a noun that is derived from a verb. In a typical use, the noun carries the main part of the meaning that is normally carried by the verb, and is preceded by a verb of general meaning, such as *do, have*, or *make*:

   > They were having *a quarrel*. (cf: They were *quarrelling*.)
   > I have made *my choice*. (cf: I have *chosen*.)

Indirect object

The indirect object typically has a **recipient** role: the person that is indirectly involved in the action, generally the person receiving something or intended to receive something, or benefiting in some way:

> They paid *me* the full amount.
> He bought *Sandra* a bunch of flowers.
> David has been showing *Andrew* his computer printout.

Subject and object complement

The complement typically has the role of **attribute**. It attributes an identification or characterization to the subject (if it is a subject complement) or the direct object (if it is an object complement):

> Susan is *my accountant*
> Ronald became *a paid agitator.*
> I have made David *my assistant.*
> The sun has turned our curtains *yellow.*

Adverbial

Adverbials have a wide range of meanings, some of which apply to adverbial complements (cf. 3.10, 3.12). Here are some typical examples:

1. **space**

   > My school is *south of the river.* (positive in space)
   > She has gone *to the bank.* (direction)

2. **time**

   > They're staying with us *for a few weeks.* (duration)
   > We come here *quite often.* (frequency)
   > Your next appointment is *on the last day of the month.* (position in time)

3. **manner**

   > The students cheered *wildly.*
   > I examined the statement *carefully.*

4. **degree**

   > I like them *very much.*
   > We know her *well.*

5. **cause**

   > My brother is ill *with the flu.*
   > They voted for her *out of a sense of loyalty.*

6. **comment on truth-value** (degree of certainty or doubt)

> They *certainly* can't finish on time.
> *Perhaps* he's out.

7. **evaluation of what the sentence refers to**

> *Luckily*, they were not hurt.
> He *unexpectedly* fell asleep.

8. **providing a connection between units**

> I was not friendly with them; *however*, I did not want them to be treated unfairly.
> We arrived too late, and *as a result* we missed her.

4

The Structures of Phrases

4.1 Kinds of Phrases

When we looked earlier (3.1) at the parts of the simple sentence, we noticed that they can be viewed in terms of either their structure or their function. In Chapter 3 we were mainly concerned with their function in the sentence, and we there distinguished functional elements such as subject and direct object. In this chapter we are mainly concerned with the internal structure of the elements. For the simple sentence, this means the structure of the various phrases that can function in the sentence as subject, verb, etc.

There are five types of phrases:

1. **noun phrase** *a peaceful result*
   (main word: noun *result*)
2. **verb phrase** *must have been dreaming*
   (main word: verb *dreaming*)
3. **adjective phrase** *very pleasant*
   (main word: adjective *pleasant*)
4. **adverb phrase** *very carefully*
   (main word: adverb *carefully*)
5. **prepositional phrase** *in the shade*
   (main word: preposition *in*)

In grammar, the technical term *phrase* is used even if there is only one word – the main word alone; for example, both *very pleasant* and *pleasant* are adjective phrases. This may seem strange at first, since in everyday use the word *phrase* applies to a group – at least two words. There is a good reason for the wider use of the term in grammar. Many rules that apply to an adjective phrase apply also to an adjective. For example, the same rules apply to the positions of *very pleasant* and *pleasant* in these sentences:

It was a $\left\{ \begin{array}{l} \textit{very pleasant} \\ \textit{pleasant} \end{array} \right\}$ occasion.

The party was $\left\{ \begin{array}{l} \textit{pleasant.} \\ \textit{very pleasant.} \end{array} \right.$

Instead of specifying each time 'adjective phrase or adjective' it is simpler to specify 'adjective phrase' and thereby include adjectives.

In the sections that follow we will be looking at the structures of the five types of phrases, but I will make several general points now. First, a phrase may contain another phrase within it. Or, to put it another way, one phrase may be **embedded** within another phrase.

[1]   We had *some very pleasant times* in Florida.
[2]   They were standing *in the shade of a large oak tree*.

In [1] the noun phrase *some very pleasant times* has the adjective phrase *very pleasant* embedded between *some* and *times*. In [2] the prepositional phrase consists of the preposition *in* and the noun phrase *the shade of a large oak tree*; in the noun phrase another prepositional phrase (*of a large oak tree*) is embedded as a modifier of *shade* and that phrase contains the noun phrase *a large oak tree*. A clause (cf. 2.3) may also be embedded in a phrase:

[3]   *The school that I attend* is quite small.

In [3] the clause *that I attend* is embedded in the noun phrase *the school that I attend*.

A second point is that phrases are defined by their structure, but they are also characterized by their potential functions. For example, a noun phrase may function (among other possibilities) as a subject, direct object, or indirect object.

Third, there is an inevitable circularity in talking about phrases and words: a noun is a word that can be the main word in a noun phrase, and a noun phrase is a phrase whose main word is a noun.

We will be examining classes of words more closely in the next chapter, but the classes must enter into the discussions of phrases in this chapter. The examples should be a sufficient indication of the types of words that are involved.

THE NOUN PHRASE

4.2   The structure of the noun phrase

The main word in a noun phrase is a noun or a pronoun. There are a number of subclasses of nouns and pronouns, but I will postpone discussion of subclasses until we come to look at word classes (cf. 5.4, 5.17).

The structure of the typical noun phrase may be represented schematically in the following way, where the parentheses indicate elements of the structure that may be absent:

(determiners)   (pre-modifiers)   noun   (post-modifiers)

Determiners introduce noun phrases. **Modifiers** are units that are dependent on the main word and can be omitted. Modifiers that come before the noun are **pre-modifiers**, and those that come after the noun are **post-modifiers**. Here are examples of possible structures of noun phrases:

noun	*books*
determiner + noun	*those books*
pre-modifier + noun	*history books*
determiner + pre-modifier + noun	*some long books*
noun + post-modifier	*books about Canada*
determiner + noun + post-modifier	*some books on astronomy*
pre-modifier + noun + post-modifier	*popular books on psychology*
determiner + pre-modifier + noun + post-modifier	*some popular books on astronomy*

All these examples can fit into the blank in this sentence:

I occasionally read ....

4.3   Determiners

There are three classes of determiners (cf. 5.26–30):

1. **pre-determiners**, e.g. *all, both, half*
2. **central determiners**, e.g. *a(n), the, those*
3. **post-determiners**, e.g. *other, two first*

Here are two examples with determiners from each class:

> all these other works
> both our two daughters

4.4   Modifiers

The noun phrase may have more than one pre-modifier or post-modifier:

> a *long hot* summer
> *acute, life-threatening* crises
> a *nasty* gash *in his chin which needed medical attention*

There are two post-modifiers in the last example because each separately modifies *gash: a nasty gash in his chin; a nasty gash which needed medical attention.* The modifier may itself be modified (cf. 4.21):

> a comfortably *cool* room
> the reduction *of violence* to children
> those eyewitnesses *willing* to testify about what they had seen

A modifier may also be discontinuous, one part coming before the noun and the other part after it:

> the easiest *children* to teach

Compare:

> the *children* (who are) easiest to teach

4.5   Relative clauses

One common type of post-modifier is the **relative clause**:

> He had a nasty gash *which needed medical attention*.

The relative clause is embedded in the noun phrase. As an independent sentence it might be:

[1]   The gash needed medical attention.

We might think of the embedding as a process that takes place in stages. The first stage puts the sentence close to the noun it will be modifying:

[1a]   He had a nasty *gash. The gash* needed medical attention.

You will notice that the two sentences share nouns (*gash*) that refer to the same thing. The next stage changes the noun phrase into a **relative pronoun** (5.24) – here *which*:

[1b]   He has a nasty gash *which* needed medical attention.

The relative pronoun *which* functions as subject in the relative clause just as *The gash* functions as subject in [1a].
    Here is another example:

[2]   The woman is an engineering student. The woman was sitting next to you.
[2a]   The woman (The woman was sitting next to you) is an engineering student.
[2b]   The woman *who* was sitting next to you is an engineering student.

    In both [1b] and [2b] the relative pronoun can be replaced by relative *that*:

[1c]   He had a nasty gash *that* needed medical attention.
[2c]   The woman *that* was sitting next to you is an engineering student.

For the choice of relative pronouns, see 5.24.

4.6   Appositive clauses

Another type of clause that is often embedded in a noun phrase is the **appositive clause**. It is introduced by the conjunction *that*, which is sometimes omitted:

> the assumption *that he will return home*
> the fact *that she rejected his offer of marriage*
> the knowledge that *she rejected his offer of marriage*
> the reason *that I am here today*

The conjunction *that* in appositive clauses differs from the relative *that* (cf. 4.5) because the conjunction does not have a function within its clause. The appositive clause can be a sentence without *that*:

[1]   You know the reason *that I am here today*.
[1a]   I am here today.

The relative clause cannot be a sentence without the relative *that*:

[2]   He has a nasty gash *that needed medical attention*.

We can convert the noun phrase containing the appositive clause into a sentence by inserting a form of the verb *be* before the clause:

[3]   the assumption *that he will return*
[3a]   The assumption *is* that he will return.

4.7   Appositives

The relation of **apposition** is also common between two noun phrases:

Paul Peterson, a rock and alpine climber, was the first to volunteer.

As with the appositional clause, we can show that *a rock and alpine climber* is appositive to (or in apposition to) *Paul Peterson* by converting the two phrases into a sentence:

Paul Peterson *is* a rock and alpine climber.

Here are some other examples of noun phrases in apposition:

vitamin B_{12}, *a complex cobalt-containing molecule*,
the witness, *a burly man with a heavy stubble*,
the first phase of the project – *an underground building topped by an above-ground glass pyramid* –
the rattlesnake, *a venomous animal capable of causing death in human beings*,

Appositives are often signalled by expressions such as *namely* and *that is to say*:

You can read the story in the first book of the Bible, *namely* Genesis.

4.8   Coordination

As with other types of phrases, we can coordinate ('link') noun phrases with *and* or *or*:

> all the senators *and* some of their aides
> law schools *or* medical schools
> my sister, her husband, *and* their three children

We can also coordinate parts of a noun phrase. Coordinated modifiers may apply as a unit:

> *wholesome and tasty* food [food that is both wholesome and tasty]
> a *calm and reassuring* gesture [a gesture that is both calm and reassuring]
> an appetizer of blackberries and raspberries [an appetizer that consists of both *blackberries and raspberries*]

Or they may apply separately:

> electric and magnetic fields [electric fields and magnetic fields]
> large or small classes [large classes or small classes]
> houses along the coast and on the lower hills [houses along the coast and houses on the lower hills]
> the chemical and the biological analysis of plants [the chemical analysis of plants and the biological analysis of plants]

A determiner may serve two or more nouns or modified nouns:

> his wife and two sons [his wife and his two sons]
> some friends and close acquaintances [some friends and some close acquaintances]
> the reactions of the students and teachers [the reactions of the students and the reactions of the teachers]

It is sometimes possible to interpret coordination of parts of phrases in more than one way:

frustrated and desperate men
(1) frustrated men and desperate men
(2) men who are both frustrated and desperate

old men and women
(1) old men and old women
(2) women and old men

their cats and other pets
(1) their cats and their other pets
(2) other pets and their cats

4.9   Complexity

Noun phrases can display considerable structural complexity. It is easy to embed in them appositional structures, clauses, and linked noun phrases. Both the subject and the subject complement in [1] are complex noun phrases:

[1]   *The government's plan, which was elaborated in a document released by the Treasury yesterday,* is *the formal outcome of the Government's commitment at the Madrid summit last year to put forward its ideas about integration.* [*The Independent*, 3 November 1989, p. 1]

Here are two other examples of complex noun phrases functioning as subject of the sentences:

[2]   *The amount of strain that the southern section of the San Andreas fault near Los Angeles can stand before it ruptures* is enormous. [*The Economist*, 28 October – 3 November 1989, p. 131]

[3]   *The prosecution and imprisonment of relatively junior policemen, most of whom were, in my view, acting under the influence of other more senior policemen,* is not the way to bring this sad and bungled affair to an end. [John Stalker, *Stalker*, p. 272. Harmondsworth, Middlesex: Penguin Books, 1988]

In [4] the complex noun phrase is subject complement and in [5] it is a direct object:

[4]   The most straightforward and favoured policy would be *a*

blanket ban on smoking except in designated smoking rooms to which smokers could retreat periodically during break or at their own discretion. [Nick Davidson, *The Independent* 3 November 1989, p. 13]

[5]   In the social and economic sphere, Gildas certainly provides *good evidence for the destruction in the second half of the fifth century of the urban framework which had supported not only the civil administration of the Romano-British diocese but also the Christian organization based until that time essentially on the bishops and clergy of the towns.* [J.N.L. Myres, *The English Settlements*, p. 19. Oxford: Clarendon Press, 1986]

4.10   Functions

The following is a brief list, with illustrations, of the possible functions of noun phrases:

1. **subject**
   The people in the bus escaped through the emergency exit.
2. **direct object**
   They are testing *some new equipment.*
3. **indirect object**
   The bank gave *her* a loan.
4. **subject complement**
   The performance was *a test of their physical endurance.*
5. **object complement**
   Many of us consider her *the best candidate.*
6. **complement of a preposition**
   The box of *chocolates* is intended for *your children.*
7. **pre-modifier of a noun or noun phrase**
   Milk production is down this year.
   He suffers from *lower back* problems.
   The matter has been referred to the *Academic Council* Executive Committee.
8. **adverbial**
   The term finishes *next week.*
   You will not succeed *that way.*

For noun phrases as dependent or independent genitives, see 5.8.

THE VERB PHRASE

4.11   The structure of the verb phrase

The typical structure of the verb phrase consists of a main verb preceded optionally by a maximum of four auxiliary verbs. The four belong to different subclasses of auxiliaries.

(aux 1)   (aux 2)   (aux 3)   (aux 4)   main verb

It is very unusual for all four auxiliaries to appear in one verb phrase, but if two or more auxiliaries co-occur they must appear in the sequence indicated in the diagram, e.g. 1+3, 1+2+4, 2+3. For the four subclasses, see 4.17 below.

4.12   Main verbs

Regular main verbs have four forms that are constructed in this way:

1. **base form:**
   The base form is what we find in dictionary entries: *laugh, mention, play.*
2. **-s form:**
   The *-s* form adds to the base form an ending in *-s: laughs, mentions, plays.*
3. **-ing participle:**
   The *-ing* participle adds to the base form an ending in *-ing: laughing, mentioning, playing.*
4. **-ed form** (past or *-ed* participle):
   The *-ed* form adds to the base form an ending in *-ed: laughed, mentioned, played.*

The addition of the endings involves some rules of pronunciation and spelling that depend on how the base form ends. For example, the *-ed* ending is pronounced as a separate syllable in *loaded* but not in *laughed*; the final consonant of the base form is doubled in the spelling of *plotted* but not in the spelling of *revolted*. Similarly, the *-s* ending is pronounced as a separate syllable and spelled *-es* in *passes*. (For the spelling rules, see A.4. in the Appendix.)

The -ed form represents two distinct functions that are differentiated in the forms of some irregular verbs:

4a. past
4b. -ed participle

Contrast the one form for *laugh* in the following sets of sentences with the two forms of *give* and *speak*:

past	She *laughed* at us.
	She *gave* us a smile.
	She *spoke* to us.

-ed participle	She has *laughed* at us.
	She has *given* us a smile.
	She has *spoken* to us.

Irregular main verbs have either fewer or more forms than regular main verbs. For example, *put* has only three forms: *put, puts, putting. Put* serves as the base form and also as the -ed form in the functions of the past and of the -ed participle:

base form	They always *put* the cat out at night.
-ed form: past	They *put* the cat out last night.
-ed form: -ed participle	They have *put* the cat out.

The irregular verb *be* has the most forms, eight in all:

base form	*be*
present	*am, is, are*
past	*was, were*
-ing participle	*being*
-ed participle	*been*

For the differences in the present forms and in the past forms of *be*, see 4.13.

4.13   Tense, person, and number

The first or only verb in the verb phrase is marked for **tense, person,** and **number**.

Tense is a grammatical category referring to the time of the situation; the tense is indicated by the form of the verb. There are two tense forms:

present and **past**. There are three persons: **first person** (the person or persons speaking or writing), **second person** (the person or persons addressed), and **third person** (others). There are two numbers: **singular** and **plural**.

For all verbs except *be*, there are two forms for the present: the *-s* form and the base form. The *-s* form is used for the third person singular, that is with *he, she, it,* and singular noun phrases as subject:

> He *plays* football every day.
> The road *seems* narrower.

The base form is used for all other subjects: *I, you, we, they,* and plural noun phrases as subject:

> I *play* football every day.
> The roads *seem* narrower.

Be has three forms for the present tense, which are distinct from the base form *be*:

> *am* – first person singular
> *is* – third person singular
> *are* – others

For all verbs except *be*, there is only one past form:

> He (*or* They) *played* football yesterday.
> The road (*or* roads) *seemed* narrower.

Be has two forms for the past:

> *was* – first and third person singular
> *were* – others

The two tenses are related to distinctions in time, but they do not correspond precisely to the difference between present and past in the real world. The present tense generally refers to a time that includes the time of speaking but usually extends backward and forward in time:

> Three and five *make* eight.

We *live* in Sydney.
I *work* in the steel industry.
They *are* my neighbours.

Sometimes the present refers to an event that is simultaneous with the time of speaking:

Here *comes* your sister.
I *nominate* Robert.

4.14 Aspect

Aspect is a grammatical category referring to the way that the time of the situation is viewed by the speaker or writer; the aspect is indicated by a combination of auxiliary and verb form. Verbs have two aspects: the **perfect** aspect and the **progressive** aspect.

The perfect of a verb combines a form of the auxiliary *have* with the *-ed* participle of that verb. The auxiliary has two present tense forms (*has, have*) and one past form (*had*). For example, the **present perfect** of *close* is *has closed* or *have closed* and the **past perfect** is *had closed*:

I *have closed* the shop for the day.
The shop *has closed* for the day.
The police *had closed* the shop months ago.

The present perfect refers to a situation set in some indefinite period that leads to the present. The situation may be a state of affairs that extends to the present:

They *have been* unhappy for a long time.
I *have lived* here since last summer.
We *have* always *liked* them.

Or it may be an event or set of events that is viewed as possibly recurring:

We *have discussed* your problems.
I *have phoned* him every day since he fell sick.
He *has read* only newspapers until now.

The past perfect refers to a situation earlier than another situation set in the past:

> We *had heard* a lot about her before we ever met her.

In many contexts, the present perfect and the past perfect can be replaced by the past.

The progressive combines a form of the auxiliary *be* with the *-ing* participle. The **present progressive** and the **past progressive** are illustrated below:

> You *are neglecting* your work.
> I *am resting* just now.
> The children *were fighting* all morning.
> We *were waiting* for you in the lobby.

The progressive indicates that the situation is in progress. It may therefore also imply that it lasts for only a limited period and that it is not ended. Contrast *I read a novel last night* (which implies that I finished it) with *I was reading a novel last night*.

4.15 Voice

Verbs have two voices: **active** and **passive**. The active is the voice that is used most commonly. The active and passive have different verb phrases in that the passive has an additional auxiliary: a form of the auxiliary *be* followed by an *-ed* participle. Here are examples of corresponding active and passive verb phrases:

Active	Passive
loves	is loved
sold	was sold
is fighting	is being fought
has reconstructed	has been reconstructed
will proclaim	will be proclaimed
may have asserted	may have been asserted
should be purifying	should be being purifed

The passive is a way of phrasing the sentence so that the subject does not refer to the person or thing responsible (directly or indirectly) for the action. The passive therefore differs from the corresponding active not only in the forms of the verb phrases but also in the positions of certain noun phrases. The direct or indirect object of the active sentence becomes the subject of the corresponding passive sentence, and the subject (if retained) appears after the verb in a *by*-phrase:

> **Active:**   *A team of detectives* (S) is investigating *the crime* (dO)
>
> **Passive:**   *The crime* (S) is being investigated *by a team of detectives.*
>
> **Active:**   *The new management* (S) has offered employees (iO) a better deal.
>
> **Passive:**   *Employees* (S) have been offered a better deal by the management.
>
> **Active:**   *Three bullets* (S) penetrated *his heart* (dO).
>
> **Passive:**   *His heart* (S) was penetrated *by three bullets.*
>
> **Active:**   *Scientists* (S) predicted *the location, extent, and strength of the earthquake* (dO) with unprecedented accuracy.
>
> **Passive:**   *The location, extent, and strength of the earthquake* (S) was predicted *by scientists* with unprecendented accuracy.

Generally the passive sentence does not contain the *by*-phrase:

> Britain's reservations on these points were duly noted.
> Most of the buildings were destroyed.
> The decision has already been taken.

The most common reason for using the passive is to avoid referring to the person performing the action. That may be because the identity of the person is not known or because it is felt to be unnecessary to identify the person (perhaps because irrelevant or obvious) or it is felt to be tactless to do so:

> He *was* immediately *admitted* to the hospital.
> The refrigerator door *has* not *been* properly *closed.*

Some *-ed* participle forms may be used as adjectives. In the following sentences the *-ed* forms are adjectives, not passive participles:

> She was *annoyed* with them.

I am *worried* about Edward.
My teachers are *pleased* with my progress.

These sentences look like passive sentences, but the *-ed* words are adjectives if one or more of these possibilities apply:

1. if they can be modified by *very* (for example, *very annoyed*);
2. if they can occur with a linking verb other than *be* (for example, *became worried*);
3. if they can be linked with another adjective (for example, *angry and worried*).

It is obviously an adjective in *Many seats were unsold when I rang the ticket office* because there is no verb *unsell*.

4.16   Expressing future time

In 4.13 I stated that verbs have only two tenses: present and past. How then do we refer to future time?

There are only two tenses in the sense that these are the two distinctions that we make through the forms of the verbs. However, there are various ways of expressing future time. One way is through the simple present tense:

My sister *chairs* the meeting tomorrow.

The most common way is by combining *will* (or the contraction *'ll*) with the base form:

He *will be* here soon.
I*'ll talk* to you next time.

Many speakers in England also use *shall* instead of *will* when the subject is *I* or *we*:

I *shall make* a note of your request.

Two other common ways are the use of *be going to* and the present progressive:

I*'m going to see* them later.
We*'re playing* your team next week.

4.17   The sequence of auxiliaries

In 4.11 I referred to the four types of auxiliaries. Here again is the diagram representing the sequence:

(aux 1) (aux 2) (aux 3) (aux 4)   main verb

If we choose to use auxiliaries, they must appear in the following sequence:

[1]   **modal** (or modal auxiliary), such as *can, may, will* (cf. 5.31)
[2]   perfect auxiliary *have*
[3]   progressive auxiliary *be*
[4]   passive auxiliary *be*

These four uses of the auxiliaries specify the form of the verb that follows:

[1]   modal, followed by base form: *may* phone
[2]   perfect *have*, followed by *-ed* participle: *have* phon*ed*
[3]   progressive *be*, followed by *-ing* participle: *was* phon*ing*
[4]   passive *be*, followed by *-ed* participle: *was* phon*ed*

Gaps in the sequence are of course normal:

[1] + [3]: will be phoning (modal progressive)
[2] + [4]: has been phoned (perfect passive)
[2] + [3]: has been phoning (perfect progressive)
[1] + [4]: can be phoned (modal passive)

The sequence does not take account of the dummy operator *do* (3.4), which is introduced when there would otherwise not be an auxiliary in the verb phrase. In this function, *do* is therefore the only auxiliary present. It is followed by the base form:

I *did* phone.
Did you phone?
I *did* not phone.
Martha phoned, and I *did* too.

There are also **phrasal auxiliaries,** which are intermediate between auxiliaries and main verbs. Here are some examples:

> Sandra *is going to* apply for the job.
> I *had better* eat now.
> My parents *are about* to leave.
> We *have got to* speak to her.
> He may *be able to* help us.
> Jennifer *is supposed to* phone us today.

Only the first word in a phrasal auxiliary is a true auxiliary, since only that word functions as an operator, for example in forming questions (cf. 3.3):

> *Is* Sandra *going to* apply for the job?
> *Had* I better eat now?
> *Is* Jennifer *supposed to* phone us today?

The phrasal auxiliaries may come together to make a long string of verbs:

> We *seem to be going to have to keep on* paying the full fee.
> They *are likely to be about to manage to start* working on our
> project.

4.18   Finite and non-finite verb phrases

Verb phrases are either **finite** or **non-finite.** A finite verb is a verb that carries a contrast in tense between present and past, and may also be marked for person and number. In a finite verb phrase the first or only verb is finite, and the other verbs (if any) are non-finite. In a non-finite verb phrase all the verbs are non-finite. *Play* and *played* are finite verbs in these sentences:

[1]   We *play* football every day.
[2]   We *played* in a football match last week.

Play is in the present tense in [1] and *played* is in the past tense in [2]. In [3] *plays* is the third person singular form of the present:

[3]   She *plays* hockey.

On the other hand, in [4] *will* is the finite verb (The past of *will* is *would*), whereas *play* is non-finite:

[4]   We *will play* some football later today.

Similarly, in [5] *have* is the finite verb and *played* is non-finite:

[5]   We *have played* football every day this week.

All the verb phrases in [1]–[5] are finite verb phrases because they begin with a finite verb.

The following are the non-finite verb forms:

1. the **infinitive**, often introduced by *to: (to) phone*
2. the *-ing* participle: *phoning*
3. the *-ed* participle: *phoned*

If one of these forms is the first or only verb in the verb phrase, the phrase is a non-finite verb phrase:

> He was afraid *to predict* the next day's weather.
> *Having stayed* in their house, I can remember how frequently they quarrelled.
> The new system, *described* in a recent report, provides criteria for evaluating scientific priorities.

The **infinitive** has the base form. It is the infinitive that is used after modals and after the dummy operator *do*:

> I may *see* you later.
> I may *be* there later.
> I did *tell* them.

Non-finite verb phrases normally do not occur as the verb phrase of an independent sentence. Contrast:

[6]   His job was *to predict* the next day's weather.
[7]   He *predicted* the next day's weather.

The verb of the sentence in [6] is *was*, not the infinitive *to predict* (cf. *To predict the next day's weather was his job*).

4.19   Mood

Mood refers to distinctions in the form of the verb that express the attitude of the speaker to what is said. Finite verb phrases have three moods:

1. indicative
2. imperative
3. subjunctive

The **indicative** is the usual mood in declarative, interrogative, and exclamative sentences:

> Roger *has known* me for a long time.
> How well *does* Rosalind *play?*
> What a heavy coat you *are wearing!*

The **imperative** has the base form. It is used chiefly as a directive to request action:

> *Stop* them!

There are two forms of the **subjunctive**: the present subjunctive and the past subjunctive. The traditional terms are misnomers, since the difference between the two is not one of tense.

The **present subjunctive** has the base form. It is used in:

1. *that*-clauses after the expression of such notions as demand or request:

[1]   We demand that he *take* the witness stand.
[2]   I accept your wish that my secretary *omit* this discussion from the minutes.
[3]   My employer insisted that I *be* on time.
[4]   I move that the meeting *be* adjourned.

In verbs other than *be*, the present subjunctive has a distinctive form only in the third person singular: the base form, which contrasts with the indicative form ending in -*s*. In other singular persons and in plurals, the base form is the same as the present tense form. Contrast [1] with [1a]:

[1a]   We demand that they *take* the witness stand.

For all persons the negative sentence need not have an operator (cf. 3.3*f*):

[1b]   We demand that $\left\{ \begin{array}{c} he \\ they \end{array} \right\}$ *not take* the witness stand.

[4a]   I move that the meeting *not be* adjourned.

In the contexts exemplified in [1]–[4] we commonly use *should* followed by the base form instead of the subjunctive:

[1c]   We demand that he *should take* the witness stand.
[3a]   My employer insisted that I *should be* on time.

Another possibility, when the verb is not *be*, is the indicative

[1d]   We demand that he *takes* the witness stand.

2. certain set expressions:

> Long *live* the Republic!
> *Be* that as it may, . . .

The past subjunctive *were* is used chiefly to convey that the speaker is not sure that the situation will happen or is happening:

[5]   If he *were* to be appointed, I would leave.
[6]   If they *were* in the city, they would contact us.
[7]   I wish you *were* here.
[8]   I wish I *were* somewhere hotter than here.

Were is also the past indicative form, so that the subjunctive and indicative are identical except where *was* is required as a past indicative – in the first and third persons singular (*I was, he was*). *Were* therefore is a distinctive form as subjunctive only in [5] and [8]. In fact, except in formal style, indicative *was* is commonly used in place of the past subjunctive in the first and third persons singular:

[5a]   If he *was* to be appointed, I would leave.
[8a]   I wish I *was* somewhere hotter than here.

4.20   Multi-word verbs

Multi-word verbs are combinations of a verb and one or more other words. They are called multi-word verbs because in certain respects they behave as a single verb.

The most frequent types of multi-word verbs consist of a verb followed by one or more **particles** (words that do not change their form) such as *at, away, by,* and *for*. The three major types of these combinations are:

phrasal verbs, e.g. *give in, blow up*
prepositional verbs, e.g. *look after, approve of*
phrasal-prepositional verb, e.g. *look down on, catch up on*

There are sometimes one-word verbs that are similar in meaning to the multi-word verbs. The one-word verbs are more formal:

phrasal verb	give in	– surrender
prepositional verb	look after	– tend
phrasal prepositional verb	put up with	– tolerate

Phrasal verbs and **prepositional verbs** are a combination of a verb and one particle, whereas **phrasal-prepositional verbs** have two particles. A prepositional verb requires an object to complete the sentence:

[1]   Peter is *looking after* his elderly parents.

A transitive phrasal verb also requires an object:

[2]   All the students have *handed in* their essays.

An intransitive phrasal verb does not require an object:

[3]   I *give up*.

We can distinguish transitive phrasal verbs from prepositional verbs by testing whether the particle can come before the object as well as after the object. The particle of a phrasal verb can take either position because it is an adverb and like most adverbs it is not confined to one position.

[2a]   All the students have *handed in* their essays.
[2b]   All the students have *handed* their essays *in*.

If the object is a personal pronoun, however, the particle in a phrasal verb normally must come after the object:

[2c]   All the students have *handed* them *in*.

On the other hand, the particle of a prepositional verb is a preposition and must always come before the object, as in [1] above and in [1a]:

[1a]   Peter is *looking after* them.

Further examples of intransitive phrasal verbs are in [4]–[6] and transitive phrasal verbs in [7]–[9]:

[4]   The discussions *went on* for a long time.
[5]   They *gave up* without a struggle.
[6]   The excitement has *died down*.
[7]   I can't *make out* their handwriting.
[7a] I can't *make* their handwriting *out*.
[8]   We should *put off* the decision until the next meeting.
[8a] We should *put* the decision *off* until the next meeting.
[9]   Cornelia has finally *brought out* her new book.
[9a] Cornelia has finally *brought* her new book *out*.

There are three types of prepositional verbs. The first type is followed by a **prepositional object**, which differs from direct and indirect objects in that a preposition introduces it:

[10]   My aunt is *looking after* my brothers.
[11]   The principal *called for* references.
[12]   Heavy smoking *leads to* cancer.

Like other objects, prepositional objects can be questioned by *who* or *what*:

[10a]   *Who* is your aunt looking after?
         My brothers.
[12a]   *What* does smoking lead to?
         Cancer.

And they can often be made the subject of a corresponding passive sentence:

[11a]   *References* were called for.

The second type of prepositional verb has two objects: a direct object and a prepositional object. The direct object comes before the particle, and the prepositional object follows the particle:

[13]   He *blamed* the accident *on* the weather.
[14]   You may *order* a drink *for* me.
[15]   I have *explained* the procedure *to* the children.
[16]   They were *making* fun *of* you.
[17]   I have just *caught* sight *of* them.

In some cases the direct object is part of an idiomatic unit, as in *make fun of* [16] and *catch sight of* [17].

The third type of prepositional verb also has two objects, but the first is an indirect object:

> They *told* us *about* your success.
> She *forgave* me *for* my rude remark.
> I *congratulated* her *on* her promotion.

The indirect object refers to a person who typically has the recipient role (cf. 3.14).

The preposition in all three types of prepositional verbs ordinarily cannot be moved from its position. But if the style is formal, in certain structures such as questions and relative clauses it may move with the object to the front. For example, the prepositional object in [13] is normally questioned like this:

[13a]   What did he blame the weather *on*?

But we could also place *on* in front, in formal style:

[13b]   *On* what did he blame the weather?

Finally, there are two types of phrasal-prepositional verbs, which have two particles (an adverb followed by a preposition). The first type has just the prepositional object:

> I have been *catching up on* my reading.
> They *look down on* their neighbours.

The second type has a direct object and a prepositional object:

I have *put* his problem *down to* inexperience.
We *put* him *up for* election.

THE ADJECTIVE PHRASE

4.21   The structure of the adjective phrase

The main word in an adjective phrase is an adjective. The structure of the typical adjective phrase may be represented in the following way, where the parentheses indicate elements of the structure that may be absent:

(pre-modifiers)   adjective   (post-modifers)

Modifiers qualify in some respect what is denoted by the adjective, and they are optional. The pre-modifer comes before the adjective and the post-modifier comes after it.

Some post-modifiers complete what is implied in the meaning of the adjective. For example, if we say *Tom is afraid* we intend this to mean that Tom is filled with fear in some respect. The post-modifier specifies in what respect:

[1]   Tom is *afraid*
$\begin{cases} \text{of spiders.} \\ \text{for his job.} \\ \text{to say anything.} \\ \text{that no one will believe him.} \end{cases}$

A few adjectives (at least in certain senses) must have a post-modifier:

[2]   Mary is *fond* of us.
[3]   I am *aware* that he is abroad.
[4]   The contract is *subject* to approval by my committee.

Some adjectives that take obligatory post-modifiers resemble verbs in their meaning:

[1a]   Tom *fears* that no one will believe him.
[2a]   Mary *likes* us.
[3a]   I *know* that he is abroad.
[4a]   The contract *requires* approval by my committee.

Here are some examples of possible structures of adjective phrases:

adjective	*happy*
pre-modifier + adjective	*very happy*
adjective + post-modifier	*happy to see you*
pre-modifier + adjective + post-modifier	*very happy that you could join us.*

4.22   Functions

These are the main possible functions of adjective phrases:

1. pre-modifier in a noun phrase
   Our *former* enemies and allies are now our *economic* competitors.
2. subject complement
   The photographs were *quite professional.*
3. object complement
   My parents made me *aware of my my filial responsibilities.*
4. post-modifier in a noun phrase
   I saw something *bizarre* on my way to school yesterday.

Indefinite pronouns, such as *somebody*, require the adjective phrase to follow them:

I bought something *quite expensive* today.
You should choose somebody older.

There are also some set expressions (mostly legal or official designations) where the adjective follows the noun:

heir *apparent*	attorney *general*
court *martial*	notary *public*

Here are a few further examples of adjective phrases as post-modifiers:

the earliest time *possible*
in years *past*
the officials *present*
the people *involved*

Central adjectives are adjectives that can fulfil all the four possible functions. There are also some adjectives that can be only pre-modifiers and others that cannot be pre-modifiers (cf. 5.13).

Adjectives can be partially converted into nouns and then like nouns can function as heads of noun phrases. Typically, such phrases refer to well-established classes of persons, such as *the handicapped, the poor, the sick, the unemployed, the young*. Nationality adjectives are commonly used in this way, too: *the British, the English, the French, the Irish*. These noun phrases are plural, even though the adjectives do not have a plural ending:

> *The sick* <u>require</u> immediate attention.
> *The British* <u>are</u> coming.

Some adjectives, particularly superlatives (cf. 5.14), function as heads of noun phrases that are abstract. These noun phrases are singular:

> *The latest* <u>is</u> that our team is winning .
> *The best* <u>is</u> yet to come.

Here are a few common examples of such phrases in set expressions:

> <u>from</u> *the sublime* <u>to</u> *the ridiculous*
> <u>out of</u> *the ordinary*
> We have much <u>in</u> *common.*
> I'm leaving <u>for</u> *good*
> I'll tell you <u>in</u> *private.*
> The situation is going <u>from</u> *bad* <u>to</u> *worse.*

THE ADVERB PHRASE

4.23   The structure of the adverb phrase

The main word in an adverb phrase is an adverb. The structure of the typical adverb phrase is similar to that of the typical adjective phrase except for the class of the main word.

(pre-modifiers)   adverb   (post-modifiers)

Here are some examples of possible structures of adverb phrases:

adverb	*surprisingly*
pre-modifier + adverb	*very surprisingly*
adverb + post-modifier	*surprisingly for her*
pre-modifier + adverb + post-modifier	*very surprisingly indeed*

4.24   Functions

Adverbs have two main types of functions, but particular adverbs may have only one of these:

1. modifier of an adjective or an adverb in phrase structure
2. adverbial in sentence structure

Here are examples of adverbs as modifiers:

1. **modifier of an adjective**
   The description was *remarkably* accurate.
2. **modifier of an adverb**
   The new drug was hailed, *somewhat* prematurely, as the penicillin of the 1990s.

Semantically, most of the modifiers are *intensifiers* (cf. 5.14). They express the degree to which the meaning of the adjective or adverb applies on an assumed scale. The most common modifier is *very*.

Adverbs are commonly used as adverbials in sentence structure:

> *Fortunately*, American automobile manufacturers are *now* concentrating on improvements in economy and safety.
> *Certainly* we should be grateful for the ways in which he *inadvertently* challenged our beliefs, *deeply* and *seriously*.

Some adverbials seem to be closely linked to the verb or perhaps the predicate, as in *She spoke vigorously* or *She spoke her mind vigorously*, but it is difficult to be precise about the scope of such adverbials. For the range of meanings of adverbials, see 3.14.

Many adverbs can function both as modifiers and as adverbials. The intensifier *entirely* is a modifier of an adjective in [1] and an adverbial in [2]:

[1]   Michael's amendment is *entirely* acceptable.
[2]   I *entirely* agree with you.

THE PREPOSITIONAL PHRASE

4.25 The structure of the prepositional phrase

The prepositional phrase is a structure with two parts:

preposition	complement

The **prepositional complement** is typically a noun phrase, but it may also be a nominal relative clause (cf. 6.9) or an -*ing* clause (cf. 6.8). Both the nominal relative clause and the -*ing* clause have a range of functions similar to that of a noun phrase.

1. complement as noun phrase
   through *the window*
2. complement as nominal relative clause
   from *what I heard* ('from that which I heard')
3. complement as -*ing* clause
   after *speaking to you*

As its name suggests ('preceding position'), the preposition normally comes before the prepositional complement. There are several exceptions, however, where the complement is moved and the preposition is left stranded by itself. The stranding is obligatory when the complement is transformed into the subject of the sentence:

> Your case will soon be attended *to*.
> This ball is for you to play *with*.
> The picture is worth looking *at*.

In questions and relative clauses the prepositional complement may be a pronoun or adverb that is fronted. In that case, the preposition is normally stranded:

> Who are you waiting *for*?
> Where are you coming *from*?
> I am the person (that) you are waiting *for*? [In relative clauses the pronoun may be omitted.]

In formal style the preposition is fronted with its complement:

> *For* whom are you waiting?
> *From* where are you coming?

I am the person *for* <u>whom</u> you are waiting.

4.26   Functions

Prepositional phrases have three main functions: post-modifier of a noun in phrase structure; post-modifier of an adjective in phrase structure; adverbial in sentence structure:

1. **post-modifier of a noun**
   I took several <u>courses</u> *in history*.
   The local council is subsidising the <u>installation</u> *of energy-saving devices*.
2. **post-modifier of an adjective**
   We were not <u>aware</u> *of his drinking problem*.
   I was <u>happy</u> *with my marks* last term.
3. **adverbial**
   In my opinion, people behave differently *in crowds*.
   In actual fact, the economy was showing signs of improvement *by 1985*.

Two or more prepositional phrases may appear independently side by side. Here is a sentence with three prepositional phrases, each a separate adverbial:

She was re-elected *in Finchley* (A) *in 1987* (A) *by a large majority* (A). One prepositional phrase may also be embedded within another, as in this prepositional phrase that post-modifies the noun *variations*:

There were <u>variations</u> *in the degree of bitterness of taste*.
The embedding can be shown in this way:

prepositional phrase	in the degree of bitterness of taste
noun phrase	the degree of bitterness of taste
prepositional phrase	of bitterness of taste
noun phrase	bitterness of taste
prepositional phrase	of taste

5

Word Classes

5.1   Open and Closed Classes

When we looked at phrases in Chapter 4, we often referred to classes of
words such as noun and adjective. Word classes are traditionally called
parts of speech. There is not a fixed number of word classes. We can set
up as many classes and subclasses as we need for our analysis. The more
detailed our analysis, the more classes and subclasses we need.

Word classes can be divided into **open classes** and **closed
classes**. Open classes are readily open to new words; closed classes are
limited classes that rarely admit new words. For example, it is easy to
create new nouns, but not new pronouns.

Listed below, with examples, are the classes that we will be examining in this chapter. They will be further divided into subclasses.

Open classes

noun	*Paul, paper, speech, play*
adjective	*young, cheerful, dark, round*
main verb	*talk, become, like, play*
adverb	*carefully, firmly, confidentially*

Closed classes

pronoun	*she, somebody, one, who, that*
determiner	*a, the, that, each, some*
auxiliary (verb)	*can, may, will, have, be, do*
conjunction	*and, that, in order that, if, though*
preposition	*of, at, to, in spite of*

There are also some more minor classes, such as the numerals (*one,
twenty-three, first*) and the interjections (*oh, ah, ouch*). And there are some

words that do not fit anywhere and should be treated individually, such as the negative *not* and the infinitive marker *to* (as in *to say*).

The conjunction *in order that* and the preposition *in spite of* are complex words even though each is written as three separate words.

5.2   Word Classes and Word Uses

In 5.1 some examples are listed in more than one class. For instance, *play* is both a noun and a verb; *that* is a pronoun, a determiner, and a conjunction. Many more examples could have been given of multiple membership of word classes. We can identify the class of some words by their form, as we will see in later sections of this chapter. But very often we can tell the class of a word only from its use in a context. *Reply* is a noun in:

[1]   I expect a *reply* before the end of the month.

It is a verb in:

[2]   You should *reply* before the end of the month.

It is particularly easy to convert nouns to verbs and to convert verbs to nouns.

Reply in [1] and [2] represents two different words that share the same form. They are two different words, though related in meaning; they are entered as separate words in dictionaries ('lexicons').

If words happen to share the same form and are not related in meaning at all, they are **homonyms**; examples are *peer* ('person belonging to the same group in age and status') and *peer* ('look searchingly'), or *peep* ('make a feeble shrill sound') and *peep* ('look cautiously'). We can make further distinctions if we wish to emphasize identity in pronunciation or identity in spelling. If homonyms share the same sound but perhaps differ in spelling, they are **homophones**; examples are *weigh* and *way* or *none* and *nun*. On the other hand, if they share the same spelling but perhaps differ in pronunciation, they are **homographs**; examples are *row* ('line of objects') and *row* ('quarrel').

A word may have more than one grammatical form. The noun *play* has the singular *play* and the plural *plays*; the verb *play* has the base form *play* and the past *played*. It is common usage to use *word* for the grammatical form, so we can say that the past of the word *see* is *saw* and we can also say that the word *saw* is spelled with a final *w*. Sometimes there is **neutralization** in form: rather than having the distinctions found in most words, some words have only one neutral form. For example, the verb *cut* represents at least three grammatical words:

present tense   I always *cut* my steak with this kind of knife.
past tense   I *cut* my finger earlier today.
past participle I have *cut* my finger.

The examples of word classes in 5.1 are 'lexical' words (listed as main entries in dictionaries), but they include any associated grammatical forms.

We recognize the class of a word by its use in context. Some words have **suffixes** (endings added to words to form new words) that help to signal the class they belong to. These suffixes are not necessarily sufficient. For example, *-ly* is a typical suffix for adverbs (*slowly, proudly*), but we also find this suffix in adjectives: *cowardly, kindly*. And we can sometimes convert words from one class to another even though they have suffixes that are typical of their original class: *an engineer, to engineer; a politic behaviour, to politic; a hopeful candidate, a hopeful.*

NOUNS   11/11/19

5.3   Noun Suffixes

A noun is a word that can be the only or main word in a noun phrase (cf. 4.2). We cannot identify all nouns merely by their form, but certain suffixes can be added to verbs or adjectives to make nouns. Here are a few typical noun suffixes with words that exemplify them:

-tion (and variants)	*education, relation, invasion, revision*
-er, -or	*camper, speaker; actor, supervisor*
-ing	*building, writing*
-ity	*mentality, normality, reality, sanity*
-ness	*happiness, compactness*

Some suffixes were part of the words when they were borrowed from other languages: *doctor, eternity, courage.*

5.4   Noun Classes

Nouns are **common** or **proper**. Proper nouns are the names of specific people, places, or occasions, and they usually begin with a capital letter: *Shakespeare, Chicago, January, Christmas*. Names may consist of more than one word: *The Hague, The New York Times, Kennedy Airport, Captain Andrews, Mount Everest*. Proper nouns are sometimes converted into common nouns: *the Thompsons I know*; the proper noun *Thompson* cannot ordinarily be made plural, but here *the Thompsons* means 'the people in the family with the name Thompson'. Common nouns are nouns that are not names, such as *capital* in:

The *capital* of the Netherlands is The Hague.

Common nouns can be subclassified in two ways:

1. type of referent: concrete and abstract
2. grammatical form: count and non-count

Concrete nouns refer to people, places, or things: *girl, kitchen, car*. Abstract nouns refer to qualities, states, or actions: *humour, belief, action*. Some nouns may be either concrete or abstract, depending on their meaning:

concrete Thomas can kick a *football* 50 yards.
abstract Jeremy often plays *football* on Saturdays.

There is a tendency for abstract nouns to be non-count.

Count nouns refer to entities that are viewed as countable. Count nouns therefore have both a singular and a plural and they can be accompanied by determiners that refer to distinctions in number:

$$
\left.\begin{array}{l} a \\ one \\ every \end{array}\right\} \text{student}
\qquad
\left.\begin{array}{l} ten \\ many \\ those \end{array}\right\} \text{students}
$$

Non-count nouns refer to entities that are viewed as a mass that cannot be counted; for example, *bread, furniture, music*. Non-count nouns are treated as singular and can be accompanied only by determiners that do not refer to distinctions in number:

$$
\left.\begin{array}{l} much \\ your \\ that \end{array}\right\} \text{information}
$$

Determiners such as *the* and *your* can go with both count and non-count nouns. Others can go only with singular count nouns (*a*) or only with plural count nouns (*those*).

Some nouns may be either count or non-count, depending on their meaning:

> There is not enough *light* in here.
> We need another couple of *lights*.
> Sandra does not have much *difficulty* with science.
> Benjamin is having great *difficulties* with arithmetic.

Nouns that are ordinarily non-count can be converted into count nouns with two types of special use:

1. When the count noun refers to different kinds:

   > The store has a large selection of *cheeses*.

2. When the count noun refers to units that are obvious in the situation.

   > I'll have two *coffees*, please. ('two cups of coffee')

5.5 Number

Count nouns make a distinction between singular and plural. The regular plural ends in -*s*. This inflection (grammatical suffix), however, is pronounced in one of three ways, depending on the sound immediately before it. Contrast these three sets:

1. *buses, bushes, churches, pages, diseases, garages*
2. *sums, machines, days, toes*
3. *tanks, patients, shocks, notes*

The plural inflection is pronounced as a separate syllable - spelled -*es* - when it follows any of the sounds that appear in the singulars of the words listed in (1); in the case of *diseases* and *garages*, a final -*e* is already present in the singular, so only an -*s* needs to be added in the plural. When -*s* is added to form the plurals *toes* in (2) and *notes* in (3), the -*es* is not pronounced as a separate syllable. There are also some other exceptions to the usual -*s* spelling. (See also A.4 in the Appendix.)

There are a few irregular plurals that reflect older English forms:

> *man – men*   *mouse – mice*
> *woman – women*   *louse – lice*

foot – feet	*brother – brethren* (in special senses)
goose – geese	*child – children*
tooth – teeth	*ox – oxen*

There are a large number of classes of other irregular plurals, many of them having foreign plurals (e.g. *stimulus – stimuli; curriculum – curricula; crisis – crises*).

5.6   Gender

Relatively few nouns are distinguished in **gender**, but there are some male nouns and female nouns; for example:

father – mother	*widower – widow*
boy – girl	*bridegroom – bride*
host – hostess	*bull – cow*
hero – heroine	*lion – lioness*

Important distinctions in gender, however, apply to the third-person singular pronouns *he, she,* and *it* (cf. 5.18).

When *he* or *she* refers to a noun, the sex of the specific person or animal is made manifest (but see 8.6):

> *The student* was absent today because *she* attended an interview for a job.

5.7   Case

Nouns make a distinction in **case**: a distinction that is based on the grammatical function of the noun. Nouns have two cases: the **common case** and the **genitive case**. The common case is the one that is used ordinarily. The genitive case generally indicates that the noun is dependent on the noun that follows it; this case often corresponds to a structure with *of*:

> *Jane's* reactions – the reactions *of Jane*

For regular nouns the genitive is indicated in writing by an apostrophe plus *s* (*student's*) in the singular and by an apostrophe following the plural *-s* inflection in the plural (*students'*):

	singular	**plural**
common case	the *student*	the *students*
genitive case	the *student's* suggestions	the *students'* suggestions

In speech, three of these forms are pronounced identically.

Irregular nouns, however, distinguish all four forms in speech as well as in writing:

	singular	**plural**
common case	the *child*	the *children*
genitive case	the *child's* suggestions	the *children's* suggestions

The same genitive inflection (*'s*) is attached to both the singular and the plural.

On the rules for placing the apostrophe after words ending in -*s*, see 7.13.

5.8   Dependent and Independent Genitives

Genitives may be dependent or independent. The **dependent genitive** functions like a possessive determiner (cf. 5.19). Compare:

> *the student's* suggestions (dependent genitive)
> t*heir* suggestions (possessive determiner)

The **independent genitive** is not dependent on a following noun. The noun may be omitted because it can be understood from the context:

> Your ideas are more acceptable than *Sandra's*. ('Sandra's ideas')
> David's comments are like *Peter's*.

But the independent genitive is also used to refer to places:

> The party's at *Alan's* tonight.
> She's gone to *the hairdresser's*.

Finally, the independent genitive may combine with the *of*-structure:

> a friend of *Martha's*
> a suggestion of *Norman's*

The independent genitive in the *of*-structure differs from the normal genitive in its meaning: *Martha's friend* means 'the friend that Martha has' (the speaker assumes that the hearer knows the identity of the friend), whereas *a friend of Martha's* means 'one of the friends that Martha has'.

MAIN VERBS

5.9   Verb Suffixes

A main verb (or, more simply, a verb) is a word that can be the main word in a verb phrase and is often the only verb (cf. 4.11). Certain suffixes are added to nouns or adjectives to make main verbs. Here are a few common verb suffixes with words that exemplify them:

-ate, iate	*chlorinate, originate, differentiate*
-en	*darken, hasten, sadden*
-ify, -fy	*codify, falsify, beautify*
-ise, -ize	*apologise, publicise, rationalize*

Like nouns, very many verbs have no suffixes: *write, walk, reveal, understand*. Many of the suffixes that characterize verbs served that function in Latin or French, and so we have words in English that were already suffixed when they were borrowed from these languages: *signify, realize*.

5.10   Regular and Irregular Verbs

I earlier (4.12) distinguished five forms of verbs. In all regular verbs (such as *laugh*) and in many irregular verbs (such as *hear*) forms 4 and 5 below are identical. In one set of irregular verbs (e.g. *cut*) forms 1, 4, and 5 are identical. The full set of five forms appears in the irregular verb *speak*.

1.	base form:	*laugh*	*hear*	*cut*	*speak*
2.	*-s* form:	*laughs*	*hears*	*cuts*	*speaks*
3.	*-ing* participle:	*laughing*	*hearing*	*cutting*	*speaking*
4.	past form:	*laughed*	*heard*	*cut*	*spoke*
5.	*-ed* participle:	*laughed*	*heard*	*cut*	*spoken*

The highly irregular verb *be* has eight forms (cf. 4.12).

Possible contexts for the five forms of *speak* are illustrated below:

1a. I *speak* French. All of them *speak* French. [present tense except for 3rd person singular, cf. 4.13]

b. I can *speak* French. Do you want to *speak* French? [infinitive, cf. 4.18]

c. *Speak* to me. [imperative, cf. 4.19]

d. She insisted that he *speak* to her. [present subjunctive, cf. 4.19]

2. She *speaks* French. [3rd person singular present tense, cf. 4.13]

3a. She's *speaking* too fast. [progressive aspect in combination with auxiliary *be*, cf. 4.14]

b. *Speaking* in public makes me nervous. [verb in *-ing* clause, cf. 6.8]

4. I *spoke* to them about your idea. [past tense, cf. 4.13]

5a. She has *spoken* to me about it. [perfect aspect in combination with auxiliary *have*, cf. 4.14]

b. English is *spoken* here. [passive voice in combination with auxiliary *be*, cf. 4.15]

c. When *spoken* slowly, the dialect is understood by other speakers of the language [verb in *-ed* clause, cf. 6.8]

5.11   Classes of Irregular Verbs

There are over 250 irregular verbs. Apart from the verb *be*, the *-s* form and the *-ing* participle can be predicted for all verbs from the base form. We therefore need list only three forms to show irregularities: the base, past, and *-ed* participle. These three forms are known as the **principal parts** of the verb. If we leave aside the verb *be*, we can group the irregular verbs into seven classes according to whether or not three features apply to their principal parts: (a) the past and *-ed* participles are identical; (b) the base vowel is the same in the other two principal parts; (c) the past and *-ed* participle have inflectional endings. If an irregular verb has inflectional endings, these may be irregular; for example, *kept* from *keep* or *spoken* from *speak*.

Table 5.1 sets out in columns the three features and shows whether they apply ('+') or not ('-') to each of the seven classes of irregular verbs. The '±' for classes II indicates that some verbs in the class do not have the specified feature. The '½' for class IV indicates that the verbs have an inflectional ending in the participle (*spoken*) but not in the past (*spoke*).

Table 5.1   Classes of irregular verbs

		Past = participle	All vowels identical	Inflections
I.	*burn, burnt, burnt*	+	+	+
II.	*saw, sawed, sawn*	–	±	+
III.	*keep, kept, kept*	+	–	+
IV.	*speak, spoke, spoken*	–	–	½
V.	*cut, cut, cut*	+	+	–
VI.	*feed, fed, fed*	+	–	–
VII.	*drink, drank, drunk*	–	–	–

I give further examples of irregular verbs in each of the classes.

I.		
	bend bent bent	*earn earnt earnt*
	build built built	*learn learnt learnt*
	have had had	*smell smelt smelt*
	make made made	*spoil spoilt spoilt*

Those in the second column also have regular variants: *earn, earned, earned.*

II.		
	mow mowed mown	*shear sheared shorn*
	show showed shown	*swell swelled swollen*

The past is formed regularly, but the participle has an *-n* inflection. Those in the second column have a different vowel in the participle, hence '±' in the table. All the verbs have regular variants for the participle: *mow, mowed, mowed.*

III.		
	buy bought bought	*dream dreamt dreamt*
	hear heard heard	*kneel knelt knelt*
	lose lost lost	*lean leant leant*
	say said said	*leap leapt leapt*

Those in the second column also have regular variants: *dream, dreamed, dreamed.*

IV.		
	blow blew blown	*see saw seen*
	break broke broken	*take took taken*
	hide hid hidden	*tear tore torn*
	lie lay lain	*write wrote written*

The participle has an *-n* inflection, but not the past, hence '½' in Table 5.1. In some verbs (e.g. *blow*) the participle has the same vowel as the base; in some (e.g. *break*) the past and participle have the same vowel; in some (e.g. *write*) all the vowels are different. The verb *beat* has the same vowel in all parts (*beat, beat, beaten*), but it may be included in this class rather than in class II because it is not inflected in the past.

V.   *burst   fit*
      hit   rid
      hurt   sweat
      let   wet

All three principal parts are identical. Those in the second column also have regular variants: *fit, fitted, fitted,* as well as *fit, fit, fit.*

VI.   *bleed bled bled   get got got*
       dig dug dug   hold held held
       find found found   strike struck struck
       fight fought fought   win won won

The past and participle are identical, but there is a change from the base vowel and no inflections. A few verbs in this class have regular variants: *light, lighted, lighted,* as well as *light, lit, lit.*

VII   *begin began begun   come came come*
       sing sang sung   run ran run

Those in the second column have the same vowel in the base and the participle. Some verbs also have variants in which the past and participle are identical: *sing, sung, sung,* as well as *sing, sang, sung.*

ADJECTIVES

5.12   Adjective Suffixes

An adjective is a word that can be the only or main word in an adjective phrase (cf. 4.21). A large number of suffixes are added to nouns and verbs to make adjectives. Here are the most common suffixes and words that exemplify them:

-able, -ible	*disposable, suitable, fashionable, audible*
-al, -ial	*normal, cynical, racial, editorial*
-ed	*wooded, boarded, aged, crooked*
-ful	*hopeful, playful, careful, forgetful*
-ic	*romantic, atmospheric, heroic, atomic*
-ical	*historical, political, paradoxical, economical*
-ish	*amateurish, darkish, foolish, childish*
-ive, -ative	*defective, communicative, attractive, affirmative*
-less	*tactless, hopeless, harmless, restless*
-ous, -eous, -ious	*famous, virtuous, erroneous, spacious*
-y	*tasty, handy, wealthy, really*

The suffix *-ed* is often used to form adjectives from noun phrases: *blue-eyed, goodnatured, open-minded, open-ended*.

Like nouns and verbs, many adjectives have no suffixes: *sad, young, happy*. Some suffixes were part of the words when they were borrowed into English: *sensitive, virtuous*.

5.13   Adjective Classes

We can divide adjectives into three classes according to their function. Used alone or with one or more modifiers, an adjective can be:

1. pre-modifier of a noun
2. subject complement
3. object complement

Adjectives are **attributive** (attributing a quality to what is denoted by a noun) when they are being used as pre-modifiers. They are **predicative** (part of the predicate) when they are being used as complements.

Central adjectives can be used in all three functions:

1. It was a *comfortable* ride.   –   **attributive**
2. The ride was *comfortable*.   } **predicative**
3. I made the bed *comfortable*.

Other examples of central adjectives: *clever, brave, calm, hungry, noisy*.
Some adjectives are attributive only:

That is *utter* nonsense.
You are the *very* person I was looking for.

Other examples: *chief, main, sheer.* Many words are restricted in this way only in particular meanings. *Old* is only attributive in:

> She is an *old* friend of mine. ('a friend for many years')

It is a central adjective in:

> She is an *old* woman.
> She is *old*.
> I consider her *old*.

Some adjectives are predicative only:

> He is *afraid* of dogs.
> I am *glad* that you are here.

Some predicative adjectives must be followed by a post-modifier (cf. 4.21): *aware* (*of* + noun phrase), *loath* (*to* + infinitive), *subject* (*to* + noun phrase). Some words have this restriction only with particular meanings. *Happy* is only predicative in:

> We are *happy* to see you.

It is a central adjective in:

> He has a *happy* disposition.
> His disposition is *happy*.
> We made him *happy*.

5.14   Gradability and Comparison

Adjectives are typically **gradable**: We can arrange them on a scale. So we can say that something is *a bit hot, somewhat hot, quite hot, very hot,* or *extremely hot*. We can also compare things and say that something is *hotter* than something else or that it is the *hottest* of a number of things.

We use **intensifiers** to indicate the point on the scale. The most common intensifier of adjectives is the adverb *very*. Other examples of intensifiers in addition to those already given include:

fairly pleasant	*entirely* happy
pretty difficult	*incredibly* dull
rather dark	*too* long

There are three degrees of comparison:

1. higher

   (a)   Ann is *politer than* Michael. (**comparative**)
   (b)   Ann is the *politest* child in the family. (**superlative**)

We have a three-term contrast: **absolute**, *polite*; **comparative**, *politer,*
– *more polite;* **superlative,** *politest,* – *most polite.*

2. same

   Ann is *as happy as* Michael.

3. lower

   (a)   Ann is *less friendly than* Michael.
   (b)   Ann is the *least friendly* child in the family.

The superlatives in (1b) and (3b) are required when the comparison involves more than two units or sets of units.

Higher degrees of comparison are expressed either through the inflections *-er* and *-est* or through the pre-modifiers *more* and *most*:

	absolute	**comparative**	**superlative**
inflection	*polite*	*politer*	*politest*
pre-modifier	*polite*	*more polite*	*most polite*

There are a few common adjectives that have irregular inflections:

good				
well	('healthy')	}	*better* –	*best*
bad	–	*worse*	–	worst
far	{	*farther*	–	farthest
		further	–	furthest

Words of one syllable generally take inflections: *older, oldest; purer,*
purest. Many words of two syllables can take either form: *politer, politest* or
more polite, most polite; noisier, noisiest or *more noisy, most noisy.* Words
that are longer than two syllables take the pre-modifiers: *more impolite,*
most impolite.

ADVERBS

5.15   Adverb Suffixes

An adverb is a word that can be the only or main word in an adverb phrase (cf. 4.23). The suffix *-ly* is commonly added to adjectives to make adverbs:

> *calmly, frankly, lightly, madly, tearfully*

If the adjective ends in *-ic*, the suffix is usually *-ically*:

> *economically, geographically, heroically, romantically*

The exception is *publicly*.

The suffix *-wise* is added to nouns to make adverbs:

> *clockwise, lengthwise, moneywise, weatherwise*

Like the other word classes, many adverbs have no suffixes. These include, in particular, most time adverbs (*now, afterwards*), space adverbs (*here, outside*), and 'linking adverbs' (*therefore, however*).

5.16   Gradability and Comparison

Like adjectives, adverbs are typically gradable and can therefore be modified by intensifiers and take comparison (cf. 5.14): *quite calmly, very calmly, less calmly, most calmly*. Most adverbs that take comparison require the pre-modifiers *more* and *most*. Those adverbs that have the same form as adjectives have the inflections (e.g. *late – later – latest*). The following adverbs have irregular inflections; the first three are identical with those for adjectives:

well	–	*better*	–	*best*
badly	–	*worse*	–	*worst*
far	{	*farther*	–	*farthest*
		further	–	*furthest*
little	–	*less*	–	*least*
much	–	*more*	–	*most*

PRONOUNS

5.17   Pronoun Classes

Pronouns are essentially special types of nouns and are the main word in a noun phrase or (more usually) the only word in a noun phrase. They fall into a number of classes, here listed with examples:

1. **personal pronouns**   *I, you*
2. **possessive pronouns**   *mine, yours*
3. **reflexive pronouns**   *myself, yourself*
4. **demonstrative pronouns**   *this, these; that, those*
5. **reciprocal pronouns**   *each other; one another*
6. **interrogative pronouns**   *who, what*
7. **relative pronouns**   *who, that*
8. **indefinite pronouns**   *some, none*

The first three classes are related in that they make distinctions in **person** (first, second, third), **gender** (masculine, feminine, and non-personal), and **number** (singular and plural). Most of them also share at least some resemblance in their sound and in their appearance (*you, yours, yourself*).

Pronouns generally substitute for a noun phrase:

> I went around the hospital with Dr Thomas. *He* was highly intelligent, austere, and warm all at the same time. *He* could perceive almost instantaneously whether a problem was a serious *one* or not.

The two instances of *He* refer back to an **antecedent** (something that came before), in this instance *Dr Thomas*. The pronouns are used to avoid repeating the noun phrase *Dr Thomas*. *One*, however, replaces the noun head *problem* (and therefore is literally a pronoun rather than a substitute for a noun phrase). Here is another example of pronoun substitution:

> A property development company has been found guilty of racial discrimination because *it* attempted to prevent blacks from buying its homes.

In this case the pronoun *it* replaces a noun phrase that is not identical with the antecedent noun phrase *A property development company*. If we did not substitute *it*, we would have to write *the property development company* (with the definite article *the*) or (more economically) *the company*.

The pronoun occasionally comes before its antecedent:

> When *she* moved into *her* own flat, Cindy seemed much more relaxed.

If we assume that the pronoun *she* and *Cindy* refer to the same person, *she* and the possessive determiner *her* (cf. 5.19) both refer forward to *Cindy*.

Pronouns can also refer directly to something that is present in the situation:

> Look at *that*!
> I'll pick *it* up.

5.18 Personal Pronouns

All the personal pronouns have distinctions in person (first, second, third). Most also have distinctions in number (singular, plural) and in case (subjective, objective, genitive). For the genitive case of the personal pronouns, see the possessive determiners (5.19).

		subjective case	**objective case**
first person			
singular		*I*	*me*
plural		*we*	*us*
second person			
singular/plural		*you*	*you*
third person			
singular	– masculine	*he*	*him*
	– feminine	*she*	*her*
	– non-personal	*it*	*it*
plural		*they*	*them*

The subjective case applies when the pronouns are the subject of a finite clause:

> *I* know that *she* lives in Coventry and that *he* lives in Birmingham.

In all other instances except the one that I am about to mention, the objective case is used:

> She knows *me* well.
> He has told *her* about me.
> You must go with *him*.

The exception is that the subjective case is also used for the subject complement. In these examples the complement follows the linking verb *be*:

> This is *he*.
> It is *I* who issued the order.

In non-formal style, however, the objective case is usual here too:

> It's *me*.

The masculine and feminine genders apply to human beings and also to other beings that are treated as persons, such as pets or perhaps some farm animals. The distinction between the two genders is made on the basis of natural distinctions in sex. Some other objects (such as ships or cars) or even personified abstractions (such as Death or Beauty) may be treated as if they were persons. Otherwise, the non-personal pronoun *it* is used. One exceptional use of *it* is for babies whose sex is unknown to the speaker.

The personal pronouns take modifiers to a limited extent:

> *you* <u>who know me</u>   *we* <u>in this country</u>
> *you* <u>there</u>   *they* <u>both</u>

5.19   Possessives

The possessives are the genitives of the personal pronouns. There are two sets. One set contains the **possessive determiners**, a subclass of determiners (cf. 5.26f.). A possessive determiner is dependent on a noun:

> Here is *your* book.

The other set of possessives contains the **possessive pronouns,** a subclass of pronouns. A possessive pronoun functions independently:

> This book is *yours.*

The possessive determiners are not pronouns, but it is convenient to deal
with them in this section because of the parallels between the two sets of
possessives.

Nouns in the genitive case also have these two functions (cf. 5.7):

> Here is *Geoffrey's* book. (dependent genitive)
> This book is *Geoffrey's.* (independent genitive)

But unlike the nouns, most of the possessives have separate forms for the
dependent and independent functions. The two sets of forms parallel the
forms for the personal pronouns (5.18).

first person
singular			*my*	*mine*
plural			*our*	*ours*

second person
singular/plural			*your*	*yours*

third person
singular	–	masculine	*his*	*his*
	–	feminine	*her*	*hers*
	–	non-personal	*its*	*its*
plural			*their*	*theirs*

5.20   Reflexive Pronouns

The reflexive pronouns parallel the personal and possessive pronouns in
person and number but have no distinctions in case. There are separate
forms for the second person singular (*yourself*) and plural (*yourselves*),
whereas there is only one form of the second person for the personal pronoun (*you*) and the possessive pronoun (*yours*).

first person
singular	*myself*
plural	*ourselves*

second person

singular   *yourself*
plural   *yourselves*

third person

singular – masculine   *himself*
          – feminine   *herself*
          – non-personal   *itself*
plural   *themselves*

The reflexives have two main uses:

1. They refer to the same person or thing as the subject does:
   They behaved *themselves* for a change.
   You'll hurt *yourself*.

2. They give emphasis to a noun phrase:
   She *herself* spoke to me.
   He wrote to me *himself*.
   I appealed to the captain *himself*.

5.21   Demonstrative Pronouns

There are four demonstrative pronouns:

singular	*this*	*that*
plural	*these*	*those*

This is for you.
You may take *those*.

The demonstratives may also be determiners (cf. 5.26*f*):

This letter is for you.

5.22   Reciprocal Pronouns

There are two reciprocal pronouns, and they have genitives:

each other	*one another*
each other's	*one another's*

The partners trusted *each other* fully.
My brother and I borrow *one another's* ties.

5.23   Interrogative Pronouns

One set of the interrogative pronouns has distinctions in gender and case:

	subjective case	objective case	genitive case
personal	*who*	*whom*	*whose*

It is normal to use *who* for both the subjective and objective cases, and to reserve *whom* for formal style (cf. 8.18). The other interrogative pronouns, *which* and *what*, have only one form. *Which*, *what*, and *whose* may also be determiners (cf. 5.26f.). We use *who* and *whom* when we refer to persons:

> *Who* is your favourite pop singer?
> *Who* (or *whom*) have they appointed?
> *Whose* is that towel?

Which can be either personal or non-personal:

> *Which* is your sister?
> *Which* (of the drinks) do you prefer?

What is normally only non-personal:

> *What* do you want?

5.24   Relative Pronouns

Relative pronouns introduce relative clauses (cf. 4.5). They also have distinctions in gender and case:

	subjective case	objective case	genitive case
Personal	*who*	*whom*	*whose*
Non-personal	*which*	*which*	*whose*
	that	*that*	

As with the interrogative pronouns (cf. 5.23), *who* is the normal form for the subjective and objective cases, whereas *whom* is used only in formal style. The relative pronoun *that*, which is gender-neutral, may be omitted in certain circumstances. The omitted pronoun is sometimes called the **zero relative pronoun**.

> the teacher *who* (or *that) taught me Chemistry*
> the house *which* (or *that* or zero) *we bought*
> the person *whom* (or, less formally, *who that*, or zero) they appointed
> the student to *whom* you gave it (formal)
> the student *who* (or *that* or zero) you gave it to

Genitive *whose* is a determiner, like *his* or *her*.

There is another set of relative pronouns that introduce **nominal relative clauses** (cf. 6.9); these are the **nominal relative pronouns**. In addition to *who*, *whom*, and *which*, they include *whoever*, *whomever* (in formal style), *whichever*, *what*, and *whatever*.

$$\text{You may take} \begin{Bmatrix} \textit{which} \\ \textit{whichever} \\ \textit{what} \\ \textit{whatever} \end{Bmatrix} \underline{\text{you wish.}}$$

> *What* I need is a period of peace and quiet.
> I'll speak to *whoever* is in charge.

Nominal relative pronouns correspond to a combination of a relative pronoun with a preceding antecedent (cf. 5.17):

> *What* I need . . . ('the thing that I need')
> . . . to *whoever* is in charge ('to the person who is in charge')

5.25   Indefinite Pronouns and Numerals

Indefinite pronouns are the largest group of pronouns. They refer to the presence (or absence) of a quantity. Most of the same words function as indefinite determiners.

Here are some examples of indefinite pronouns:

> *Many* have replied to the advertisement and *several* have been interviewed.
> You take *one* and I'll take the *the other*.

No one was absent today.
More will be arriving later.
You can have *both*.
Either will do for me.
There are *fewer* here today.
Everybody was pleased with the speech.

The *some*-set of indefinite pronouns contrasts with the *any*-set:

some	*any*
someone	*anyone*
somebody	*anybody*
something	*anything*

The *any*-set is normal in negative contexts. Contrast:

She has *some* close friends.
She doesn't have *any* close friends.

Some implies a specific quantity, though the quantity is not specified. *Any* does not imply a specific quantity; the quantity is without limit. The *any*-set is also normal in questions unless a positive reply is expected:

Did *anyone* call for me?
Did *someone* call for me?

Two uses of indefinite *one* deserve special mention:

1. *One* has the meaning 'people in general':

If *one* is concerned about the increasing deterioration of the environment, *one* must be prepared to accept a lower standard of living.

2. *One* is a substitute for a noun:

A: Do you want an ice cream?
B: I think I'll take a small *one*.

Unlike most pronouns, *one* in the response by B substitutes for a noun, not a noun phrase. It is the main word in the noun phrase *a small one*.

Many of the indefinite pronouns may be post-modified. *Of*-phrases are particularly common:

somebody <u>else</u>   *neither* <u>of us</u>
several <u>in our group</u>   *half* <u>of your class</u>
something <u>quite funny</u>   *a few* <u>of my friends.</u>

Numerals may be used as pronouns. Here are two examples of **cardinal numerals** as pronouns:

> *Twenty-two* were rescued from the sinking ship.
> *Three* <u>of the children</u> wandered off on their own.

The **ordinal numerals** (first, second, third, ...) combine with *the* in this function:

> *The first* of <u>my children</u> is still at school.

DETERMINERS

5.26   Classes of Determiners

Determiners introduce noun phrases. The three classes of determiners are defined by the order in which they come:

1. **pre-determiners**
2. **central determiners**
3. **post-determiners**

Here are examples with determiners from each class:

> *all* (1) *those* (2) *other* (3) problems
> *once* (1) *every* (2) *two* (3) weeks

Many words may be either determiners or pronouns:

pronoun	*Some* have left.
determiner	*Some* <u>people</u> have left.
pronoun	I need *more*.
determiner	I need *more* <u>money</u>.

| pronoun | *All* are forgiven. |
| determiner | *All* <u>faults</u> are forgiven. |

| pronouns | You may borrow *this*. |
| determiner | You may borrow *this* <u>pencil</u>. |

5.27   Central Determiners

The central determiners fall into several subclasses. We cannot combine central determiners to introduce the same noun phrase.

1. **definite article** (cf. 5.28)   *the*
2. **indefinite article** (cf. 5.28)   *a* or (before a vowel sound) *an*
3. **demonstratives** (cf.5.21)   *this, that, these, those*
4. **possessives** (cf. 5.19)   *my, our, your, his, her, its, their*
5. **interrogatives** cf. 5.23)   *what, which, whose*
                                                     What <u>day</u> is it?
                                                     Whose <u>coat</u> are you wearing?
6. **relatives** (cf. 5.24)   *which, whose, whatever, whichever* . . . ,
                                                   at *which* <u>point</u> I interrupted him . . . ,
                                                   whose <u>student</u> I used to be.
                                                   You can use it for *whatever* <u>purpose</u> you wish.
7. **indefinites** (cf. 5.25)   *some, any, no, enough, every, each, either, neither*

5.28   The Articles and Reference

We can apply three sets of contrast in the reference of noun phrases:

1. **generic** and **non-generic**
2. **specific** and **non-specific**
3. **definite** and **non-definite**

Generic/non-generic reference

Noun phrases are **generic** when they refer to a class as a whole:

> *Dogs* make good pets.

They are **non-generic** when they refer to individual members of the class:

Bring in *the dogs*.

For generic reference, the distinction between singular and plural is neutralized, and so is the distinction between the definite and indefinite articles. In their generic use, all of the following are roughly similar in meaning:

[1]   *An American* works hard.
[2]   *Americans* work hard.
[3]   *The American* works hard.
[4]   *The Americans* work hard.

Depending on the contrast, [3] and [4] can also be interpreted non-generically to refer to individual Americans.

Specific/non-specific reference

Noun phrases are **specific** when they refer to some particular person, place, thing, etc. In [5] *an Australian* refers to a specific person (even if unknown to the speaker):

[5]   Patrick has married *an Australian*. (some Australian)

In [6], on the other hand, *an Australian* does not refer to anybody specific:

[6]   Patrick would not dream of marrying *an Australian*. (any Australian)

Sentence [7] is ambiguous between the two interpretations:

[7]   Patrick intends to marry *an Australian*.

It may mean that Patrick has a specific person in mind (perhaps unknown to the speaker), or that he has the ambition to marry someone from Australia though he has nobody in mind at present.

As we will shortly see, both the indefinite article *a* and the definite article *the* are readily available for specific reference. For non-specific reference, indefinite *a* is usual but definite *the* also occurs:

[8]   Patrick intends to marry *the first Australian he meets*.

Generic reference is always non-specific. Some non-generic reference may also be non-specific, as in [6] and [8].

Definite/indefinite reference

The definite article *the* is used to signal that a noun phrase is **definite**. Noun phrases are definite when they are intended to convey enough information to identify what they refer to. If they are not so intended, they are **indefinite**. The identification may come from several sources:

1. The phrase refers to something uniquely identifiable by the speaker and hearer from their general knowledge or from their knowledge of the particular situation:

   > *the sun; the sea; the Church*
   > *The Prime Minister* is speaking on *the radio* this evening.
   > I must feed *the dog.*
   > *The door* is locked.
   > *The boss* wants you.

2. The phrase may refer to something mentioned previously:

   > Nancy introduced me to a young man and his wife at the reception. *The young man* was her nephew.

   At the first mention of the young man, the sentence refers to him by the indefinite phrase *a young man.*

3. The information may be identified by modifiers in the noun phrase:

   > I wonder whether you would mind getting for me *the blue book on the top shelf.*

Noun phrases may be definite even though they are not introduced by the definite article. For example, in a particular situation, personal pronouns (*I, you,* etc) and names are uniquely identifiable and so are the demonstrative pronouns (cf. 5.21). Other determiners, such as the demonstrative determiners (cf. 5.27), may also signal that the noun phrase is definite.

5.29   Pre-determiners

There can also be pre-determiners before the central determiners. These include the multipliers (*double, twice, three times,* . . .) and the fractions (*half*, *one-third*, . . .):

> *double* <u>her fee</u>
> *half* <u>a loaf</u>

They also include the words *all*, *both*, *such*, and *what*:

> *all* <u>their problems</u>
> *such* <u>a mess</u>
> *what* <u>a good idea</u>

These can also occur without a central determiner:

> *all* <u>stations</u>
> *both* <u>children</u>
> *such* <u>jokes</u>

Such is exceptional in that it can combine with other pre-determiners (*all such jokes*) and can come after a central determiner (*no such jokes*) and even a post-determiner (*many such jokes*).

5.30   Post-determiners

Post-determiners can come after the central determiners. They include the cardinal numbers and the ordinal numbers:

> <u>the</u> *three* largest rooms
> <u>our</u> *first* apartment

They also include *many*, *few*, and *little*:

> <u>my</u> *many* good friends
> <u>the</u> *little* furniture that I have

The ordinal and cardinal numerals can co-occur:

> the *first two* weeks

The post-determiners can occur without other determiners:

> He has *few* <u>vices</u>.
> We saw *two* <u>accidents</u> on our way here.

AUXILIARIES

5.31 Classes of Auxiliaries

Auxiliaries come before the main verb in a verb phrase. The **primary auxiliaries** are *be, have,* and *do.* They are different from each other and from the other auxiliaries. Their uses are:

1. *be* for (a)   the **progressive**: *was playing* (cf. 4.14)
          (b)   the **passive**: *was played* (cf. 4.15)
2. *have* for the **perfect**: *has played* (cf. 4.14)
3. *do* as the **dummy operator**: *did play* (cf. 4.17)

   The remaining auxiliaries are the **modal auxiliaries** or, more simply, the **modals**. The central modals are:

present	*can*	*may*	*will*	*shall*	*must*
past	*could*	*might*	*would*	*should*	

Like other verbs, most of the modals have a tense distinction between present and past (the exception being *must*), but the past forms are often used for present or future time:

We $\left\{ \begin{array}{l} may \\ might \end{array} \right\}$ come along after dinner.

I $\left\{ \begin{array}{l} can \\ could \end{array} \right\}$ help you later.

5.32 Meanings of the Modals

The modals express two main types of meaning:

1. human control over events, such as is involved in permission, intention ability, or obligation

   You *may* leave now. ('I give you permission to . . . ')
   I *could* speak Greek when I was young. ('I knew how to . . . ')
   You *must* go to bed at once. ('I require you to . . . ')

2. judgement whether an event was, is, or will be likely to happen

   They *may* be on the aeroplane by now. ('It is possible that they are . . . ')
   That *could* be your mother. ('It is possible that it is . . . ')
   It *must* be past midnight. ('It is certainly the case that it is . . . ')
   Joan *may* have heard the result by now. ('It is possible that Joan has   . . . ')

5.33   Conjunctions

There are two classes of conjunctions:

1. **coordinators,** or **coordinating conjunctions**
2. **subordinators,** or **subordinating conjunctions**

Coordinators link units of equal status. The central coordinators are *and, or,* and *but*:

> I enjoy novels *and* short stories best of all.
> I can *and* will speak!
> The device seals a plastic shopping bag *and* equips it with a handle.
> You may pay by cash *or* credit card.
> He was apologetic, *but* he refused to intervene.

The coordinators may be reinforced by **correlative** expressions: *both . . . and; either . . . or; not only . . . but also:*

> *both* Susan *and* her brother
> *either* tea *or* coffee
> *Not only* was the speech uninspiring, *but* it was *also* full of illogical statements.

The marginal coordinator *nor* may be reinforced by the correlative *neither*:

> I have *neither* seen the movie *nor* read the book.

Subordinators introduce subordinate clauses (cf. 6.9):

> The negotiations succeeded *because* both sides bargained in good faith.
> *If* you like the service, tell the manager.

Here are some common subordinators:

after	before	till	where
although	if	unless	while
as	since	until	
because	that	when	

Some subordinators consist of more than one word: *except that* and *as long as,* for example.

Some words are both subordinators and prepositions. If the word introduces a finite clause, it is a subordinator; if it introduces a phrase, it is a preposition:

subordinator	I saw her *after* <u>I had my interview.</u>
preposition	I saw her *after* <u>the interview.</u>

5.34   Prepositions

Prepositions introduce a prepositional phrase, and are followed by a prepositional complement (cf. 4.25). The preposition links the complement to some other expression. If it links the complement to the rest of the sentence or clause, the prepositional phrase may be placed in any of various positions:

I had an argument *in* <u>a supermarket.</u>
All the members of the team, *in* <u>my view</u>, contributed equally to the victory.
By <u>that time</u> I was feeling sleepy.

It may also link the complement to a phrase:

He became personal assistant *to* <u>the managing director of the company</u>.
The government suppressed all information *about* <u>the epidemic.</u>

Here are some common prepositions:

about	before	during	over	until
above	behind	for	past	up
across	below	from	since	with
after	beside	in	than	without
against	between	inside	through	
among(st)	but	into	till	
around	by	off	to	
as	despite	on	toward(s)	
at	down	out	under	

Some prepositions consist of more than one word; for example, *because of, in spite of, in addition to*.

Many of the words listed as single-word prepositions are also adverbs or conjunctions.

6

Sentences and Clauses

6.1   Sentence types

In 2.4 I listed the four major types of sentences that are associated with four major uses in communication:

1. declaratives for statements
2. interrogatives for questions
3. imperatives for directives
4. exclamatives for exclamations

Most of the sentences that we have looked at so far have been declaratives. In the sections that follow we will examine the other three types of sentences.

6.2   Questions

There are two main types of interrogative sentences:

1. **Yes-no questions** begin with a verb. They require **subject-operator inversion**; that is, a reversal of the order of subject and verb (the order that is normal in declaratives). The verb that appears before the subject is an operator (cf. 3.3*f*):

> *Should* (op) *the government* (S) cut income taxes?
> *Does* (op) *this shop* (S) open 24 hours every day?

They are called *yes–no* questions because they expect the answer *yes* or *no*. They may in fact be answered in other ways; for example, *Certainly; Perhaps; I don't know; What do you think?*

2. **Wh-questions** begin with an interrogative word or phrase:

> *Why* should the government cut income taxes?

On which days does this shop open 24 hours?

They are called *wh*-questions because most of the interrogative words begin with *wh*- (the exception is *how*). The interrogative phrases contain an interrogative word such as *which* in *On which days*. The interrogative word in *wh*-questions represents a missing piece of information that the speaker wants the hearer to supply.

Wh-questions generally require subject–operator inversion too. The exception occurs when the interrogative word or phrase is the subject, and in that case the normal subject–verb order applies:

> *Who* has taken my car?
> *Which bus* goes to Chicago?

There are also several other types of questions.

3. **Declarative questions** have the form of a declarative sentence but the force of a question. They are signalled by a rising intonation in speech and by a question mark in writing:

> You know my name?
> He's got the key?

4. **Alternative questions** present two or more choices, and the hearer is expected to reply with one of them. One type of alternative question resembles the form of *yes-no* questions:

> Should the government reduce its deficit by raising income taxes or by cutting expenditure?

The other type resembles *wh*-questions:

> Which do you want, coffee or tea?

5. **Tag questions** are attached to sentences that are not interrogative. They invite the hearer to respond in agreement with the speaker:

> The government should cut income taxes, *shouldn't it*?
> You haven't said anything yet, *have you*?

Tag questions have the form of *yes-no* questions. They consist of an operator and a pronoun subject that echo the subject and operator of the sentence. The tag question is usually negative if the sentence is positive, and positive if the sentence is negative. Tag questions can be attached to imperative sentences; generally in these the subject is *you* and the operator is *will*:

> Don't tell him, *will you?*
> Make yourself at home, *won't you?*

6. **Rhetorical questions** do not expect a reply since they are the equivalent of forceful statements. If the rhetorical question is positive it has negative force, and if it is negative it has positive force. The questions may resemble either *yes-no* questions or *wh*-questions:

> Is there anything more relaxing than a hot bath? ('Surely there isn't . . . ')
> Haven't you eyes? ('Surely you have eyes.')
> Who could defend such a view? ('Surely no one could . . . ')

6.3   Imperatives

Imperative sentences usually do not have a subject. If there is no auxiliary, the verb has the base form:

> *Take* a seat.
> *Pass* me the bottle.
> *Make* us an offer.

Modal auxiliaries do not occur with imperatives, and the only auxiliary that occurs with any frequency is passive *be* (usually in the negative):

> Don't be carried away with the idea.

You may be added as a second person subject:

> *You* make us an offer.

Occasionally, a third person subject is used:

> *Somebody* make us an offer.
> *Those in the front row* sit down.

First and third person imperatives may be formed with *let* and a subject:

> *Let us* go now.
> *Let's* not tell him.
> Don't *let's* talk about it.
> *Let me* think what I should do.
> *Let nobody* move.

6.4   Exclamatives

Exclamatives begin with *what* or *how*. *What* introduces noun phrases; *how* is used for all other purposes. The exclamative word or (more commonly) phrase is fronted:

> *What* a good show it was! ('It was an extremely good show.')
> *What* a time we've had!
> *How* hard she works!
> *How* strange they look!
> *How* time flies! ('Time flies extremely fast')

Exclamative sentences express strong feeling. More specifically, they indicate the extent to which the speaker is impressed by something. *What* and *how* are intensifiers expressing a high degree.

6.5   Speech acts

When we say or write something, we are performing an action. This action expressed in words is a **speech act**. The intended effect in a speech act is the communicative purpose of the speech act.

In Section 2.4 I referred to four major communicative uses associated with the four major types of sentences. We have already seen (cf. 6.2) that a sentence type may have a communicative use other than the one normally associated with it: a declarative question is a declarative sentence with the force of a question; a rhetorical question, on the other hand, is an interrogative sentence with the force of a statement.

There are many more than four types of communicative purpose.

Directly or indirectly, we may convey our intention to promise, predict, warn, complain, offer, advise, and so on. The communicative purpose of a speech act depends on the particular context in which the act is performed. Here are some sentences, together with plausible interpretations of their purpose if they are uttered as speech acts:

> It's getting late. (request for someone to leave with the speaker)
> Tell me your phone number. (inquiry – request for information)
> There is a prospect of heavy thunderstorms later in the day.
>   (prediction)
> I'm afraid that I've broken your vase. (apology)
> Break it, and you'll pay for it. (warning)
> Do you want a seat? (offer)
> I nominate Tony Palmer. (nomination)
> Enjoy yourself. (wish)
> Don't touch. (prohibition)
> I won't be late. (promise)
> It would be a good idea to send a copy to the manager. (advice)

The purpose may be merely to make a friendly gesture, where silence might be interpreted as hostility or indifference:

> It's a nice day, isn't it? (ostensibly information)
> How are you? (ostensibly an inquiry)

6.6   Compound sentences

A **multiple sentence** is a sentence that contains one or more clauses (structures that can be analysed in terms of sentence elements such as subject). If the multiple sentence consists of two or more coordinated clauses, it is a **compound sentence**. The coordinated clauses are normally linked by a coordinator (or coordinating conjunction). The central coordinators are *and, or* and *but*:

[1]   She is a superb administrator, and everybody knows that.
[2]   Lawns are turning green, flowers are blooming, and summer time is returning.
[3]   Send it to me by post or bring it around yourself.
[4]   They have played badly every year since 1985, but this year may be different.

Compound sentences have two or more **main clauses**, each with independent status. We cannot therefore speak of, say, the subject of the sentence. In [1] for example, there is no subject of the sentence as a whole: the subject of the first main clause is *she* and the subject of the second main clause is *everybody*. In [2] there are three subjects of main clauses: *lawns, flowers,*and *summer time*.

Instead of linking main clauses with a coordinator, we can often juxtapose them (place them side by side), and link them with a semicolon:

[1a]   She is a superb administrator; everybody knows that.
[4a]   They have played badly every year since 1985; this year may be different.

If we put a full-stop between them, we have two orthographic sentences.

We sometimes avoid repeating identical expressions across coordinated clauses by **ellipsis** (the omission of essential grammatical units that can be supplied by the hearer from the context):

The adults ate chicken, the teenagers hamburgers, and the youngest children pizza. (The verb *ate* is omitted in the second and third clauses.)

Last year we spent our holiday in Spain, the year before in Greece. (The expression *we spent our holiday* is ellipted in the second clause.)

6.7   Complex sentences

A **complex sentence** is a multiple sentence in which are embedded one or more **subordinate clauses**:

[1]   Everybody knows *that she is a superb administrator.*
[2]   He saw the trouble *that idle gossip can cause.*
[3]   I am happy *that you are joining our company.*

In [1] the clause functions as a sentence element: the direct object. In [2] it is a modifier in a phrase: the post-modifier of the noun *trouble*. In [3] it is also a modifier in a phrase: the post-modifier of the adjective *happy*.

Subordinate clauses are often introduced by a subordinator (or subordinating conjunction, cf. 5.33), particularly if the clauses are finite.

A complex sentence can be analysed in terms of sentence elements such as subject and verb. In [1] the subject is *Everybody*, the verb is *knows*, and the direct object is the subordinate *that*-clause. In the subordinate clause, which is introduced by the subordinator *that*, *she* is the subject, *is* is the verb, and *a superb administrator* is the subject complement.

6.8   Non-finite and verbless clauses

Non-finite and verbless clauses are generally subordinate clauses. **Non-finite clauses** have a non-finite verb (cf. 4.18); **verbless clauses** are without a verb.

There are three types of non-finite clauses, depending on the form of the first verb in the verb phrase:

1. *-ing* clauses (or *-ing* participle clauses)

    [1] *Just thinking about the final round* put him in a combative mood.

2. *-ed* clauses (or *-ed* participle clauses)

    [2] *Dressed in street clothes*, the patients strolled in the garden.

3. infinitive clauses
    (a)   with *to*

    [3] They wanted *to pay for their meal.*

    (b)   without *to*

    [4] We helped *unload the car.*

    Here are two examples of verbless clauses:

    [5] *Though fearful of road conditions*, they decided to go by car.
    [6] *Weary and almost out of money*, we drove into a petrol station off the motorway.

Non-finite and verbless clauses can be regarded as reduced clauses, reduced in comparison with finite clauses. They often lack a subject, and verbless clauses also lack a verb. However, we can analyse them in terms of sentence elements if we reconstruct them as finite clauses, supplying the missing parts that we understand from the rest of the sentence:

[2]   Dressed in street clothes, (V + A)
[2a]   They were dressed in street clothes. (S + V + A)

[4]   unload the car. (V + dO)
[4a]   We unloaded the car. (S + V + dO)

[5]   Fearful of road conditions, (sC)
[5c]   They were fearful of road conditions. (S + V + sC)

Non-finite and verbless clauses may have their own subject:

> He nervously began his speech, **his voice** (S) *trembling and* **his face** (S) *flushed.*
> They trudged by the river in the deep snow, **their heads and their hands** (S) *bare.*

If they do not have a subject, their subject is generally interpreted as being identical in its reference with that of the subject of the sentence or clause in which they are embedded. This rule applies to sentences [2]-[6]. For [1] we deduce that the reference of the subject of *thinking* is identical with that of the object *him*.

Non-finite and verbless clauses are sometimes introduced by subordinators. In [5] the subordinator *though* introduces the verbless clause.

We have seen (3.7-12) that the choice of the verb determines the choice of other sentence elements. For example, a transitive verb requires a direct object. The verb also determines the form of the element, including whether it allows a clause and what type of clause. For example, the transitive verb *like* may have as its direct object a noun phrase, an infinitive clause, or an *-ing* clause:

I like
{
vanilla ice cream.
to shop at Harrods.
shopping at Harrods.
}

The transitive verb *prefer*, on the other hand, takes as a direct object a noun phrase, an infinitive clause, an *-ing* clause, or a *that*-clause:

I prefer
{
vanilla ice cream.
to shop at Harrods.
shopping at Harrods.
that we shop at Harrods.
}

6.9   Functions of subordinate clauses

Subordinate clauses have three main sets of functions:

1. **Nominal clauses** have a range of functions similar to that for noun phrases (cf. 4.10). For example:

subject	*Achieving the perfect crew cut* is no easy task.
subject complement	The only problem in design is *to relate design to people's needs.*
direct object	I believe *that a hot, humid summer has benifited the movie business.*
prepositional complement	I listened to *what the candidates had to say.*

Nominal relative clauses are clauses that are introduced by nominal relative pronouns (cf. 5.24). Whereas relative clauses post-modify nouns, nominal relative clauses have the same functions as noun phrases:

He gave his children *what they wanted* (dO).
Whoever said that (S) does not understand the question.

2. **Modifier clauses** function as modifiers in phrases. One common kind of modifier is the **relative clause** (cf. 4.5), which post-modifies a noun:

Drugs *that are used in chemotherapy* damage a patient's healthy cells as well.

Non-finite clauses function as reduced relative clauses:

The firemen battled an inferno *fuelled by toxic chemicals.* ('that was fuelled by . . . ')
Scientists found no evidence *to suggest that neutrinos have mass.* ('that would suggest that . . . ')
I was engaged in a programme of laborious research *involving many chemical reactions.* ('that involved . . . ')

Another common kind of modifier is the **comparative clause** introduced by *than* or *as*:

She is a better doctor *than I am.*
He spoke more rashly *than he used to do.*
Norman plays as fiercely *as I expected.*

A third kind is a post-modifier of an adjective:

> Roger was afraid *to tell his parents.*

3. **Adverbial clauses** function as the adverbial element in sentence or clause structure (cf. 3.9f):

> *If a heart attack occurs,* the electronic device automatically orders charges of electricity *to jolt the heart back into a normal rhythm.*
> *Reflecting on the past three years,* she wondered whether she could have made better choices.
> *When in Rome,* do as the Romans do.

6.10 Sentence complexity

The earlier division of multiple sentences into compound sentences and complex sentences (cf. 6.6f) is an oversimplification. It indicates at the highest level within the sentence a distinction between coordination and subordination of clauses. But these two types of clause linkage may mingle at lower levels. A compound sentence may have subordination within one of its main clauses. In this compound sentence, the second main clause is complex:

[1]   Mite specialists have identified 30,000 species of mites, *but* they believe *that* these represent only a tenth of the total number.

In [1], *but* introduces a main clause and *that* introduces a subordinate clause within the main clause. The *that*-clause is subordinate to the *but*-clause and not to the sentence as a whole: the *but*-clause is *superordinate* to the subordinate *that*-clause.

A complex sentence may contain a hierarchy of subordination:

[2]   They refused (A) *to say* (B) *what they would do* (C) *if the strikers did not return to their jobs.*

In [2] each of the subordinate clauses extends from the parenthesized letter that marks it to the end of the sentence: (A) is a direct object that is subordinate to the sentence as a whole and superordinate to (B); (B) is a direct object that is subordinate to (A) and superordinate to (C); (C) is an adverbial clause that is subordinate to (B).

The next example is a complex sentence whose subordinate clauses are coordinated:

[3]   They claimed *that the streets are clean, the rubbish is regularly collected, and the crime rate is low.*

In [3] the three coordinated subordinate clauses together constitute the direct object of the sentence.

In the final example, the compound sentence has both subordination and coordination at lower levels.

[4]   The Great Lake states warned pregnant women and nursing mothers to avoid eating certain Great Lakes fish, *and* they advised the rest of us to avoid certain large fatty species and to limit the consumption of other fish.

The two main clauses are linked by *and* (underlined in the sentence). The first main clause contains a non-finite subordinate clause (beginning *to avoid*) in which is embedded another non-finite subordinate clause (*eating . . . fish*). The second main clause contains two coordinated non-finite subordinate clauses (*to avoid . . . and to limit . . .*). The relationship of coordination and subordination in [4] is represented in Figure 6.1.

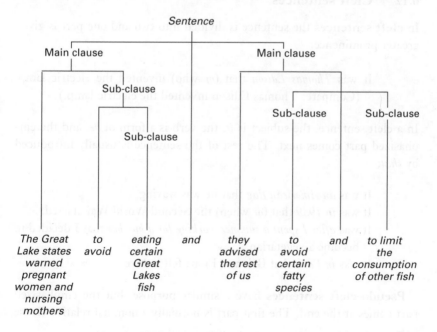

Figure 6.1   Coordination and Subordination

6.11   *There*-structures

In the remaining sections of this chapter we will examine some common structures that depart from the basic sentence patterns.

The first is the **there-structure**. *There* is put in the subject position and the subject is moved forward to a later position:

> *There* is nobody outside. (Cf. Nobody is outside.)
> *There* are some topics that are best discussed in private. (Cf. Some topics are best discussed in private.)
> *There* are several countries that have asked the Secretary-General for an emergency session of the Security Council.
> *There* is somebody knocking on the door.

The effect of this structure is to present the postponed subject and the rest of the sentence as new information and thereby to give the sentence (in particular the subject) greater prominence. The postponed subject is normally an indefinite pronoun (cf. 5.25) or a noun phrase with an indefinite determiner (cf. 5.27).

6.12   Cleft sentences

In **cleft sentences** the sentence is divided into two and one part is given greater prominence:

> It was *Thomas Edison* that (*or* who) invented the electric lamp. (Compare: Thomas Edison invented the electric lamp.)

In a cleft sentence, the subject is *it*, the verb is a form of *be*, and the emphasized part comes next. The rest of the sentence is usually introduced by *that*:

> It was *an American flag* that he was waving.
> It was *in 1939* that (*or* when) the Second World War started.
> It was *after I spent a summer working for a butcher* that I decided to become a vegetarian.
> It was *in Paris* that Bob and Fiona fell in love.

Pseudo-cleft sentences have a similar purpose, but the emphasized part comes at the end. The first part is normally a nominal relative clause (cf. 6.9) introduced by *what*. The verb *be* links the two parts of this SVC structure:

> What I want *is* a good sleep.
> What he did *was* open my letters.
> What I'm going to do *is* see the principal.

6.13   Anticipatory *it*

It is unusual to have a nominal clause as the subject of the sentence:

[1]   *That the season has started so early* seems a pity.

Instead, the subject is usually moved to the end (the *postponed subject*) and its position is taken by *it* (the *anticipatory subject*):

[1a]   *It* seems a pity *that the season has started so early*.

Here are some other examples:

> *It* is likely *that we'll be moving to Glasgow.*
> *It* doesn't matter to me *who pays my ticket.*
> *It's* impossible *to say when they are arriving.*
> *It* has not been announced *whether negotiations between the employers and the strikers have broken down.*

The exception is that nominal *-ing* clauses are natural in the normal subject position:

> *Having a good self-image* keeps me sane.
> *Finding rattlesnake dens* provided rare excitement.

Part II

The Applications

7

Punctuation

7.1   Punctuation rules

The rules for punctuation are conventions that have been developed by printers and publishers. In large part, punctuation helps the readers to understand the written communication by breaking it down into smaller components. The conventions also contribute to the appearance of the printed page, notably through paragraphing.

The conventions establish a measure of consistency for writers. Some conventions are obligatory: if we break them, we have made mistakes in punctuation. Others are optional: we can make better or worse choices in particular circumstances, depending on the effects we wish to convey. To that extent, punctuation is an art.

Some punctuation marks are intended to represent pauses that we should make in our reading. In [1] below, the author has chosen to enclose three words in brackets to indicate that they are to be read with pauses on either side. The effect of the separating pauses is rhetorical: they emphasize the addition of *or may not*:

[1]   The bowls may (or may not) be Anglo-Saxon, but the ornament of the mounts is of importance in the development of later Anglo-Saxon arts. [David M. Wilson, *Anglo-Saxon Art*, p.16. London: Thames & Hudson, 1984]

But we do not always insert punctuation marks where we pause in speech. We would be likely to read or speak the sentence in [2] with a pause (or a break in our intonation) after the word *arise* (and perhaps other pauses too):

[2]   The only way to make sure that misunderstandings such as the one described above could not arise would be to make sure that the context actually used by the hearer was always identical to the

117

one envisaged by the speaker. [Dan Sperber & Deirdre Wilson, *Relevance*, p. 17. Oxford: Basil Blackwell, 1986]

The punctuation system, however, does not allow a comma after *arise*. There is a punctuation rule that forbids a comma between the subject and predicate unless the comma is the first of a pair of commas, as in [3]. Here parenthetic *such as the Morse code* is separated by a pair of commas:

[3]   A simple code, such as the Morse code, may consist of a straight-forward list of message-signal pairs. [*Relevance*, p. 4]

The rule forbidding a comma after *arise* in [2] depends on the grammar of the sentence: the analysis of the sentence into subject and predicate. Some punctuation rules involve grammar and others involve meaning. We will be looking at such rules in the sections that follow.

7.2   Sentence fragments and fragmentary sentences

A **sentence fragment** is a set of words that is punctuated as a sentence even though it is not grammatically an independent sentence. Experienced writers can set a tone in their writing that allows them to violate the rules of punctuation through their intentional use of sentence fragments. When inexperienced writers violate these rules, their readers are given the impression that the writers do not know the rules. On the whole, it is safer for writers to avoid using fragments in formal writing until they are experienced enough to sense when it is appropriate to use them. Below are three types of sentence fragments to avoid. In each instance, if we replace the full stop, we also need to change the preceding capital to lower case.

1. **subordinate clauses**
    Boy's bullying has always attracted attention. Because it is crudely obvious. [Replace the full stop with a comma.]
    The percentage or letter-marking system is better than the pass/fail system. Because marks motivate students to work harder. [Omit the full stop or replace it with a comma.]
    I woke up late the next morning. My head throbbing and my stomach burning. [Replace the full stop by a comma or a dash.]
2. **loosely joined phrases**
    The kit comes complete with an instruction leaflet. All for £18.50. [Replace the full stop with a comma or a dash.]
    Our class was rowdy during our last year at school. Especially during

the last two months. [Replace the full stop with a comma or a dash.]
Some parents are making an effort to deal with the problem of
teenage drinking. An effort that can help reduce alcoholism and
road accidents. [Replace the full stop with a comma.]
3. **coordinated expressions**
   Some of his students became interested in environmental problems.
   And later helped in the battle against environmental pollution.
   [Replace the full stop with a comma.]
   They have abandoned their homes. And taken all their possessions
   with them. [Delete the full stop or replace it with a comma.]
   He gossiped about other people's relationships. And even his own.
   [Replace the full stop with a comma or a dash.]

Sentence fragments are occasionally used in print, particularly in
advertising, to suggest an afterthought or a dramatic pause, as in this extract from an advertisement for intercity trains:

> Suddenly, a brilliant thought might strike. An idea for a game
> that could be bigger than Trivial Pursuits.

Fragmentary sentences are sentences that are grammatically incom-
plete but can be completed from the verbal context (cf. 2.2). In written
dialogue they are particularly common for responses, and their use in such
contexts is perfectly appropriate:

> A: What did she tell you?
> B: *To help myself to food.* ('She told me to help myself to food.')
>
> A: I heard you passed your driving test.
> B: *After failing three times.* ('I passed it after failing three times.')

Fragmentary sentences are also common and appropriate in fictional description and narration, representing informal speech:

> Outside it drizzled. No taxi. [Doris Lessing, *A Man and Two
> Women*, p. 17. London: Grafton Books, 1965]

In the next example (from a novel), all the sentences except the first are
fragmentary. The first sentence (ending in a semicolon) provides the clue
to their interpretation. For most of them we would supply an initial *She
was*, *She had* or *She had a* to make them grammatically complete:

Dr von Haller looked younger than I; about thirty-eight, I judged, for though her expression was youthful there was a little gray in her hair. Fine face; rather big features but not coarse. Excellent nose, aquiline if one wished to be complimentary but verging on the hooky if not. Large mouth and nice teeth, white but not American-white. Beautiful eyes, brown to go with her hair. Pleasant low voice and a not quite perfect command of colloquial English. Slight acccent. Clothes unremarkable, neither fashionable nor dowdy, in the manner Caroline calls 'classic'. Altogether a person to inspire confidence. [Robertson Davies, *The Deptford Trilogy*, p. 282. Harmondsworth, Middlesex: Penguin Books, 1977]

My final examples of fragments come from a book on art:

All the features admired and described by poets and writers are encountered in the material which survives. *Sometimes triumphantly, as with the greater Gospel Books; sometimes subtly, as in the use of gold inlaid in silver.* Much, it is true, is now lost. *Painting, for example.* [David M. Wilson, *Anglo-Saxon Art*, p. 10. London: Thames & Hudson, 1984]

7.3   Run-on sentences and comma splices

In [1] we have two separate sentences:

[1]   I used to be afraid of him. I have since got to know him well.

We can join them into one sentence by simply putting a semicolon between them:

[1a]   I used to be afraid of him; I have since got to know him well.

The general rule is that if we juxtapose sentences, as in [1] and [1a] , we must use a major punctuation mark. The major punctuation marks are full stops, question marks, exclamation marks, colons, semicolons, and dashes. If we fail to use any mark at all the resulting error is a **run-on sentence**, as in [1b]:

[1b]   I used to be afraid of him I have since got to know him well.

[Correct by inserting a major punctuation mark after *afraid of him*.]

If we use a comma instead of a major mark, the resulting error is a **comma splice**, as in [1c]:

[1c]   I used to be afraid of him, I have since got to know him well. [Replace the comma with a major punctuation mark.]

Here are further examples of run-on sentences:

It did not matter to me whether or not I had made an impact on the world I just wanted to learn as much as possible. [Insert a major punctuation mark after *the world*.]

Ask the first person you see if they will help you I am sure they will. [Insert a major punctuation mark after *help you*.]

And here are further examples of comma splices:

I visited them in their new home, it was a large apartment with a living room, kitchen, dining alcove, and two bedrooms. [Replace the comma after *home* with a major punctuation mark.]

I drifted towards vegetarianism, it was only partly for moral reasons. [Replace the comma after *vegetarianism* with a major punctuation mark.]

Comma splices are most likely to occur when a linking adverb (e.g. *therefore, nevertheless*) or a linking prepositional phrase (e.g. *in spite of that, as a result*) comes between the two sentences. A semicolon is the normal major punctuation mark if the two sentences are combined:

[2]   They lost the battle, *nevertheless* they were determined to continue the war. [Correct by replacing the comma with a major punctuation mark.]

[3]   The supply of houses grew more slowly than the number of new households, as a result there was a giddy rise in prices. [Correct by replacing the comma with a major punctuation mark.]

These linking expressions do not have to come between the two sentences. They can be moved elsewhere in the second sentence, as in [2a] and [2b]:

[2a]   They lost the battle; they were determined, *nevertheless,* to continue the war.

[2b]   They lost the battle; they were determined to continue the war *nevertheless.*

There is one exception to the general rule. We may use commas between juxtaposed sentences if they are short and are similar in their structure, as in [4]:

[4]   The first set of rules prescribes what counts as a proper sentence of the language, the second prescribes how one sentence can be derived from another. [D.W. Hamlyn, *A History of Western Philosophy,* p. 308. London; Penguin Books, 1988]

The sentence may consist of just two parallel clauses involving a kind of comparison, as in [5] and [6]:

[5]   The sooner he finishes, the better he will feel.
[6]   The more they earned, the more they wanted.

7.4   Coordinated main clauses

Instead of juxtaposing sentences, we can often link them with a coordinator as two main clauses within one sentence. When we use a coordinator, we can put merely a comma between the clauses. In [1d] below, the coordinator *but* follows a comma:

[1d]   I used to be afraid of him, but I have since got to know him well.

The central coordinators are *and, or,* and *but.* The marginal coordinators, which resemble the central coordinators in that they must come between the clauses, can also be used merely with a preceding comma: these are *for, nor, so* ('therefore'), *then* ('after that'), and *yet.* Here are examples with the three central coordinators and the other linking words:

They were highly successful in the competition for grant

support, *and* each grant provided jobs for technicians and other workers.

He ought to admit that he is responsible for what he is doing, *or* he ought not to do it all.

The legal profession does not seem to have changed much, *but* in fact it has become much more democratic.

Peace is by no means assured, *for* several cabinet ministers are opposed to key paragraphs in the draft treaty.

He is not a furniture designer, *nor* is he a shopkeeper.

A storm damaged their radio, *yet* they were able to send messages.

She was refused admission, *so* she complained to the manager.

Check that the pilot is alight, *then* push the knob inwards and turn to the setting that you require for cooking.

The central coordinators may also link clauses without a punctuation mark, particularly if one or more of the clauses are short:

We've all been asked to take more personal responsibility *and* people have responded to that challenge.

My father has never been remote *and* he has never been suffocating.

We may want to use major punctuation marks between coordinated main clauses because they are long, because we want to emphasize that each clause is a separate unit, or because one or more of the clauses has internal commas:

They're bored with TV; *and* they're bored with films; *and* they're bored with stereo systems; *and* they're bored with athletics.

She thinks that the data on which the current view is based are biased by the fact that many of the measurements were made near urban areas, which tend to be warmer. But the measurements at sea are unreliable too, especially the older ones.

On the other hand, we should not use a full stop or a semicolon to separate a subordinate clause from the main clause. Using a full stop results in a sentence fragment (cf. 7.2), and a similar mistake results from using a semicolon:

> He told the police that she has moved; although in fact she had died. [Replace the semicolon with a comma.]

7.5   Direct speech

We use **direct** speech when we report the actual words that somebody has said or written. It is normal to enclose direct speech in two pairs of either single or double quotation marks, an opening one or pair and a closing one or pair. Single quotation marks are more common.

In dialogue, direct speech often comes with a **reporting clause**, such as *she said*. Sentences [1]–[3] illustrate the usual punctuation of direct speech with a reporting clause when the direct speech is a declarative sentence. The reporting clause can appear in one of three positions:

[1]   He said to us, 'The solution is in your hands'.
[2]   'The solution is in your hands,' he said to us.
[3]   'The solution,' he said to us, 'is in your hands'.

When we report the original in our own words, we use **indirect speech**:

> He told us that the solution was in our hands.

Rules for punctuating direct speech

The following are the rules for punctuating direct speech with a reporting clause:

(a)   initial reporting clause, as in [4]
It is usual to put a comma after the reporting clause and before the initial quotation marks:

[4]   She told them, 'We should not waste food when millions are starving'.

We may use a colon instead of a comma, particularly if the direct speech contains more than one sentence:

[5]   He turned to me and said: 'For the first time in my life I understood who I was and what I was doing and why I was doing it'.

If the quotation is indented, it is not necessary to use quotation marks, since the layout is a sufficient indication of direct speech.

If the quotation ends the sentence, we put a full stop, a question mark, an exclamation mark, or a dash before the final quotation marks. The full stop is illustrated in [1], [3], [4], and [5]. The other three marks are illustrated in [6]–[8]:

[6]   The reporter asked, 'Has the general arrived?'
[7]   The crowd cried, 'Long live the President!'
[8]   She said, 'I have done my share, but you – '

The dash in [8] indicates that the speaker has stopped in mid-sentence.

If the question mark or exclamation mark belongs to the sentence as a whole (not to the direct speech), it goes outside the closing quotation marks:

[9]   Did she say, 'It is against my religious principles'?
[10]   He actually said, 'I am too busy to see you'!

In the rare situation when the question mark or exclamation mark belongs both to the sentence and to the direct speech, use only one mark and put it before the quotation marks:

Did she say, 'Is it against your religious principles?'

(b)   final reporting clause, as in [2]
If the direct speech sentence would ordinarily end in a full stop, put a comma before the quotation marks:

[11]   'I'm not yet ready,' he replied.

Otherwise, use a question mark or exclamation mark as appropriate:

[12]   'Do you know the way?' she asked.
[13]   'Lights!' he screamed.

The sentence may continue after the reporting clause:

[11a]   'I'm not yet ready,' he replied, and put down the telephone.
[11b]   'I'm not yet ready,' he replied; then he picked up the telephone.

(c)   medial reporting clause, as in [3]
The medial clause combines punctuation features associated with the initial and final reporting clause. The punctuation *before* the medial clause is the same as for the final reporting clause:

[14]   'I'm not yet ready,' he replied. 'You go ahead without me.' (cf [11])
[15]   'Do you know the way?' she asked. 'I'm lost.' (cf. [12])
[16]   'Lights!' he screamed. 'Give me lights!' (cf. [13])

If the reporting clause interrupts a sentence, use a comma even if the sentence would ordinarily have no punctuation:

[17]   'When you are ready,' he said, 'let me know'. (cf: *When you are ready, let me know*.)
[18]   'I know,' he said, 'that they suspect me'. (cf. *I know that they suspect me*.)

The punctuation after the medial reporting clause depends on whether the first part is an independent sentence. If it is, a full stop follows the reporting clause, as in [14]–[16]. If the reporting clause interrupts the sentence where the sentence would ordinarily have a comma or no punctuation, as in [17] and [18], then a comma follows the clause. If the reporting clause is placed where the sentence would ordinarily have a semicolon, the semicolon follows the reporting clause:

[19]   'The first two attempts to amend the constitution by convention succeeded,' the senator said; 'the next two attempts failed.'

The punctuation at the end of the sentence is the same as for the initial reporting clause. We therefore have a full stop after the closing quotation marks in [17]–[19], and an exclamation mark in [16]. In [14] and [15], however, the full stop comes before the quotation marks because they enclose an independent sentence. Here are two further examples:

[20]   'Did you say,' she asked, 'that she would see me now?'

[21]   'I have done my share, ' she said, 'but you –'

(d)   in general
It is normal to start a new paragraph when there is a change of speaker, whether or not the direct speech is accompanied by a reporting clause:

> 'What was written in the letter?' she asked.
> 'I can't tell you. I couldn't read it.'
> 'Why not?'
> 'It was in Spanish.'

Use double quotation marks for a quotation within a quotation if you have used single quotation marks for the main quotation:

> 'I said I'd take the job. Then I went to bed and thought, "What am I doing?" I don't want my children to say "He was a good football coach". I want them to think that I tried to do more than that.'

If the quotation is not in full, the punctuation mark that follows it comes after the quotation marks:

> The Colonel says he regards 'the past 20 years just as an introduction'.
> He described the pleasure of seeing how deserts had become 'not the Garden of Eden exactly, but a bit greener', though he made it clear that self-fulfilment was not his aim.

Partial quotations draw attention to a significant part of what was said, and they may therefore be very brief:

> The newspapers carried a report on a famine of 'biblical proportions' in Ethiopia.
> Sometimes the party sounds a little too enthusiastic about enforcing majority 'rights'.

In the last example the effect of inserting the quotation marks is to suggest that the writer does not accept responsibility for the appropriateness of the expression 'rights' in this context.

7.6   Citations

We use words in a special way when we refer to them as words. Compare [1] with [2]:

[1]   They are in love.
[2]   *Love* can be either a verb or a noun.

In [1] *love* is used in the normal way. In [2] it is the word *love* that is being discussed. When a word or phrase is cited – quoted or mentioned rather than used in the normal way – it is either put in double quotation marks or underlined. (Underlining in writing is the equivalent of italics in print.) If you are going to use many such citations or if you need quotation marks for other purposes, it would be clearer to use underlining rather than quotation marks. Definitions and translations of words and phrases are usually in single quotation marks:

> *Perennial* 'perpetual' or 'recurring' has its roots in the Latin *per* ('through') and *annus* ('year').

Titles of works are also a special use of language. If the works are published or produced separately (for example, books, magazines, movies, musical compositions), they are underlined. But if the titles are for part of a larger work (for example, articles, chapters, short stories, songs), they are enclosed in single or double quotation marks:

> I read the report in the *New York Times*.
> You can find that character in *A Streetcar Named Desire*.
> My favourite Beatles song is 'Eleanor Rigby'.

Contrast:

> *Hamlet* is a complex play.
> Hamlet is a complex character.

7.7   Questions

The general rule is that a question mark comes at the end of an interrogative sentence:

> Is our nation prepared for further sacrifices?

The rule also applies to tag questions (cf. 6.2):

> She's in quite a good frame of mind, *isn't she?*

It extends to declarative questions, which have the structure of a declarative sentence but function as a question (cf. 6.2):

> You know the rules?

It is usual to put an exclamation mark at the end of an exclamatory question to ensure that it is read as an exclamation:

> Haven't you grown!
> Am I thirsty!

It is usual to put a full stop at the end of a question beginning *Would you* that is intended as a polite request, particularly if the sentence is long. This usage is common in official letters. In this context the writer expects the fulfilling of the request, not a reply to the question:

> Would you please send me a copy of the instructional book that should have been enclosed with the microwave oven.

Do not use a question mark for an indirect question (a question in indirect speech). Contrast the direct question in [1] with the indirect question in [2]:

[1]   He asked, 'Who wants to speak?'
[2]   He asked who wanted to speak.

7.8   Restrictive and non-restrictive relative clauses

Relative clauses post-modify nouns (cf. 4.5):

[1]   the house *that they bought last year*
[2]   a student *who belongs to our group*
[3]   the place *where we first met*

The three examples above are **restrictive** relative clauses. Restrictive clauses identify more closely what the nouns refer to. The *house* in [1] might be in contrast with the *house that they used to live in*. The *student* in [2] might be in contrast with a *student who belongs to another group*. The *place* in [3] might be in contrast with a *place where we met last week*.

Non-restrictive relative clauses do not identify. They offer additional information:

[4]   their present house, *which they bought last year*,
[5]   Jean, *who belongs to our group*,
[6]   San Francisco, *where we first met*,

The *house* in [4] is identified by *their present*. The person in [5] and the place in [6] are identified by their names. Names rarely need further identification, but it is possible to use a restrictive clause if further identification is necessary, as in [7]:

[7]   The Jimmy Robinson *who was in my primary school class* has just become a bank manager.

Restrictive clauses should not be punctuated. Non-restrictive clauses, on the other hand, should be enclosed in punctuation marks. The usual punctuation is a pair of commas, as in [8], unless a major punctuation mark (cf. 7.3) would ordinarily appear at the end of the non-restrictive clause, as in [9] and [10]:

[8]   The regulations, *which took effect last fall*, list over 500 industrial processes and materials as hazardous.
[9]   Americans are becoming like Europeans, *who prefer to buy goods that last a long time*.
[10]   I have grown tired of my old stereo, *which I bought 12 years ago*; however, I can't afford to buy a new one.

Dashes or parentheses are sometimes also used to enclose non-restrictive clauses. Dashes indicate dramatic pauses and parentheses separate the clause more distinctly.

Non-restrictive relative clauses may refer back not only to a noun, but also to a previous part of the sentence:

He failed his driving test, *which must be discouraging*. ('His having failed . . . must be discouraging.')
She reads financial publications, *which is unusual for a 15-year-old*.

('Reading financial publications is unusual for a 15-year-old.')

The distinction between restrictive and non-restrictive applies also to reduced relative clauses – those that correspond to relative clauses. Contrast the restrictive clause in [11] and the non-restrictive clause in [12]:

[11]   research *involving chemical reactions* ('that involves chemical reactions')

[12]   his recent research, *involving chemical reactions,*

Here are further examples of restrictive clauses.

It is impossible to find a teacher *who is happy with the facilities at her school.*

The team has developed a fungicide *that acts as a toxic barrier when it is applied to a vine's bare wood.*

He imagines building sites *in which workers have been replaced by smart machines.*

The threat to the premises stems from a change in the planning laws *pushed through by the government in 1987 but only now taking effect.*

Governments in Western Europe are not the only ones *grappling with the problems of monetary integration.*

For the course on current European politics, these are the best books *to read.*

The rents available to workers in the airline industry *can be substantial.*

Here are further examples of non-restrictive clauses:

The Brady cactus, *which is small and single-stemmed,* retracts its head into the soil during dry hot spells.

The technology has opened up astonishing new possibilities, *many of which are already being exploited.*

Human infants pass through a critical period, *lasting a few years,* during which they acquire language.

The foreigners, *treated by the rebels as guests rather than as hostages,* were allowed to escape the next day.

My aunt, *who is frightened of flying,* had a very unpleasant experience on an aeroplane recently.

7.9   Restrictive and non-restrictive apposition

Apposition expresses a relationship of some equivalence between two units (cf. 4.6*f*):

> The civil servants often switch from *English, the official language,* to their native languages.

The relationship can be demonstrated by linking the two units with the verb *be*:

> *English* is *the official language.*

The second unit is generally *appositive* to the first.

Like relative clauses (cf. 7.8), appositives are restrictive or non-restrictive: restrictive appositives identify more closely the preceding noun, whereas non-restrictive appositives offer additional information. And as with relative clauses, restrictive appositives are not punctuated, whereas non-restrictive appositives are enclosed in punctuation marks, normally a pair of commas but occasionally dashes or parentheses. Appositives may be either noun phrases or clauses.

Here are examples of restrictive appositives:

> *My brother* Tom is an architect.
> Do you know the meaning of the word *'pejorative'*?
> I heard on the radio the news *that the party leader had been re-elected.*
> The fact *that she likes the job* suggests that she will remain here for a long while.

Here are examples of non-restrictive apposition:

> The genuine American hamburger, *a ground beef patty served on a bun,* was invented at the beginning of the twentieth century.
> The most reliable indication of Islam's revival is the observance of the hajj, t*he pilgrimage to Mecca that devout Muslims are expected to make at least once in their lifetime.*
> Scientists have discovered two sets of hydrothermal vents (*ocean hot springs*).
> His greatest service – *the issue that made him famous* – was the way he defused the crisis.

The agency ignored <u>their objection</u>, *that the antipollution measures would greatly increase the cost of the products.*

Berkeley scientists have finally realized <u>the medieval alchemist's dream</u>: *transmuting a base metal into gold.*

Like non-restrictive relative clauses, non-restrictive appositives can refer back to a previous part of the sentence, not merely to a noun phrase:

The scientists wanted their research to be useful, *an indication of their desire to work for the benefit of humanity.*

Retail prices were begining to rise, *an early warning of inflation.*

7.10 Adverbial clauses

Clauses that function as adverbials in sentence structure are **adverbial clauses** (cf. 6.9). Adverbial clauses occur initially, medially, and finally. Medial position – the position between the subject and the verb – occurs relatively infrequently. When adverbial clauses are punctuated, the normal punctuation marks are commas. In medial position, the clauses are enclosed in a pair of commas.

Adverbial *-ing* and *-ed* clauses (cf. 6.8) are generally punctuated, whatever their position:

Feeling unadventurous, I ordered chicken soup for my first course.

My parents, *needing money for extensive house repairs,* applied for a second mortgage.

His colleague worked in the corporate section, *selling art to big firms.*

When asked to speak, he complained about the poor service.

My wife, *not easily pleased,* declared that the play was excellent.

It is peaceful to float down a river, *carried effortlessly by the current.*

Medial finite clauses are always punctuated:

The members of the committee, *when they read his report,* demanded his resignation.

Initial finite and infinitive clauses (cf. 6.8) are often punctuated:

If the negotiations are held in public, they are likely to fail.

As the canoe drew near, the design on its prow became visible.
To qualify for entry, the conversion must have been completed since January 1, 1980.

The punctuation of final finite and infinitive clauses depends on their relationship to the rest of the sentence. If they specify the circumstances of the situation, they are not punctuated:

Call me *if you decide not to come with us.*
Security has been heightened *since a porter was mugged.*
I recognized her talents *before anyone else did.*
People often phone *to thank me for my advice.*

If they provide additional information or a comment, they are punctuated:

She walked fast, *so that she arrived before us.*
They expelled him from the country, *although he had not been charged with a crime.*
I have been studying every day past midnight, *since I want to graduate this year.*
He was self-conscious in his casual clothes, *as if he had appeared without socks for a formal reception.*
It's too large, *if I may say so.*
The suit doesn't fit him, *to tell you the truth.*

The same applies to verbless clauses (cf. 6.8):

If in difficulty, phone me.
Her father, *when a hotel manager,* had to work overtime every night.
The procedure was simple, *though somewhat unpleasant.*

If the sentence is negative, the absence of punctuation indicates that the negation includes the adverbial clause. The distinction is particularly sharp for a *because*-clause:

[1]　He didn't go there *because his sister was going to be there.*

The absence of a comma before the *because*-clause in [1] suggests the interpretation 'He did go there, but not because his sister was going to be there'. On the other hand, the presence of a comma stops the negation from applying to the *because*-clause, as in [2]:

[2]   He didn't go there, *because his sister was going to be there.*

The interpretation of [2] is 'He did not go there, and he decided not to because his sister was going to be there'. The same interpretation applies if the *because*-clause is fronted:

[2a]   *Because his sister was going to be there,* he didn't go there.

Adverbials other than clauses are often separated by commas if they provide a comment or have a linking function:

> *Unfortunately,* we were unable to attend your party.
> It was, *quite frankly,* a very boring speech.
> She was, *in fact,* a mathematical genius.
> None of the children liked the puppet show, *to my surprise.*
> Do you know her, *by the way?*
> His opinion, *however,* does not carry any weight.
> Rhetoric has started wars; *on the other hand,* rhetoric has stopped wars.
> *In summary,* his idea was neither original nor correct.

7.11   Vocatives and interjections

Vocatives are phrases – commonly names – that directly address the person spoken to. Vocatives resemble adverbials in their range of positions and are always separated by commas:

> *Mr Chairman,* I want to second the motion.
> Can you tell me, *Caroline,* what I have to do next?
> Turn on the light for me, *Jean.*

Similarly, interjections and other reaction expressions are isolated by commas:

> *Oh,* we didn't expect to see you so soon.
> *Well,* what's your explanation?
> *Yes,* the finals will be next week.
> *OK,* we're ready.

7.12   Avoidance of misunderstanding

Commas may be needed to prevent readers from misunderstanding the sentence, even if only momentarily:

> Above all, discrimination is ethically indefensible. [Not *all discrimination.*]
> After cleaning, position the cutter centrally over the retaining clip and push downwards. [Not *After cleaning position.*]
> When architectural changes occur, clearly society is changing. [Not *occur clearly.*]
> To be honest, workers don't stay there long. [Not *honest workers.*]
> In most parts of the country *you* replaced *thou*, and *ye* was rarely used. [Not *you replaced thou and ye.*]

If the same verb appears twice, a comma is inserted between the two verbs:

> What she thinks her role on the committee is, is likely to influence her decisions.

7.13   Genitives of nouns

In writing we indicate that nouns are genitive (cf. 5.7) by using an apostrophe. The general rules for forming the genitive are:

1. If the noun is singular, add *'s*.

the student	the student's expectations
the woman	the woman's options
David	David's brothers

2. If the noun is plural and ends in *-s*, add just an apostrophe.

the students	the students' expectations
my sisters	my sisters' friends
his parents	his parents' address

3. If the noun is plural and does not end in *-s*, add *'s*.

the women	the women's suggestions
the people	the people's decision
the police	the police's reactions

There is some variation among writers about singular nouns ending in -*s*. On the whole, it is safer to follow the general rule and add '*s*:

The boss's daughter	Charles's video
Burns's poetry	Dickens's novels

The traditional exceptions, which take just the apostrophe are:

1. the genitive of *Jesus* and *Moses*
    Jesus' teaching   Moses' blessing

2. names of more than one syllable that end in -*s* and have an 'eez' sound:
    Socrates' death   Xerxes' defeat

In the fixed expressions *for . . . sake* where the noun in the middle ends in an 's' sound, the noun traditionally takes just the apostrophe:

    for goodness' sake   for appearance' sake

7.14   Genitives of pronouns

Certain indefinite pronouns (cf. 5.25) have a genitive ending in '*s*. These are *one*, compounds ending in -*one* (e.g. *someone*), and compounds ending in -*body* (e.g. *somebody*):

one's friend	anybody's idea
nobody's fault	someone's move

In the combinations with *else*, '*s* is added to e*lse*:

    someone else's coat   no one else's mistake

The indefinite pronoun *other* follows the general rule for nouns: the genitive singular is *other's* and the genitive plural is *others'*:

each other's letters	the others' problems (the problems of
one another's children	the others)

Possessive pronouns (cf. 5.19) ending in -*s* should not have an apostrophe:

hers   its   yours
his   ours   theirs

On the possible confusion of homophones such as *its* and *it's*, see A.7.

8

Usage Problems

SUBJECT–VERB AGREEMENT

8.1 The general rules

The verb agrees with its subject in number and person. The agreement applies whenever the verb displays distinctions in person and number. For all verbs other than *be*, the distinctions are found only in the present tense, where the third person singular has the -*s* form and the third person plural – like the first and second persons – has the base form:

[1] The noise distracts them.
[2] The noises distract them.

The verb *be* makes further distinctions in the present and introduces distinctions in the past. For the convenience of the present discussion, I display the set of present and past forms for *be*:

present tense	singular	plural
1st person	*am*	
2nd person	*are*	*are*
3rd person	*is*	

past tense	singular	plural
1st person	*was*	
2nd person	*were*	*were*
3rd person	*was*	

The distinctions for third person agreement with *be* are illustrated in [3] and [4] for the present and in [5] and [6] for the past:

[3] The noise is distracting them.

139

[4]   The noises are distracting them.
[5]   The noise was distracting them.
[6]   The noises were distracting them.

The agreement affects the first verb in the verb phrase, whether it is a main verb as in [1]–[2] or an auxiliary as in [3]–[6]. Modal auxiliaries (cf. 5.31), however, do not make distinctions in number or person:

The noise
The noises } may distract them.

If the subject is a noun phrase, the main noun determines the number of the phrase:

The *noise* of the { demonstration / demonstrators } *is* distracting them.

The *noises* of the { demonstration / demonstrators } *are* distracting them.

It is a mistake to allow the verb to be influenced by an adjacent noun that is not the main noun.

Noun phrases coordinated with *and* are generally plural, even though the individual noun phrases are singular:

The President and the Vice-President were at the ceremony.

Clauses are generally singular:

That he needs a shave is obvious.
Playing handball relaxes me.
To make mistakes is only human.

The rule of number agreement between subject (S) and verb applies to all finite clauses, whether they are main clauses or subordinate clauses:

Inflation (S) *is* decreasing, and *productivity* (S) *is* rising.
Nature (S) *has* arranged that *no two flowers* (S) *are* the same, even though *they* (S) *appear* very similar.

8.2   *And*

The subject is plural if it consists of two or more phrases that are linked by *and*, even if each is singular:

> Your kitchen, your living-room, and your dining-room *are* too small.

It is also plural if *and* is implied though not actually present:

> Your kitchen, your living-room, your dining-room, *are* too small.

It is plural when one of the main nouns is implied though not actually present:

> British and American English *are* dialects of one language. (British English and American English are . . .)
> Both the first and the second prize *were* won by students at our school. (Both the first prize and the second prize were . . .)

On the other hand, if the linked units refer to the same thing, the subject is singular:

> The first serious poem I read in grade school and one I later studied in high school *was* 'Ozymandias' by Shelley. (The first serious poem was identical with the one later studied.)
> A conscientious and honest politician *has* nothing to fear. (A politician who is both conscientious and honest has . . .)

In some instances, two linked units may be viewed as either a combination (and therefore singular) or as separate units (and therefore plural):

> Bread and butter *is* good for you. (Bread with butter on it is . . .)
> Bread and butter *have* recently gone up in price. (Both bread and butter have . . .)

If the noun phrases are introduced by *each* or *every*, the subject is singular:

> Every student and every instructor *has* to show an ID card to borrow books from the library.

> Each adult and each child *was* given a sandwich.
> Every bank and store *was* closed that day.

See 8.4 for *with* and other linking expressions.

8.3   *Or, nor*

If the noun phrases are linked by *or, either . . . or,* or *neither . . . nor,* the verb may be singular or plural. When both phrases are singular, the verb is singular:

> No food or drink *was* provided.
> Either pollen or dust *causes* his allergy.
> Neither the time nor the place *was* appropriate.

When both phrases are plural, the verb is plural:

> Either the miners or the mineowners *have* to make concessions.

When one phrase is singular and the other plural, usage guides prefer the verb to agree in number with the phrase closest to it:

> Three short essays or one long essay *is* required.
> Neither your brother nor your sisters *are* responsible.

The plural is very often used in conversation regardless of which phrase precedes the verb.

When the linked units are pronouns that require different verb forms, it is better to avoid having to make a choice. Instead, rephrase the sentence:

> Neither you are responsible for the arrangements, nor am I.
> Neither of us is responsible for the arrangements.

8.4   *With*

When a singular noun phrase is linked to a following noun phrase by a preposition such as *with*, the subject is singular even though the preposition is similar in meaning to *and*:

> His sister, together with her two youngest children, *is* staying with them.

The subject is singular because the main noun is singular. Other prepositions used in a similar way include *as well as* and *in addition to*:

> The teacher, as well as the students, *was* enjoying the picnic.

In the following sentence, the preposition is *after*:

> One person after another *has* objected to the proposed reform.

8.5   Collective nouns

A collective noun refers to a group of people or things. Some common
examples are:

administration	enemy	herd
army	firm	jury
audience	family	mob
class	fleet	nation
committee	gang	public
crew	government	swarm
crowd	group	team

When members of the group are viewed as a unit, singular verbs and singular pronouns are usual:

> The audience *was* very noisy.
> The public *has* a right to know.
> The jury *has* retired for the night, but *it* will resume *its* delibera-
> tions early tomorrow.

Plural verbs and plural pronouns are used when the members of the group
are viewed as individuals:

> All the team *are* in *their* places. (All the members of the team are
> ...)
> The committee *have* not been able to agree among *themselves*
> whether to approve the proposed changes.

8.6   Indefinite pronouns

Most indefinite pronouns (cf. 5.25) take singular verbs:

> Everybody *is* now here.
> Someone *has* borrowed my comb.

In formal writing, use singular verbs even when a plural phrase follows the pronouns:

> Either of them *is* prepared to help you.
> Each of our friends *has* taken the course.

Several indefinite pronouns (*none, all, some, any*) and the fractions may be either singular or plural. If they refer to one thing, they take a singular verb:

> Some (of the material) *is* not suitable for children.
> Half (the county) *is* under water.
> All (the fruit) *has* been eaten.
> None (of the crop) *was* in danger.

If they refer to more than one person or thing, they take a plural verb:

> Some (of the pages) *are* missing.
> Half (of the members) *have* voted in favour of the amendment to the constitution.
> All (my friends) *were* abroad.
> None (of us) *have* heard about the new regulation.

None is also used with a singular verb:

> None (of us) *has* heard about the new regulation.

Problems sometimes arise in the choice of pronouns or determiners for which singular indefinite pronouns are the antecedent. The traditional choice for formal writing is a masculine pronoun or determiner, according to what is required in the context:

[1]   Everybody wanted a room of *his* own.
[2]   Does anyone think *he* can solve this problem?

It is also the traditional choice when noun phrases are introduced by indefinite determiners such as *every* or *any* (cf. 5.26*f*) or when the phrases refer to a class of people:

[3]   Every student has handed in *his* work on time.

[4]   A good musician receives more invitations to perform than *he* can manage.

Changes in attitude have led many to avoid using the masculine to refer to both male and female. It is generally possible to rephrase the sentence to avoid suggesting a sexist bias. One way is to avoid using a pronoun or possessive determiner, as in [1a]; another way is to make the subject plural, as in [2a]–[4a]:

[1a]   Everybody wanted a separate room.

[2a]   Do a*ny of you* think you can solve the problem?

[3a]   *All students* have handed in *their* work on time.

[4a]   *Good musicians* receive more invitations to perform than *they* can manage.

8.7   Quantity phrases

Plural phrases of quantity or extent take singular verbs when the quantity or extent is viewed as a unit:

Ten pounds *is* enough.
Two years *seems* too long to wait.
Five miles *was* as far as they would walk.

Otherwise, a plural is used:

Two years *have* passed since I was last here.
Twenty-seven pounds *were* stolen from his wallet.

8.8   Singular nouns ending in -*s*

Nouns ending in -*ics* are singular when they refer to a field of study, for example *civics, economics, linguistics, mathematics, physics, statistics*:

Statistics *is* one of the options in the degree course.

Economics *was* my favourite subject at school.

Some of these nouns are used in a different sense and may then be plural:

Your statistics *are* inaccurate.
The acoustics in this hall *have* been improved.

Names of diseases that end in -*s* are generally treated as singular, for example *measles, mumps, rickets*:

Measles *is* a highly infectious disease.

Names of games that end in -*s* are singular, for example *billiards, darts, draughts, dominoes*:

Dominoes *is* the only game I play at home.

Individual pieces have singular and plural forms:

You've dropped a *domino* on the floor.
The *dominoes are* on the floor.

8.9   Who, which, that

The relative pronouns *who, which,* and *that* have the same number as the nouns they refer to. The singular is correct in the following sentences:

I have written a letter for the student who *is* applying for a job in our department. (The student is applying . . .)
You need special permission to borrow a book which *is* kept in the reference section. (The book is kept . . .)
They noted the tension that *has* begun to mount in the city. (The tension has begun to mount . . .)

The plural is correct in the following sentences:

People who *live* in glasshouses shouldn't throw stones. (The people live in glasshouses.)
The weapons which *were* found during the search were produced

as evidence in court. (The weapons were found . . .)
She reported on the motions that *were* passed at the meeting.
(The motions were passed . . .)

The same rule of agreement applies when the relative pronoun refers to a personal pronoun:

> You who *are* my closest friends know best what needs to be done. (You are my closest friends)
> It is I who *am* to blame. (I am to blame)
> It is he who *is* responsible for organizing the event. (He is responsible . . .)

In less formal contexts, constructions beginning *It's* . . . will take objective forms of the pronouns (cf. 8.13) and third person verb forms:

> It's *me* who*'s*/who *was* to blame.
> It's *us* who *are*/*were* to blame.

8.10 What

You may use either a singular verb or a plural verb with the pronoun *what*. The choice depends on the meaning:

> What worries them is that he has not yet made up his mind. (The thing that worries them . . .)
> They live in what *are* called ranch houses. (in houses that *are* called . . .)

Similarly, use either the singular or the plural with *what*-clauses, according to the meaning:

> What they need *is* a good rest. (The thing that they need is . . .)
> What were once painful ordeals *are* now routine examinations. (Those things . . . are now . . .)

8.11 There is, there are

In speech it is common to use a singular verb after introductory *there* (cf. 6.11) even when the subject (which follows the verb) is plural:

There's two men waiting for you.

In formal writing, follow the general rule:

There *is* somebody waiting for you.
There *are* two men waiting for you.

8.12   Citations and titles

Citations and titles always take a singular verb, even though they consist of plural phrases:

'Children' *is* an irregular plural.
The Power and the Glory is a novel set in Mexico.
The Four Feathers was one of the first novels I read as a child.

CASE

8.13   Subject complement

When the subject complement is a pronoun, it is usually in the objective case: *It's me, That's him.* Such sentences tend to occur in speech or written dialogue. Subjective forms as in *It is I* and *This is he* are felt to be pedantic, though they may be used in formal contexts in constructions such as *It is I who am to blame, It is he who is responsible* (cf. 8.9).

8.14   Coordinated phrases

In 5.18 I stated the rules for the selection of subjective and objective cases in pronouns: we use the subjective case for the subject and (in formal style) for the subject complement; otherwise we use the objective case. Errors of case may arise when a pronoun is coordinated with a noun or another pronoun:

[1]   *You and her* will take charge. (Correct to *You and she.*)
[2]   I think *Bob and me* have the right approach. (Correct to *Bob and I.*)
[3]   Everybody knows *Nancy and I.* (Correct to *Nancy and me.*)
[4]   The tickets are for *you and I.* (Correct to *you and me.*)

The errors do not occur when there is only one pronoun. You can therefore test which form is correct by using just the second pronoun:

[1a]   *She* will take charge. (*She* is subject.)
[2a]   I think *I* have the right approach. (*I* is subject of the subordinate
        clause.)
[3a]   Everybody knows *me*. (*Me* is direct object.)
[4a]   The tickets are for *me*. (*Me* is complement of the preposition *for*.)

There is a similar possibility of error when *we* or *us* is accompanied by a
noun:

> They complained about the way *us* students were behaving.
> (Correct to *we students*. Cf.: *the way we were behaving*.)
> They will not succeed in pushing *we Australians* around. (Correct
> to *us Australians*. Cf.: *pushing us around*.)

8.15   After *as* and *than*

In formal writing, *as* and *than* are always conjunctions in comparisons.
The case of the pronoun depends on its function in the comparative
clause, though the verb may be absent:

[1]   They felt the same way as *he*. (*He* is subject.)
[2]   She works faster than *we*. (*We* is subject.)
[3]   They paid him more than *me*. (*Me* is indirect object.)
[4]   He likes me more than *her*. (*Her* is direct object.)

You can test which form is correct by expanding the comparative clause:

[1a]   They felt the same way as *he* did.
[2a]   She works faster than *we* do.
[3a]   They paid him more than they paid *me*.
[4a]   He likes me more than he likes *her*.

In less formal contexts, the objective forms are normal even when the
pronoun is subject:

[1b]   They felt the same way as *him*.
[2b]   She works faster than *us*.

8.16   After *but*

But meaning 'except' is a preposition. In formal writing, the pronoun following the preposition *but* should be in the objective case:

> I know everybody here but *her*.
> Nobody but *me* can tell the difference.

8.17   After *let*

Use the objective case after *let*:

> Let *us* examine the problem carefully.
> Let *them* make their own decisions.

Take care that a coordinated pronoun is objective:

> Let *you and me* take the matter in hand.
> Let *Bob and her* say what they think.

8.18   *Who, whom*

Whom is not often used in everyday speech. In formal writing, however, retain the distinction between subjective *who* and objective *whom*:

> She is somebody *who* knows her own mind. (Cf.: *She* knows her own mind.)
> She is somebody on *whom* I can rely. (Cf.: I can rely on *her*.)

Parenthetic clauses like *I believe* and *I think* should not affect the choice of case:

[1]   I recently spoke to somebody *who* I believe knows you well. (Cf.: *She* knows you well, I believe.)

[2]   I recently spoke to somebody *whom* I believe you know well. (Cf.: You know *her* well, I believe.)

The following example is different:

[3]   She is somebody *whom* I consider to be a good candidate for

promotion. (Cf.: I consider *her* to be a good candidate for promotion.)

I consider in [3] is not parenthetic. It cannot be omitted like *I believe* in [1] and [2]. *Whom* in [3] is the direct object of *consider*.

Similarly, retain the distinction between subjective *whoever* and *whomever* in formal writing:

> *Whoever* wants to see me should make an appointment with my secretary. (Cf.: *She* wants to see me.)
> You can show the report to *whoever* wants to see it. (Cf: *She* wants to see it.)
> I will offer advice to *whomever* I wish. (Cf.: I wish to offer advice to *her*.)

8.19 Case with *-ing* clauses

An *-ing* participle clause may have a nominal function (i.e. a function similar to one possible for a noun phrase). If the subject of the clause is a pronoun, a name, or other short personal noun phrase, it is preferable to put it into the genitive case:

> They were surprised at $\left\{\begin{array}{c} Gerald's \\ his \end{array}\right\}$ refusing to join the strike
> He was afraid of *my* protesting against the new rule.
> I dislike *Robert's* seeing x-rated movies.
> Do you know the reason for *your sister's* breaking off the engagement

Use the common case for long noun phrases:

> I remember *a car with a broken rear window* being parked alongside our house.
> They were annoyed at *the students and staff* demonstrating against cuts in student loans.

Use the common case for non-personal nouns:

> I am interested in *the car* being sold as soon as possible.

Except in formal writing, the subject is often in the common case (for nouns) or objective case (for pronouns):

They were surprised at $\left\{ \begin{array}{l} Gerald \\ him \end{array} \right\}$ refusing to join the strike

In all styles, use the genitive when the clause is the subject:

My forgetting her name amused everybody.

In all styles, use the common case (for nouns) or objective case (for pronouns) after verbs of perception, such as *see*, or certain other verbs, the most frequent of which are *find*, *keep*, and *leave*:

I kept *them* waiting.

AUXILIARIES AND VERBS

8.20   Problems with Auxiliaries

When it follows a modal (cf. 5.31), the auxiliary *have* is often pronounced like *of* and is therefore sometimes misspelled *of*. The correct spelling is *have* after the modals in these sentences:

I *should have* said something about it long ago.
Somebody else *would have* paid.
You *might have* helped me.
She *could have* become the mayor.

The semi-modal *had better* is often rendered as *'d better* or *better* in speech: *He better not be there*. Use the full expression in formal writing.

Ought to should be the first verb in the verb phrase. Combinations such as *didn't ought to* and *hadn't ought to* are not standard.

8.21   *Lie, lay*

The intransitive verb *lie* ('be in a reclining position') and the transitive verb *lay* ('place') are often confused, because the past tense of *lie* is *lay* and the present tense of *lay* is *lay* or *lays*. Here are the forms of the two verbs:

present tense	*lie, lies*	*lay, lays*
-ing participle	*lying*	*laying*
past tense	*lay*	*laid*
-ed participle	*lain*	*laid*

Here are examples of sentences with these verbs:

lie   Is she *lying* on the sofa?
The children *lay* asleep on the floor.
I have *lain* in bed all morning.

lay   Are you *laying* a bet on the next race?
He *laid* his head on his arms.
The hens have *laid* a dozen eggs this morning.

8.22   Present tense

Standard written English requires the *-s* inflection for the third person singular and no inflection elsewhere (cf. 8.1 for the verb *be*):

Johns say*s*.	I say.
She know*s*.	We know
The dog bite*s*.	They bite.
It do*es*.	You do.

Forms such as *I says, you knows,* and *it do* are heard in casual conversation, but they are not standard forms and should therefore be avoided unless they represent non-standard speech in dialogue.

Negative contractions sometimes cause difficulties. The standard contraction of *does not* is *doesn't (she doesn't)*, not *don't*. Negative *ain't* is commonly heard in casual conversation as a contraction of various combinations, including *am not, is not, have not,* and *has not*, but it is not a standard form.

8.23   Past and *-ed* participle

Regular verbs have the same form for the past and the *-ed* participle:

He *laughed* loudly.
He hasn't *laughed* so much for a long time.

Some irregular verbs have different forms:

> She *spoke* to me about it.
> She has *spoken* to me about it.

Except in written representations of non-standard speech, do not write non-standard forms for the past and *-ed* participle:

> I *done* my assignment. (Correct to *did*.)
> We *seen* the movie last week. (Correct to *saw*.)
> He was *shook* up by the news. (Correct to *shaken*.)
> I must have *knew* her. (Correct to *known*.)

Some verbs have variant forms that are acceptable for both past and *-ed* participle: *dreamed, dreamt; kneeled, knelt; lighted, lit; shined, shone*. The past and *-ed* participle of *hang* is generally *hanged* in the sense 'suspend by neck until dead' and is *hung* when it refers to pictures *hung*.

8.24   Past and past subjunctive

The past subjunctive is used to refer to situations that are very unlikely or that are contrary to the facts (cf. 4.19):

> I wish she *were* here.
> He behaves as though he *were* your friend.
> Suppose she *were* here now.
> If I *were* you, I wouldn't tell him.

The only past subjunctive is *were*, which is used for the first and third person singular of the verb *be* in formal English. In less formal style the simple past *was* is generally used in the same contexts:

> I wish she *was* here.
> If I *was* you, I wouldn't tell him.

For the plural and the second person singular of *be* and for verbs other than *be*, the simple past is used to refer to situations in the present or future that are very unlikely or that are contrary to fact. One very common context is in conditional clauses, clauses that express a condition on which something else is dependent:

If they *were* graduating next year, they would need to borrow less money. (But they probably will not be graduating next year.)

If she *lived* at home, she would be happier. (But she does not live at home.)

If I *came* to your party, I would need a new dress. (But I probably won't come to your party.)

The verb in the main clause is always a past modal, usually *would*.

If the situations are set in the past, the past perfect is used in the conditional clause and a past perfect modal, usually *would have*, in the main clause:

If we *had been* there yesterday, we *would have seen* them. (But we were not there yesterday.)

If he *had been given* a good mark, he *would have told me*. (But it seems that he was not given a good mark.)

If the auxiliary in the conditional clause is *were*, *had*, or *should*, we can omit *if* and front the auxiliary:

Were she here now, there would be no problem.

Had we stayed at home, we would have met them.

Should you see him, give him my best wishes.

8.25   Multiple negation

Standard English generally allows only one negative in the same clause. Non-standard English allows two or more negatives in the same clause:

double negation	They did*n't* say *nothing*.
corrected	They said *nothing*.
	They did*n't* say *anything*.
triple negation	*Nobody never* believes *nothing* I say.
corrected	*Nobody ever* believes *anything* I say.
double negation	I did*n't* like it, *neither*.
corrected	I did*n't* like it, *either*.

Negative adverbs include not only the obvious negative *never*, but also *barely, hardly, scarcely*:

double negation	I ca*n't hardly* tell the difference.
corrected	I *can hardly* tell the difference.

Standard English allows double negation when the two negatives combine to make a positive. When *not* modifies an adjective or adverb with a negative prefix (*unhappy, indecisively*), it reduces the negative force of the word, perhaps to express an understatement:

It was a *not unhappy* occasion. ('a fairly happy occasion')
She spoke *not indecisively*. ('fairly decisively')

Occasionally both the auxiliary and the main verb are negated:

You ca*n't not* obey her instructions. ('It's not possible for you not to obey her instructions.')

Other negative combinations also occasionally occur:

Nobody has *no* complaints. ('There is nobody that has no complaints'; 'Everybody has some complaints.')

ADJECTIVES AND ADVERBS

8.26   Confusion between Adjectives and Adverbs

It is occasionally not obvious whether to use an adjective or a related adverb. One rule is to use an adjective if the word is the subject complement after a linking verb (cf. 3.8). The adjective characterizes the subject:

She looked *angry*.
She feels *bad*.
I don't feel *well*.
He sounded *nervous*.
The flowers smell *sweet*.
The food tastes *good*.

The adverb *badly* is often used with the linking verb *feel*, but in formal writing use *feel bad*. *Well* in *I don't feel well* is an adjective meaning 'in good health'. It is an adverb in 'He didn't play *well*.'

If the word characterizes the manner of the action denoted by the verb, use an adverb in formal writing:

> She writes *well*. (not *good*)
> He hurt his neck *badly*. (not *bad*)
> Your dog is barking *loudly*. (not *loud*)
> If the job is done *satisfactorily*, I will give him other jobs (not *satisfactory*)

Some words can have the same form for both the adjective and the adverb: *early*, *fast*, *hard*, *late*, *slow*, *quick*, *long*, and words in *-ly* that are formed from nouns denoting time (*hourly*, *daily*). The adverbs *slow*, *quick*, and *deep* also have parallel adverb forms in *-ly*: *slowly*, *quickly*, and *deeply*. These three adverbs formed without the *-ly* suffix are mainly used with imperatives:

> Drive *slow*,
> Come *quick*,
> Dig *deep* into your pocket for a donation.

Both *direct* and *directly* are adverbs in the senses 'in a straight line' or 'without anything intervening':

> Bring it *direct* to me.

8.27 Comparison

Most adjectives and adverbs are *gradable* (cf. 5.14): we can view them as being on a scale of less or more. Gradable words allow comparison (*less foolish*, *more quickly*) and modification by intensifiers that show how far they are along the scale (*somewhat foolish*, *very quickly*). Some adjectives and adverbs are not gradable; for example, we cannot say *more medical* or *very previously*.

Writers vary on whether certain adjectives or adverbs are gradable. Those who treat them as non-gradable think that they express the highest degree (*excellent*) or that they cannot be measured on a scale (*uniquely*). The most common of these disputed words are *complete(ly)*, *perfect(ly)*, *unique(ly)*. Yet even in formal writing we find expressions such as *a more perfect union* or *the most extreme poverty*. If you are in doubt, it is better not to treat these words as gradable in formal writing.

Use the comparative for two only (*the older of the two girls*) and the superlative for more than two (*the oldest of the three girls*).

The comparative of the adjective *bad* and the adverb *badly* is *worse* (not *worser*); the superlative is *worst* (not *worsest*).

Fewer goes with count nouns and *less* with non-count nouns:

fewer { demonstrators / mistakes / votes }   less { help / sunlight / time }

Less is often used with count nouns, but this use is a mistake in formal writing.

8.28   *Only*

Where you put *only* in a sentence may affect how the reader understands the sentence. In speech you can make your intention clear through your intonation, but when you write, it is best to put *only* next to the word or phrase it refers to:

> *Only children* can swim in the lake before noon. (not adults)
> Children can *only swim* in the lake before noon. (not fish)
> Children can swim *only in the lake* before noon. (not in the pool)
> Children can swim in the lake *only before noon*. (not in the afternoon)

There are other words that you need to position with care: *also, even, just, and merely.*

8.29   Dangling modifiers

Absolute clauses are non-finite or verbless adverbial clauses that have their own subjects:

> *All their money having been spent on repairs*, they applied to the bank for a loan.
> He nervously began his speech, *his voice trembling and his face flushed*.

They strolled by the river, *their heads bare*.

If adverbial clauses have no subject of their own, their implied subject is generally the same as the subject of the sentence:

> *Having spent all his money on a vacation to Hawaii*, Norman applied to the bank for a loan. (Norman has spent all his money on a vacation to Hawaii.)

A **dangling modifier** has no subject of its own, and its implied subject cannot be identified with the subject of the sentence though it can usually be identified with some other phrase in the sentence:

dangling	*Being blind*, a dog guided her across the street.
corrected	Being blind, she was guided across the street by a dog.
dangling	*Although large enough*, they did not like the apartment.
corrected	Although the apartment was large enough, they did not like it.
dangling	*After turning the radio off*, the interior of the car became silent.
corrected	After she (or *I*, etc.) turned the radio off, the interior of the car became silent.
dangling	*When absent through illness*, the company pays you your full salary for six months.
corrected	When you are absent through illness, the company pays you your full salary for six months.
dangling	*Being an excellent student*, her teacher gave her extra work to do.
corrected	Since she was an excellent student, her teacher gave her extra work to do.

9

Style

9.1   Style in writing

In normal unprepared conversation we have only a very limited time to monitor what we say and the way we say it. We have much more time when we write, and generally we have the opportunity to revise what we write. Sometimes we are happy with our first decision, but very often we think of new things as we write and perhaps want to change both what we write and how we write it.

In our revisions we can draw on the resources that are available to us in various aspects of the language. Our writing style reflects the choices we make. In this chapter we will be looking at the choices we make in grammar. In particular, we will be considering how we can ensure that we convey our message effectively.

EMPHASIS

9.2   End-focus

It is normal to arrange the information in our message so that the most important information comes at the end. We follow this principle of *end-focus* when we put such information at the end of a sentence or clause. In contrast, the beginning of a sentence or clause typically contains information that is general knowledge, or is obvious from the context, or may be assumed as given because it has been mentioned earlier.

The following paragraph appeared in the middle of an article on the immigration to Canada of large numbers of wealthy Hong Kong Chinese. The influx was encouraged by the Canadian government but resented by many Canadians. The final part of each sentence (italicized here, but not in the original) conveys the most important information:

160

People who strive to become better-off in their own country are '*upwardly mobile*'. If they are willing to climb on an aeroplane and be a stranger in a strange land they become '*economic refugees*'. Should their adopted home desperately need an injection of cash and entrepreneurial skill, then they are termed '*immigrant investors*'. But perhaps they *shouldn't expect to be welcome*. [Keith Wheately in *The Sunday Times Magazine*, December 17, 1989, p. 22]

If we put a subordinate clause at the end, it receives greater emphasis. For example, [2] emphasizes the action of the committee members, whereas [2a] emphasizes their feelings:

[2]   *Although they were not completely happy with it*, the committee members adopted her wording of the resolution.

[2a]   The committee members adopted her wording of the resolution, *although they were not completely happy with it*.

Similarly, the pairs that follow show how we can choose which information comes at the end by the way we phrase the sentence:

[3]   The American public is not interested in *foreign policy*.

[3a]   Foreign policy does not interest *the American public*.

[4]   On guard stood *a man with a gun in each hand*.

[4a]   A man with a gun in each hand stood *on guard*.

[5]   Teenagers are *difficult to teach*.

[5a]   It is difficult to teach *teenagers*.

9.3   Front-focus

If we place an expression in an abnormal position, the effect is to make the expression more conspicuous. It is abnormal for the verb and any objects or complements to come before the subject. If these are fronted, they acquire greater prominence:

Attitudes will not change overnight, but *change* they will.

Marijuana they used occasionally, but *cocaine* they never touched.

Easily recognizable was the leader of the wolf pack.

The same applies if an adverbial that normally follows the verb is fronted and therefore comes before the subject:

> *Out* you go.
> *Here* they are.
> *Into the office* I marched.
> *On the highest storey* we lived.

When a negative adverbial is fronted, it gains stronger emphasis. The operator comes before the subject, as in questions:

> *Never* have so many youngsters been unemployed.
> *Under no circumstances* will they permit smoking in public areas.

9.4   *There*-structures and cleft sentences

There-structures give greater prominence to the subject (cf. 6.11):

> There were some students who refused to show their ID card.

They are particularly useful when the only other elements are the subject and the verb *be*:

> There are no simple solutions.
> There was no reason to be annoyed.
> There is more than one kind of octane rating.

Cleft sentences (cf. 6.12) provide greater prominence to one part of the sentence by placing it after a semantically empty subject (*it*) and a semantically empty verb (*be*):

> It was *a human error* that caused the explosion.
> It is *the ending* that is the weakest part of the novel.

Similar effects can be achieved by using a nominal relative clause (cf. 6.9) or a general abstract noun:

> What caused the explosion was *a human error*.
> The thing that caused the explosion was *a human error*.
> What he forgot to do was to *lock the front door*.

9.5   Parenthetic expressions

Parenthetic expressions are marked by intonation in speech and by punctuation in writing. The effect of the interruption is to give greater prominence to the previous unit:

> *Freud,* of course, thought that he had discovered the underlying causes of many mental illnesses.
> The record business is *not,* in actual fact, an easy business to succeed in.
> *In Australia,* for example, the kangaroo is a traffic hazard.
> *The unions,* understandably, wanted the wage increase to be adjusted to rising inflation.

CLARITY

9.6   End-weight

Where there is a choice, it is normal for a longer structure to come at the end. This principle of **end-weight** is in large part a consequence of the principle of end-focus (cf. 9.2), since the more important information tends to be given in fuller detail.

A sentence is clumsy and more difficult to understand when the subject is considerably longer than the predicate. We can rephrase the sentence to shift the weight to the end:

> **clumsy**   *The rate at which the American people are using up the world's supply of irreplaceable fossil fuels and their refusal to admit that the supply is limited* is the real problem.
>
> **improved**   The real problem is *the rate at which the American people are using up the world's supply of irreplaceable fossil fuels and their refusal to admit that the supply is limited.*

Similarly, if there is a considerable difference in length among the units that follow the verb, the longer or longest unit should come at the end:

clumsy   The discovery of a baby mammal in Siberia has provided *biochemists, anthropologists, immunologists, zoologists, and paleontologists* with ample material.

improved   The discovery of a baby mammal in Siberia has provided ample material for *biochemists, anthropologists, immunologists, zoologists, and paleontologists.*

Other examples follow where a rephrasing is desirable because of the principle of end-weight:

clumsy   Einstein's theories have made *many important technological developments which we now take for granted* possible.

improved   Einstein's theories have made possible *many important technological developments which we now take for granted.*

clumsy   *The value of trying to identify the problem and to provide the tools necessary to make the education of these children a success* is not questioned.

improved   No one questions *the value of trying to identify the problem and to provide the tools necessary to make the education of these children a success.*

clumsy   *That the recession will be longer, deeper, and more painful than was expected only a few weeks ago* is very possible.

improved   It is very possible *that the recession will be longer, deeper, and more painful than was expected only a few weeks ago.*

clumsy   *A pronunciation set of symbols to enable the reader to produce a satisfactory pronunciation* is used.

improved   *A pronunciation set of symbols* is used *to enable the reader to produce a satisfactory pronunciation.*

9.7   Misplaced expressions

We show where an expression belongs by where we place it. For example, [1] and [1a] as written sentences are likely to be understood differently because of the different positions of *immediately afterwards*:

[1]   *Immediately afterwards* I remembered having met her.

[1a]   I remembered having met her *immediately afterwards*.

A sentence is more difficult to understand when an expression is mis-placed, even if there is no danger of misinterpretation. The [a] sentences in the pairs that follow give a corrected placement:

[2]   He had not realized how slim she had become *before he saw her*.
[2a]   *Before he saw her*, he had not realized how slim she had become.
[3]   They knew what I meant *quite well*.
[3a]   They knew *quite well* what I meant.
[4]   She told him that it was all a joke *in a calm voice*.
[4a]   She told him *in a calm voice* that it was all a joke.

Sometimes a sentence has more than one interpretation because an expression is positioned where it might belong in either of two directions. In [5] *on several occasions* may go with *He said* or with *he suffered from headaches:*

[5]   He said *on several occasions* he suffered from headaches.

One way of showing it belongs with *He said* is to insert the conjunction *that* after it, since *on several occasions* will then be outside the boundaries of the subordinate clause:

[5a]   He said *on several occasions* that he suffered from headaches.

The second interpretation is elicited in [5b]:

[5b]   He said that he *occasionally* suffered from headaches.

For [6], we can ensure the correct interpretation by moving *again* to un-ambiguous positions, as in [6a] and [6b]:

[6]   I told them *again* the meeting had been postponed.
[6b]   I *again* told them the meeting had been postponed.
[6b]   I told them the meeting had *again* been postponed.

For [7], it might be best to rephrase the sentence, as in [7a] and [7b]:

[7]   Writing *clearly* is important.

[7a]   It is important to write clearly.

[7b]   It is clear that writing is important.

Similarly, [8a] and [8b] clarify the intended meaning of the writer of [8]:

[8]   Looking at the ages of the subjects *first* proved not to be very useful.

[8a]   It proved not to be very useful to look *first* at the ages of the subjects.

[8b]   *At first* it proved not to be very useful to look at the ages of the subjects.

9.8   Abstract nouns

It is often possible to make a sentence clearer by rephrasing it to replace abstract nouns (or at least some of them) with verbs or adjectives:

clumsy   Since the *decriminalization* of public *drunkenness*, people have been avoiding Broadway Park, where drunks have been congregating.

improved   Since it is no longer a crime to be drunk in public, people have been avoiding Broadway Park, where drunks have been congregating.

clumsy   The report evaluates the *effectiveness* of government regulations in terms of the *extent* to which exposures to carcinogenic substances have been reduced.

improved   The report evaluates how effective government regulations have been in reducing exposures to carcinogenic substances.

clumsy   They should lessen their *self-centredness* and increase their *assistance* to others.

improved   They should be less self-centred and more helpful to others.

General abstract nouns are often redundant. In such cases you can easily leave them out by rephrasing the sentence:

redundant If the fox population were not controlled by *the fox-*

	hunting method, other techniques would have to be employed.
improved	If the fox population were not controlled by *fox-hunting,* other techniques would have to be employed.
redundant	The charge that the industry is making excessive profits does not stand on *a valid foundation.*
improved	The charge that the industry is making excessive profits is not *valid.*
redundant	*The entertainment aspect* of reading is *a factor* in addition to the *informative experience* of reading.
improved	Reading provides *entertainment* as well as *information.*
or	Reading is *entertaining* as well as *informative.*

Some longwinded phrases with general words such as *fact* are better replaced by simpler conjunctions or prepositions:

longwinded	I went with my friends to see the film *in spite of the fact that* I dislike war films.
improved	I went with my friends to see the film *even though* I dislike war films.

Other examples are *on account of the fact that* and *due to the fact that* (both of which can be replaced by 'because'), *apart from the fact that* ('except'), *as a consequence of* ('because of'), *during the course of* ('during'), *in the neighbourhood of* ('near'), *with the exception of* ('except').

9.9   Modifiers in noun phrases

Readers may find it difficult to work out the meaning of a noun phrase that has two or more modifiers. If we are writing about American history, it may be obvious what we mean by *American history teachers.* But if the context fails to make the meaning unambiguous, we should use prepositions to show the relationships: *teachers of American history* or *American teachers of history.*

Even if there is no ambiguity, a long noun phrase such as *annual human rights progress statements* is better written with prepositions that indicate the words that belong together: *annual statements on the progress on human rights.*

9.10   Subordination

It is sometimes better to split up a long complex sentence:

[1]   *Because* many minor revisions were still required in the second draft of the document, contact with individual committee members was made by phone or letter, *as* the committee had been dissolved by the board and was soon to be replaced by an entirely new committee made up of members from a different department within the university.

One way of improving the readability of [1] is to divide it into two or more sentences, since one of the problems with [1] is that it contains two clauses (introduced by *because* and *as*) that separately give reasons for contacting committee members:

[1a]   Many minor revisions were still required in the second draft of the document. Committee members were individually contacted by phone or letter for their views on the draft, since the committee had been dissolved by the board. An entirely new committee was soon to be formed consisting of members from a different department within the university.

In [2] the problem is the string of *that*-clauses:

[2]   She rehearsed the speech *that* she was to give to the committee *that* distributed funds *that* had been allocated for training the unemployed.

We can replace the last two *that*-clauses by converting them into nonfinite clauses, as in [2a]:

[2a]   She rehearsed the speech *that* she was to give to the committee *distributing* funds *allocated* for training the unemployed.

9.11   Parallelism

Parallel structures provide a pleasing balance between the parallel units, and they emphasize meaning relationships between the units such as equivalence and contrast.

Parallelism often involves coordination. The coordinate units must be

similar in type. Here is an example of faulty parallelism, where the units
are wrongly coordinated.

faulty	They discontinued the production of the paint because *the results of the field tests were unsatisfactory* and *a lack of interested customers.* (clause and noun phrase)
corrected	They discontinued the production of the paint because *the results of the field tests were unsatisfactory* and *there was a lack of interested customers.*
or	They discontinued the production of the paint because of *the unsatisfactory results of the field tests* and *a lack of interested customers.*
faulty	You will find long lines *in the bookstore* and *to pay your tuition.* (prepositional phrase and infinitive clause)
corrected	You will find long lines *in the bookstore* and *at the cashier.*

The relative pronoun *that* is generally an alternative to *which* or *who*. It
is a fault to switch from *that* to *which* or *who*, or vice versa. The fault is
illustrated in the following sentence; it can be corrected by using either
which or *that* in both instances.

Scientists are still trying to explain the UFO *which* was seen over
Siberia in 1908 by thousands of witnesses and *that* caused an ex-
plosion like that of an H-bomb.

In a series of three or more coordinated units, we can often choose
whether to repeat words from the first unit or to leave them out. But we
should be consistent:

faulty	*The* colour of her hair, look of self-assurance, and *the* aristocratic bearing match those in the painting of the beautiful woman staring from the wall of the living room. (determiner in the third unit, but not in the second)
corrected	*The* colour of her hair, *the* look of self-assurance, and *the* aristocratic bearing . . .
or	*The* colour of her hair, look of self-assurance, and aristocratic bearing . . .

faulty	His collages derive from *both* art *and* from popular culture.
corrected	His collages derive from *both* art *and* popular culture.
or	His collages derive *both* from art *and* from popular culture.
faulty	They *neither* will help *nor* hinder her attempts to persuade the workers to join the trade union.
corrected	They will *neither* help *nor* hinder . . .
faulty	We realized that we had to make a decision, *either* marry *or* we go our separate ways.
corrected	We realized that we had to make a decision, *either* marry *or* go our separate ways.

Similarly, expressions that compare or contrast must also introduce parallel units:

faulty	The lung capacity of non-smokers exposed to tobacco smoke in offices is *measurably less than* non-smokers in smoke-free offices.
corrected	. . . is *measurably less than* that of non-smokers in smoke-free offices.
faulty	I *prefer* the novels of Hemingway *to* Faulkner.
corrected	I *prefer* the novels of Hemingway *to* those of Faulkner.
or	I *prefer* Hemingway *to* Faulkner.

Both correlatives must be present in comparative structures of the type *The more, the merrier*:

faulty	If the cost of raw materials keeps rising, *the more* manufacturers will raise their prices.
corrected	*The more* the cost of raw materials rises, *the more* manufacturers will raise their prices.
or	If the cost of raw materials keeps rising, manufacturers will raise their prices.

9.12   Repeated Sounds

Avoid putting words near each other if they sound the same or almost the same but have different meanings. The lack of harmony between sound and sense may be distracting and sometimes even confusing. I suggest some alternatives in parentheses:

> Industries and the professions are *finding* it increasingly difficult to *find* people qualified in basic writing skills. (Replace *find* by *recruit* or *hire*.)
>
> The *subject* of my paper is the agreement between *subject* and verb in English. (Replace the first *subject* by *topic*.)
>
> At this *point* I should *point* out that I left of my own free will. (Replace *point out* by *mention*.)
>
> The television *show showed* how coal was mined in the United States. (Replace *showed* by *demonstrated*.)

9.13   Pronoun Reference

A pronoun may refer to something in the situation (*this* in *Give this to your mother*), but generally it refers back to another word or phrase – its antecedent (cf. 5.17). The reference to an antecedent should be clear:

> **unclear**   The students worked during the vacation for individuals who were fussy about *their* work.
>
> **clarified**   *The students* worked during the vacation for individuals who were fussy about *the students'* work.
>
> **or**   The students worked during the vacation for *individuals* who were fussy about *their own* work.

You need to be particularly careful when you intend the pronoun to refer to more than a phrase:

> **unclear**   Some people believe that *a person is successful only when he acquires enormous wealth* and they cannot be persuaded otherwise. But *that* is not always true.
>
> **clarified**   Some people believe that *a person is successful only when he acquires enormous wealth* and they cannot be persuaded otherwise. But wealth is not always a true measure of success.

Do not use a pronoun to refer vaguely to an antecedent that is implied but is not actually present. Replace the pronoun with a suitable noun phrase:

vague   The airlines and the airports are unable to cope with the flood of passengers. Delays and frustration affect travellers daily. No one saw *it* coming.

clarified   The airlines and the airports are unable to cope with the flood of passengers. Delays and frustration affect travellers daily. No one anticipated *the problem.*

You can sometimes improve a sentence by rephrasing it to omit a pronoun:

unnecessary pronouns   In our textbook *it* says that we should make sure that the reference of the pronoun is clear.

improved   Our textbook says that we should make sure that the reference of pronouns is clear.

CONSISTENCY

9.14   Pronoun agreement

Pronouns should agree with their antecedents in number (cf. 5.17):

faulty   Get *a university map* because *they* really help.
corrected   Get *a university map* because *it* really helps.
faulty   *A manager* should consider several factors when determining how *they* will deal with inefficient employees.
corrected   *Managers* should consider several factors when determining how *they* will deal with inefficient employees.
faulty   When *one partner* in a marriage says *they* will not compromise, the marriage is in danger.
corrected   When *one partner* in a marriage says *he or she* will not compromise, the marriage is in danger.

Be consistent in the use of pronouns. Use the same pronouns to refer to the same persons:

inconsistent	Every day *you* are bombarded with advertisements. It is up to *us* to decide what is worth buying.
corrected	Every day *you* are bombarded with advertisements. It is up to *you* to decide what is worth buying.
or	Every day *we* are bombarded with advertisements. It is up to *us* to decide what is worth buying.

The inconsistency in the next example follows from the inconsistent switch from passive to active:

inconsistent	A coordinating conjunction should be used to join two main clauses when *you* want to give them equal emphasis.
corrected	*You* should use a coordinating conjunction to join two main clauses when *you* want to give them equal emphasis.
or	A coordinating conjunction should be used to join two main clauses when equal emphasis is required.

9.15   Tense consistency

Be consistent in your use of tenses:

A day later you *start* thinking about the essay and then you *realized* that you *had* been neglecting it. (Replace *realized* with *realize* and *had* with *have*.)

Mr William Sanders *is* a loyal and efficient man. He rarely *left* the house until all his work *was* done. (Replace *left* with *leaves* and *was* with *is*.)

For the most part they well *understood* the problems, once *being* undergraduates themselves. (Replace *once being* with *having once been*.)

Although I *worked* until midnight, I *can't* finish all my assignments. (Replace *can't* with *couldn't*)

If you *had* gone to the bookshop before the semester *started*, you *would be* able to buy all your course books. (Replace *would be* with *would have been*.)

10

Literary Analysis

10.1   The Language of Literature

Most of what we find in the language of literature – particularly in prose fiction and drama – we also find in other uses of language. Writers select from what is available in the language as a whole. Poetry, however, often departs from the norms of language use in two respects: (1) in deviations from the rules and conventions of ordinary language, and (2) in excessive regularities. For that reason, I will be drawing my examples from poetry. At the same time, it must be said that some poets are more inclined than others to keep close to everyday uses of language, perhaps even to simulate the style of natural conversations.

The deviations that we encounter in poetry are located in various aspects of the language. Poetry is distinctive visually: It is set out in lines that do not go right across the page. Spaces may be left between sets of lines to indicate the beginnings of new sections, and lines within sections may be indented in various ways to indicate connections of some kind, perhaps in rhyme or metrical pattern. The traditional verse convention is for each line to begin with a capital letter, but some modern poets defy this convention. Some modern poets also defy the ordinary language conventions of spelling and punctuation. In this respect, e.e. cummings is particularly idiosyncratic: for example, he regularly writes the first person singular pronoun as 'i' and he sometimes inserts a punctuation mark in the middle of a word.

Poets often create new words. These tend to follow the normal rules for word-formation rather than being deviant. Some eventually enter the general language. But new words are surprising at their first appearance and they may never be admitted to the general vocabulary, particularly when they are based on word-formation rules that are little used. Gerard Manley Hopkins seems to have invented *unfathering* ('depriving of a father'). He describes how the snow 'Spins to the widow-making unchilding *unfathering* deeps'. The new word and its sense are prepared for by the more transparent *widow-making* and the parallel *unchilding* (an existing word, though uncommon). Hopkins has combined the prefix *un-* with a noun to form a verb *unfather* in a deprivative sense. This is a rule of word-formation that is little used. Even more rare is the formation of a negative noun by prefixing *un-* to an existing noun. Thomas Hardy introduces the noun *unhope* as the final word in the last stanza of 'In Tenebris':

> Black is night's cope;
> But death will not appal
> One who, past doubtings all,
> Waits in *unhope*.

We find very few nouns with the prefix *-un;* two for example, are *untruth* and *unrest*. Hopkin's *unfathering*, and Hardy's *unhope* remain **nonce-words** (words coined for a single occasion); they have not entered the vocabulary stock of the language.

Conversion is a common process for the formation of new words. We *butter* bread, take a *look, calm* somebody. In these everyday examples, words have changed from their original word-class to a new word-class without any change in their form: *Butter* is a verb derived from a noun ('put butter on'), *look* is a noun derived from a verb, and *calm* is a verb derived from an adjective. Poets sometimes introduce nonce-formations through conversion. Hopkins converts the adjective *comfortless* into a noun in 'groping round my *comfortless*' and the abstract non-count noun *comfort* into a concrete count noun in 'Here! creep, Wretch, under a *comfort*'. cummings takes conversion to an extreme by converting the past form *did* and its negative *didn't* into nouns in 'he sang his *didn't* he danced his *did*'.

Sometimes the poet's lexical innovations are **compounds,** the combination of two words into one: Hopkin's *selfyeast* in '*selfyeast* of spirit a dull dough sours'; T.S. Eliot's *sea-girls; thought-fox* in the title of a poem by Ted Hughes; and *gift-strong* in John Berryman's 'when he was young and *gift-strong*'.

Poets often introduce unusual collocations of words, which may require figurative interpretations. Examples abound. Here are just a few:

> The child's *cry* / *Melts* in the wall. (Sylvia Plath)
> Bitter *memory* like *vomit* / *Choked* my throat. (Gary Snyder)
> Your *lips* are *animals* (Anne Sexton)

This *grandson* of *fishes* (Robert Bly)
across the *castrate lawn* (Richard Wilbur)
hopeless cathedrals (Allen Ginsberg)

Some deviations are grammatical. Departures from normal word order are common in poetry. In the following line from Walt Whitman the direct object *Vigil strange* is fronted, an occasional unusual order in non-poetic language (cf. 9.3).

Vigil strange I kept on the field one night

Also abnormal is the order *vigil strange* rather than *strange vigil*, since adjectives generally come before the nouns they modify. In the next example from W.H. Auden, the direct object *A white perfection* is abnormally placed between the subject *Swans in the winter* and the verb *have:*

Swans in the winter air
A white perfection have

In another example, from Wallace Stevens, the phrase *upon a hill* is extracted from the first of a pair of coordinated clauses (*I placed a jar in Tennessee upon a hill)* and placed after the second clause:

I placed a jar in Tennessee
And round it was, *upon a hill.*

In addition, the subject complement *round* is fronted from its normal position (*it was round*).

Finally, in these lines from a sonnet by Gerard Manley Hopkins, the verb *find* is abnormally omitted in the first of two coordinated clauses:

. . . than blind
Eyes in their dark can day or thirst can find
Thirst's all-in-all in all a world of wet.

The sense is 'than blind eyes can *find* day in their dark?'

Excessive regularities are expressed in the systematic organization of features that otherwise occur unsystematically in the language. Poetry is often marked by patterns of sound; for example, metre, rhyme, and alliteration. The alliteration of *l* in this stanza from Philip Larkin's poem 'Toads' is so abundant that it could not occur by chance in the ordinary use of language:

> Lots of folk live on their wits:
> Lecturers, lispers,
> Losels, loblolly-men, louts –
> They don't end as paupers.

The alternative lines end with identical sounds: *ts* in *wits* and *louts,* and *pers* in *lispers* and *paupers.*

Another type of patterning is **parallelism**. Parallel structures exhibit grammatical, lexical, and semantic similarities. Here is an example of close parallelism from 'Little Gidding' in T.S. Eliot's 'Four Quartets':

> We die with the dying:
> See, they depart, and we go with them.
> We are born with the dead:
> See, they return, and bring us with them.

In the next example, from the end of one of John Donne's sonnets, the final two lines are parallel. This parallelism takes the form of **chiasmus,** a reversal of the order of the two parts of the parallel structures: the *except-*clause comes first in one line, and second in the other line.

> Take me to you, imprison me, for I,
> Except you enthrall me, never shall be free,
> Nor ever chaste, except you ravish me.

The two clauses in the first line are also parallel. Grammatically, both clauses are imperative, starting with an imperative verb followed by a direct object. Lexically, both clauses have the same pronoun *me* as direct object, and the verbs *take* (in this structure) and *imprison* are partial synonyms. Semantically, both clauses express the poet's request to God (the subject that is understood from the previous context) to take control of him.

One useful approach to literary analysis is to start by looking for the language features that deviate from what we know to be normal in language. This approach is explored in the following section.

10.2   Foregrounding

Literary language, especially poetic language, is distinguished by the consistency with which it uses **foregrounding**. The term *foregrounding* is a visual metaphor; it refers to the language features that stand out from the background of normal use. One of the objectives that literary analysts of the language of literature may set for themselves is to find interpretations of foregrounding. As in all literary criticism, there is scope for more than one interpretation, but some interpretations are more plausible than others.

I take as my first example a poem by Thomas Hardy, entitled 'In Tenebris' ('In Darkness'). It has a Latin epigraph from Psalm 102, which is rendered in the King James version 'My heart is smitten, and withered like grass.' The complete poem follows:

> Wintertime nighs;
> But my bereavement-pain
> It cannot bring again:
> Twice no one dies.
>
> 5   Flower-petals flee;
> But, since it once hath been,
> No more that severing scene
> Can harrow me.
>
> Birds faint in dread:
> 10   I shall not lose old strength
> In the lone frost's black length:
> Strength long since fled!
>
> Leaves freeze to dun;
> But friends can not turn cold
> 15   This season as of old
> For him with none.
>
> Tempests may scath;
> But love can not make smart
> Again this year his heart
> 20   Who no heart hath.
>
> Black is night's cope;
> But death will not appal
> One who, past doubtings all,
> Waits in unhope.

The poem is divided into six stanzas. The stanza division is made more conspicuous than usual by the indentation of the first and last lines, which are shorter than the middle lines. Sound patterning reinforces the feeling that each stanza is a unit: the two shorter lines rhyme and the two longer lines rhyme, and no rhymes are repeated across stanzas. The metrical scheme is iambic (unstressed syllable followed by stressed syllable), but contrary to the iambic norm every stanza begins with a stressed syllable.

The parallelism in appearance and sound has its analogy in a parallelism in sense. The stanzas elaborate the comparison expressed in the epigram from the Psalms: a comparison between desolation in nature and desolation in personal feelings. The first line of each stanza portrays a negative image from nature, an image that conjures up loss or danger. The next three lines relate this image to a negative human experience.

Negation is foregrounded in the poem, which is replete with negative words (*no one, no more, none, not, no*) and words with negative connotations (such as *wintertime, bereavement-pain, flee, lose, black, death*). The final word is the nonce-formation *unhope*, which we examined in the previous section. It makes a stronger impact than a possible synonym such as *despair* might have. As the negative of *hope*, it intimates the absence of any feeling of hope: a state beyond hope. The contrast with *hope* is underlined by the collocation *Waits in unhope*, which brings to mind the normal collocation *waits in hope*. In its strategic position as the final word of the poem, *unhope* is the climax to a series of preceding negative expressions.

The negation motif chimes with the imagery and themes of the poem. In each stanza the comments that follow the nature imagery allude to previous experiences of pain and despair. The consequences of past adversities have been permanent, so that a repetition of the adversity can no longer affect the poet. The final stanza refers to the ultimate adversity – death. But even death 'will not appal'.

In the first half of the poem, the poet treats the experiences as personal to him by using the first person pronouns *I, me, my*. In the second half, his pain and despair are distanced through the use of the third person pronouns *him* and *his* and (in the final stanza) the indefinite pronoun *one*. Through the change in pronouns, the poet generalizes from his own experiences to the human condition.

My reference to the change in pronouns in the Hardy poem provides a useful transition to a more startling foregrounding of pronouns in the 23rd Psalm, here given in the King James Version:

1.   The LORD is my shepherd; I shall not want.

2.   He maketh me to lie down in green pastures:
he leadeth me beside the still waters.

3.   He restoreth my soul: he leadeth me in the
paths of righteousness for his name's sake.

4.   Yea, though I walk through the valley of the
shadow of death, I will fear no evil: for thou
art with me; thy rod and thy staff they comfort
me.

5.   Thou preparest a table before me in the
presence of mine enemies: thou anointest my head
with oil; my cup runneth over.

6.   Surely goodness and mercy shall follow me all
the days of my life: and I will dwell in the house
of the LORD for ever.

In 'In Tenebris', the background from which the multiplicity of negative expressions is foregrounded is the language as a whole. In the 23rd Psalm, on the other hand, the norms that form the background lie within the poem: the dominant selection of pronouns to refer to the two main persons in the poem. In Psalm 23 the psalmist and the Lord are predominantly portrayed in a *I–he* relationship. The psalmist addresses the Lord in the third person: *The LORD is my shepherd . . . ; He maketh me to lie down . . . .* But in verses 4 and 5 there is a change to an *I–thou* relationship: *for thou art with me . . . ; thou anointest my head . . . .* In verse 6 the psalmist reverts to the dominant *I–he* relationship: *I will dwell in the house of the LORD for ever.* The changes foreground the *person* relationship in the psalm, which tallies with the theme of the psalm: the psalmist's trust in God and in his *personal* relationship with God.

The theme is also expressed in the metaphorical relationships: the psalmist as a sheep and the Lord as his shepherd (verses 1–2); the psalmist as a traveller and the Lord as his guide (3–4); and the psalmist as a guest and the Lord as his host (5–6). The metaphorical progression represents a growing confidence and a deepening personal relationship from complete dependence (of the sheep on his shepherd) to near-equality (of the guest with his host). The change of pronouns to an *I–thou* relationship coincides with the references to danger: the evil in the valley of the shadow of death and the presence of enemies during the meal. At these times, the psalmist feels the greatest need for the Lord's protection; he expresses his confidence in the Lord's nearness by switching to the *thou-* pronouns. In the final verse the psalmist is most self-confident, assured of staying in the house of the Lord for ever, and it is then that he can feel comfortable again with using the third-person reference to the Lord.

My final example of foregrounding involves departures from both external and internal norms. The poem, given in full below, is by Gerard Manley Hopkins. It is titled 'Heaven-Haven' and subtitled 'A nun takes the veil'. The subtitle provides the situational context for the poem. The title not only points to the theme of the poem (heaven as haven), but also introduces the linguistic device that dominates the poem, close parallelism: The two words *heaven* and *haven* fall short of complete identity by just one vowel sound as well as one letter:

1.   I have desired to go
2.   Where springs not fail,
3.   To fields where flies no sharp and sided hail
4.   And a few lilies blow.

5.   And I have asked to be
6.   Where no storms come,
7.   Where the green swell is in the havens dumb,
8.   And out of the swing of the sea.

The close parallelism in grammatical structure between the two stanzas calls attention to itself. The last three lines in each stanza refer to places that are characterized by the negatives *not* and *no* and by words that have negative connotations.

The closeness of the parallelism also foregrounds the differences between the two stanzas. The first stanza opens with *I have desired to go* and the second stanza with *I have asked to be*. *Desire* is ambiguous between two meanings: the stative 'wanted' and the dynamic 'asked' (cf. 3.14). In the 'asked' interpretation, the line is closer in meaning to the opening line of the second stanza. Both lines then describe a past request. The present perfect *have desired* and *have asked* indicate that the request is relevant to the present time of the poem, whereas the simple past *I desired* and *I asked* might suggest that the person is no longer interested in having the request granted. On the other hand, in the 'wanted' interpretation, *I have desired* points to a feeling that has extended over a period of time to the present but has not necessarily been translated into the action of making a request. The ambiguity is mimetic of ambivalence. The ostensible speaker is a woman about to become a nun, and she expresses some feeling of ambivalence about taking the veil. The change from the ambiguous *desired* to the unambiguous *asked* suggests a progression in the poem.

Similarly the switch from *desired to go* to a*sked to be* marks a progression: the dynamic *go* points to a striving, whereas the stative *be* indicates a state of rest. There are other differences between the stanzas that suggest a similar advance. There is more deviation from grammatical norms in the first stanza, perhaps mimetic of the striving: the archaic negation without *do* in *springs not fail* (instead of *springs do not fail*), the fronting of the verb in *flies no sharp and sided hail,* and the separation of the two parts of the compound in *sharp and sided hail* (instead of s*harp-sided hail*).

There is a difference between where the speaker has desired to go and where she has asked to be. The first stanza describes a countryside with springs and fields. It alludes to material needs (*springs not fail*) and pleasures (*a few lilies blow*). The second stanza describes a place of peace and quiet, the haven of the poem's title. The tension in the first stanza – conveyed in large part by the grammar – is resolved in the final stanza. The first stanza indicates a desire for positive things, even though negatives are used: springs that do not fail, fields without hail, and the presence of a few lilies. The second stanza calls for the absence of storms and tides: the ideal is the absence of conflict.

In the next section we will explore the type of foregrounding that derives from ambiguity.

10.3   Ambiguity

In the everyday uses of the spoken language and in most writing, ambiguity is a fault to be avoided because it may cause confusion or misunderstanding. Poets, however, introduce ambiguity intentionally to convey simultaneous meanings.

Puns, which are based on multiple interpretations, are employed playfully in poetry as in jokes and advertisements, though they may also have a serious purpose. This final stanza, from a poem by John Donne, contains two puns, one on *Sun* and the other on *done*:

> I have a sin of fear, that when I have spun
>   My last thread, I shall perish on the shore;
> Swear by thyself, that at my death thy *Sun*
> Shall shine as it shines now, and heretofore:
>   And, having done that, thou hast *done,*
>   I have no more.

Religious poetry traditionally puns *Sun* with *Son,* Christ the son of God, blending the associations of natural light with the associations of spiritual light. The second pun is personal, on the name of the poet: *thou hast done* combines the meaning 'you have finished' with 'you have Donne'. The last two lines of the poem echo a refrain in the previous stanzas:

> When thou hast done, thou hast not done,
> > For I have more.

The poet tells God that when He has forgiven the sins he enumerates He has not finished because he has more sins. At the same time, the pun conveys the added meaning that God has not taken possession of Donne because he has more sins. It is through Christ that at his death the poet will be fully forgiven by God and taken by God.

Grammatical ambiguities are also found in poetry. They are generally more difficult to analyse than lexical ambiguities. The first example comes from T.S. Eliot's *The Waste Land,* in an extract from the section called 'The Fire Sermon':

1. At the violet hour, when the eyes and back
2. Turn upward from the desk, when the human engine waits
3. Like a taxi throbbing waiting,
4. I Tiresias, though blind, throbbing between two lives,
5. Old man with wrinkled female breasts can see,
6. At the violet hour, the evening hour that strives
7. Homeward, and brings the sailor home from sea,
8. The typist home at teatime, clears her breakfast, lights
9. Her stove, and lays out food in tins.

The subject of this sentence, *I Tiresias* (line 4), is followed by two adverbials: a verbless clause *though blind* and a non-finite clause *throbbing between two lives.* Then comes an appositive (cf. 4.7): *Old man with wrinkled female breasts.* This seems at first reading to be appositive to *two lives:* one life is an old man, the other perhaps a woman *with wrinkled female breasts.* But the absence of a description of a second life suggests that the reader has been sent on a false trail. The phrase is then reassigned as appositive to the subject of the sentence *I Tiresias.* We have two grammatical analyses of the function of the appositive; the second supersedes the first, but the effect of the first lingers. Tiresias is the old man with wrinkled female breasts and the throbbing between two lives is the uneasy straddling of male and female in Tiresias. The grammatical straddling between two analyses reinforces the imagery.

A second false trail is set by what follows the verb *can see* (line 5). Is *see* here intransitive ('Tiresias has the ability to see'), or is it transitive ('Tiresias can see somebody or something')? If it is transitive, we expect a direct object to follow later in the sentence. The reader is kept in suspense for several lines. The phrase beginning with *the evening hour* is appositive to *the violet hour* (line 6). *The evening hour* is modified by a relative clause whose predicates are coordinated: *that strives / Homeward, and brings the sailor home from sea*. It looks as if what follows shares the verb *brings* and is coordinated, though the coordinator *and* is implied and not absent; *brings the sailor home from sea, / The typist home at teatime*. The parallelism of *the sailor home* and *The typist home* and the commas after *sea* and *teatime* encourage that initial reading. Yet as we read on, we see that *The typist* has its own set of coordinated predicates: *clears her breakfast, lights / Her stove, and lays out food in tins* (lines 8–9). *The typist* could therefore be the subject of a new sentence. Alternatively, *The typist home at sea* might indeed be coordinated with *the sailor home from sea*, and the predicates that follow might be a relative clause (cf. 4.5) with the relative pronoun *who* omitted, though the omission would be very odd in the ordinary use of language: *brings ... / The typist home at teatime, [who] clears / her breakfast, lights / Her stove, and lays out food in tins*.

Let us now turn back to the question whether *see* in line 5 is intransitive or transitive. The question is in fact not resolved, since the grammatical status of *see* depends on the interpretation of *The typist home at teatime* (line 8). If this phrase begins a new sentence, *see* is intransitive. If it is coordinated with *the sailor home from sea* (line 7), *see* is still intransitive. But there is yet a third possibility. The phrase may be the subject of a *that*-clause (whose conjunction *that* is omitted) which functions as direct object of a transitive *see*: *I Tiresias ... can see / At the violet hour ... [that] / The typist home at teatime, clears her breakfast, lights / Her stove, and lays out food in tins*. This interpretation, which is discouraged by the comma after *teatime*, is given some support by a parallel sentence five lines later:

> I Tiresias, old man with wrinkled dugs
> Perceived the scene, and foretold the rest –
> I too awaited the expected guest.

Yet the analysis of these lines is also not straightforward. The sentence is parallel if *Perceived the scene, and foretold the rest* is the predicate of the sentence (*I Tiresias* ... / *Perceived* ...). But the absence of a comma after *dugs* allows the possibility that the line is a relative clause with omitted *who* (*I Tiresias* ... [*who*] / *Perceived* ...).

We have seen that the phrase *The typist home at teatime* faces both ways and that as a result there are three possible interpretations of lines 8–9 that depend on three grammatical analyses. The grammatical ambiguities mimic the paradox of Tiresias, a man who has wrinkled female breasts and a blind man who can see.

The next example of ambiguity comes from the first four lines of a sonnet by Gerard Manley Hopkins. In these lines, the poet calls on himself to turn away from a cycle of self-accusations with which he is tormenting himself:

1. My own heart let me more have pity on; let
2. Me live to my sad self hereafter kind,
3. Charitable; not live this tormented mind
4. With this tormented mind tormenting yet.

Line 1 starts with the fronted *My own heart*, the complement of the preposition *on* (cf. 4.25). Later in the line occurs the unusual positioning of *more*. The oddity of the position of *more* foregrounds the word and is the cause of its grammatical ambiguity. *More* may be an adverb ('more often') or an adjective modifying *pity*. As an adverb, it should come at the end and be accompanied by some time expression such as *now* or *than before*: 'Let me have pity on my heart more than before'. As an adjective, it should precede *pity*: 'Let me have more pity on my heart'. The basis of comparison for the adjective is left vague, but two possibilities suggest themselves: 'Let me have more pity on myself than on others' or Let me have more pity on myself than I have had before'. The second possibility is closer to the interpretation indicated if *more* is an adverb, and it receives support from the word *hereafter* in the parallel sentence that follows.

Live in line 2 seems to be treated as a linking verb, with the adjectives *kind*, / *Charitable* as subject complement (cf. 3.8). In normal use, *live* is an intransitive or a transitive verb, so we would ordinarily expect it to occur with adverbs rather than adjectives (*They lived happily ever after*, not *They lived happy ever after*). The grammatical deviation is highlighted by the postponement of the adjectives to the end instead of the normal order as in 'Let me live hereafter kind, charitable to my sad self'. The unusual structure with a subject complement contributes to the ambiguities of the parallel contrasting sentence in lines 3–4.

The ambiguities lie in the grammatical function of *this tormented mind*. According to one interpretation the phrase is a subject complement, parallel to *kind, / Charitable,* and then *let me* is implied from the preceding sentence: *let / Me live to my sad self hereafter kind, / Charitable; [let me] not live this tormented mind / With this tormented mind tormenting yet.* If we use *be* as the linking verb, a simple example of this structure might be *Let me be kind to myself, not be a tormentor.* As in the preceding sentence, it is odd to have *live* as a linking verb.

In a second interpretation, *this tormented mind* is the subject of the intransitive verb *live* and is parallel to *me* in the preceding sentence; only *let* is carried over. The grammatical oddity in this interpretation is that the subject is placed after the verb. If we repositioned the subject in the normal order, we would have *[let] this tormented mind not live with this tormented mind tormenting yet.*

In the third interpretation, *this tormented mind* is the direct object of the transitive verb *live*, and *let me* is implied from the preceding context. The first part of the sentence might be rephrased 'Let me not live this tormented mind.' But as a transitive verb, *live* is highly restricted in the direct objects it may take. We would normally expect a noun phrase with *life* as its main word ('Let me not live this tormented life'), as in the expressions *live a hard life, live a good life.*

The verb *torment* is ordinarily a transitive verb, but no direct object follows it in line 4. One interpretation is that *this tormented mind* is the object implied from line 3: *With this tormented mind tormenting [this tormented mind] yet.* The effect is to suggest an endless cycle of tormentor and tormented, with the poet as a self-tormentor. Alternatively, *torment* is exceptionally here intransitive, and the sense is 'This tormented mind is still experiencing torment'. Compare *My leg is hurting.*

All the interpretations that I have offered for these four lines co-exist and, in doing so, enrich the poem. The dislocations in grammar mimic the psychological dislocations that the poet describes.

The final example comes from the first eight lines of a sonnet by John Milton. The context of the sonnet is the onset of blindness in Milton and his reaction to his disability.

1. When I consider how my light is spent,
2. Ere half my days in this dark world and wide,
3. And that one Talent which is death to hide
4. Lodged with me useless, though my Soul more bent
5. To serve therewith my Maker, and present

6.   My true account, lest he returning chide,
7.   Doth God exact day labour, light denied,
8.   I fondly ask; . . .

There are various places where multiple interpretations are possible, but I will focus on the last three lines of the octet. In lines 4– 6 Milton asserts his eagerness to present God with a 'true account' of his life, *lest he returning chide* ('lest God when He returns – or when He replies – rebukes me'). On an initial reading the question in line 7 seems to be asked by God: *Doth God exact day labour, light denied* ('Does God require casual labour when light is denied?'). The question then appears to be a rhetorical question that God asks in rebuking the poet, and as a rhetorical question it seeks no answer (cf. 6.2). It implies the strong assertion that of course God does not exact day labour when light is denied. However, when the reader reaches line 8, it becomes transparent that the fronting of the question before the reporting clause has laid a false trail. The question is not asked by God, but by the poet: *I fondly ask* ('I foolishly ask'). The question now emerges as a genuine *yes-no* question, which the poet immediately evaluates as a foolish question. The folly of the question is underlined by the previous reading of it as a rhetorical question, which makes the question unnecessary. Because God's assertion of His justice is replaced by the poet's questioning of God's justice, the poet's question is seen to be insolent and presumptuous. The effect is obtained through the succession of two analyses of the grammar of lines 6–7: the initial misinterpretation is immediately followed by an accurate second interpretation. The poet's foolish question is answered in the final line of the sonnet:

They also serve who only stand and wait.

Appendix: Spelling

A.1   Spelling, pronunciation, and meaning

English spelling is difficult because the pronunciation of a word is not always an accurate guide to its spelling. Two reasons account for most of the discrepancy between pronunciation and spelling.

One reason is that our spelling system is essentially a mixture of two systems: the system used in England before the Norman Conquest in 1066 was mixed with a new system introduced by the Norman-French scribes. We therefore find two spellings for the same sound (as in the final sound of *mouse* and *mice*) or two sounds for the same spelling (as in the first sound of *get* and *gem*). Later borrowings of words from foreign languages – particularly from French, Latin, and Greek – brought additional spellings; you will recognize as unusual such spellings as the *ch* of *chorus*, the *ph* of *philosophy*, the *g* of *genre*, the *oi* of *reservoir*, and the *oup* of *coup*. Some spellings were changed to bring words nearer to the form they had in other languages, and the changes introduced letters that have never been pronounced in English. One example is the *b* in debt: the *b* was present in the Latin word from which the French equivalent came, but English borrowed the word from French when French no longer had a *b*. Other examples of such changes are the *b* in *doubt*, the *l* in *salmon*, and the *p* in *receipt*.

The second reason for the discrepancy between pronunciation and spelling is that spellings have generally remained fixed while pronunciations have changed. During the Middle Ages the few who could write might spell the same word in more than one way; they did not think that only one spelling was correct. When the first printers introduced printing into English in the late fifteenth century they began to establish stable spellings. However, during that century important sound changes took place in English vowels. Those changes and later sound changes are generally not reflected in our spellings. In the centuries that followed, printers continued to work toward a uniform and stable system of spelling,

188

and then the major dictionaries of the eighteenth century established a standard spelling that is close to our present system. On the whole, printers and dictionaries have been a conservative force, preserving old spellings when sounds have changed. We therefore find spellings like the *gh* of *night* and the *k* of *know*, which retain letters for sounds that we no longer make. Or we find different spellings for the same sound, such as *ea* in *meat* and *ee* in *need*, because at one time those combinations represented different sounds. Or the sound changed differently in different words, so that the same spelling represents for us two different sounds, such as *oo* in *book* and *flood*.

To some extent our spellings take account of meaning. Sometimes we lose in the spelling-sound relationship but gain in the spelling-meaning relationship.

In the first place, we often distinguish **homophones** (different words pronounced in the same way) by spelling them differently. Here are a few common homophones that we distinguish through spelling:

son – sun	peace – piece
sent – cent – scent	right – write

You will find a list of homophones in A.7.

Secondly, we often use a similar spelling for parts of words that are related in meaning even though we pronounce them differently. The *-ed* inflection, for example, has the same grammatical functions in *developed*, *published*, and *revolted*, but the inflection is pronounced in three different ways. The spelling may also show that some sets of words are related where the pronunciation obscures the relationship. For example, we spell the first two syllables of *nation* and *national* identically, but the first vowel is pronounced differently in the two words. Similarly, the first three vowels of *photography* are different from the vowels of *photograph*, but our spelling connects the two words. We pronounce the words in these sets differently because we shorten vowels that are stressed weakly or not at all. Usually the unstressed or weakly stressed vowel is pronounced like the second vowel of *nation*. Some common one-syllable words we pronounce in more than one way; in the rapid pace of normal conversation we do not stress them and therefore we shorten their vowels. For that reason we have at least two pronunciations of words like *can*, *does*, and *your*. Sometimes we go further and drop the vowel completely; when we are not writing formally, we can then show the omission by contractions of some words, such as *'m* for am, *'s* for *is* or *has*, and *'ll* for *will*.

A final advantage of the relationship between spelling and meaning is that one spelling of a word may represent different pronunciations, but the spelling shows that it is the same word. English is an international language that is spoken differently in different countries. Even within England we do not find a uniform pronunciation; the pronunciation of a word may vary from one area to another or between groups within the same area. For example, some say *roof* with a long *u* sound, others with a short *u* sound; some pronounce the final *r* in words like *car*, others do not; some pronounce the vowel in *cup* like that in *luck*, others like that in *put*. Those spellings give some indication of pronunciation, but if we spelled words exactly as we pronounced them, people with different pronunciations of a word would spell the word in different ways. Our spelling usually indicates a shared meaning; it does not necessarily represent an identical pronunciation.

A.2   Spelling variants

English spelling, like English punctuation, is a convention that is helpful to the reader. Spelling mistakes distract and irritate readers. Good spelling is usually considered a sign that the writer is educated.

The spelling of the vast majority of words is now fixed. However, you will encounter some variant spellings in your reading or in dictionaries. For example, you may find *realise* and *realize, archaeology* and *archeology, judgment* and *judgement, adviser* and *advisor*. Do not use more than one spelling in a piece of writing, since inconsistencies are distracting. If you are used to a recognized and acceptable variant, keep to it. If not, select a dictionary and follow its spellings consistently. Consult the introduction to your dictionary to find out if it signals the preferred spelling when there are variants.

Some spelling variants are exclusively British or are more common in British writing. For example, British spelling uses the *-ise* and *-isation* endings (*civilise, civilisation*) as well as the *-ize* and *-ization* endings that are normal for American spelling (*civilize, civilization*). Here are some common American spellings and the usual British spellings for the same word:

American	British
behavior	behaviour
center	centre
check	cheque

color	colour
draft	draught
jail	gaol
harbor	harbour
jewelry	jewellery
labor	labour
meter	metre
neighbor	neighbour
pajamas	pyjamas
rumor	rumour

Because of the constant movement of publications between America and Britain, the national spelling distinctions are becoming acceptable variants in the two countries and also in other English-speaking countries.

The rest of the Appendix falls into three parts. Sections A.3–6 contain common spelling rules. Section A.7 lists sets of words that are spelled differently but are pronounced either identically or similarly. Section A.8 contains an alphabetical list of words that are frequently misspelled.

A.3   Spelling rules for short and long vowel sounds

1.   Doubling of consonant after short vowel

The vowels *a, e, i, o, u* have both long and short pronunciations; for example, the vowel *a* has a long pronunciation in *rate* and a short pronunciation in *rat*. The following general rule applies if the vowel is stressed.

Generally, a **long** vowel is followed by a single consonant plus a vowel:

$$V + C + V: \quad \text{\textbf{long} vowel} + \text{consonant} + \text{vowel}$$

and a **short** vowel is followed by a double consonant; at the end of the word, a **short** vowel can be followed by just a single consonant:

$$V + C + C: \quad \text{\textbf{short} vowel} + \text{consonant} + \text{consonant}$$
$$V + C: \quad \text{\textbf{short} vowel} + \text{consonant (end of word).}$$

Examples:

Long vowel	Short vowel		
	middle	end	
V + C + V	V + C + C	V + C	V + C + C
tape, taping	matter, tapping	tap	camp
scene, scenic	message, begging	beg	sell
ripe, ripen	blizzard, shipping	ship	miss
hope, hopeful	bottom, hopping	hop	fond
amuse amusement	suffer, cutting	cut	much

The rule is particularly useful when you add a suffix or inflectional ending to a word (cf. A.4 (1)).

2.   addition of final -e to indicate long vowel

A final silent -e is used to indicate that the preceding stressed vowel is long:

Long vowel	Short vowel
V + C + e	V + C
mate, debate	mat
theme, extreme	them
fine, polite	fin
robe, explode	rob
cute, amuse	cut

Here are some common exceptions, where the preceding vowel does not have the regular pronunciation:

> have; there, where; were; come, done, love, none, one, some; lose, move, prove, whose; gone; give, live (verb)

The general rule applies also in the sequence V + C + le. Hence, in *gable* the vowel *a* is long whereas in *gabble* it is short. Other examples of the long vowel in this sequence:

Long vowel			
V + C + le			
able	cycle	noble	table
bible	idle	rifle	title

A.4   Suffixes

A suffix is an ending added to a word that produces another word; for example, the suffix *ful* is added to *help* to produce *helpful*. An inflection is a type of suffix that is added to the end of a word to produce another form of the same word; for example, we add *-s* to the noun *book* to produce the plural *books*, and we add *-ed* to the verb *walk* to produce the past *walked*. The general rules for suffixes in (1)–(3) below apply also to inflections, and the examples include words with inflections added to them.

1.   doubling of consonant before suffix

We often double a final consonant when we add a suffix beginning with a vowel.

Double the final consonant before a suffix beginning with a vowel:

1. if the word ends in a single consonant, and
2. if a single vowel comes before the consonant, and
3. if the syllable before the suffix is stressed.

Condition (3) always applies if the suffix is added to a monosyllabic word.

suffix added to monosyllabic word	*polysyllabic word: suffix follows stressed syllable*
stop + ed → stopped	permit + ed → permitted
swim + ing → swimming	prefer + ed → preferred
big + er → bigger	forget + ing → forgetting
red + ish → reddish	begin + ing → beginning
drug + ist → druggist	occur + ence → occurrence
win + er → winner	

The vowel before the consonant is a short vowel (cf. A.3).

In the following sets of related words, the final consonant is doubled when the suffix follows a stressed syllable, but not when it follows an unstressed syllable. The contrasts illustrate the stress rule:

suffix follows stressed syllable	*suffix follows unstressed syllable*
deferred, deferring	deference
inferred, inferring	inference
preferred, preferring	preference
referred, referring	reference

A few monosyllabic words ending in -s have irregular variants without the doubling; for example: *busses, buses; bussed, bused; bussing, busing; gasses, gases*. A few polysyllabic words ending in -s have irregular variants with the doubling, even though the final syllable before the suffix is unstressed; for example: *biased, biassed; focusing, focussing*.

Do not double the final consonant before a suffix:

1. if the word ends in two consonants:
    finding, lifted, recorded, resistance, oldest
2. if there are two vowels:
    meeting, rained, beaten, trainer, repeated, appearance
3. if the stress is not on the last syllable of the word to which the suffix is added:
    limit − limiting; deliver − delivered; differ − difference

Exceptions for words of two or more syllables:

(a) Some words, most of them ending in *l*, have a double consonant even though the suffix is not stressed; for example, *marvellous, modelling, traveller, quarrelled, gossipping, worshipping, handicapped, diagrammed*.

(b) Final *c* is usually spelled *ck* when a suffix is added to indicate the *k* sound: *mimic − mimicking; panic − panicky; picnic − picnicked; traffic − trafficked*.

2.   dropping of final −e before suffix

Drop the final silent -e before a suffix beginning with a vowel:

have + ing → having	explore + ation → exploration
debate + ed → debated	cure + able → curable
fame + ous → famous	refuse + al → refusal

Exceptions where the *e* is kept before a vowel:

1. Keep the *e* in *dyeing* (from *dye*) and *singeing* (from *singe*) to distinguish the words from *dying* (from *die*) and *singing* (from *sing*).
2. Keep the *e* in *ce* and *ge* before a suffix beginning with *a* or *o* to preserve the *s* and *j* sounds: *enforceable, noticeable, peaceable, traceable, advantageous, courageous, knowledgeable*.

Do not drop the *e* before a suffix beginning with a consonant:

movement, forceful, hopeless, strangely

Exceptions where the *e* is dropped before a consonant:

1. *argument, awful, duly, truly, wholly*
2. *abridgment, acknowledgment,* and *judgment*; these words have more common variants with the *e.*

3. change of *-y* to *-i* before suffix

When a word ends in a consonant plus *y*, change the *y* to *i* before any suffix except *-ing* or *'s*:

happy + ly → happily	study + es → studies
amplify + er → amplifier	mystery + ous → mysterious
beauty + ful → beautiful	ratify + cation → ratification
apply + ed → applied	empty + ness → emptiness

Exceptions where the *y* after a consonant is kept:

1. A few words of one syllable keep the *y* before a suffix: *dryness, shyness, slyness.*
2. The *y* is kept in *busyness* to distinguish it from *business.*

Keep the *y* before *-ing*: *studying, applying.*
Keep the *y* before *'s*: *the spy's name, July's weather.*
Keep the *y* in most words that end in a vowel + *y*:

employ + er → employer	play + ful → playful
annoy + ance → annoyance	destroy + s → destroys
spray + ed → sprayed	pay + ment → payment

Exceptions where the *y* after a vowel is changed to *i*:

daily, laid, paid, said, slain

4. plurals of nouns and *-s* forms of verbs

Similar rules apply for making the plurals of regular nouns and the *-s* forms of regular verbs. Indeed, many words can be either nouns or verbs.

1. General rule: add *-s*:

noun plurals	*verb -s forms*
street → streets	speak → speaks

eye → eyes   bring → brings
winter → winters   write → writes

2. If the ending is pronounced as a separate syllable (like the sound in *is*), add -*es*:

noun plurals	verb -s forms
church → churches	touch → touches
box → boxes	buzz → buzzes
bush → bushes	wash → washes

When the word already ends in an -*e*, add just -*s*:

noun plurals	verb -s forms
base → bases	curse → curses
judge → judges	trace → traces

3. If the word ends in a consonant plus *y*, change *y* to *i* and then add -*es*:

noun plurals	verb -s forms
worry → worries	carry → carries
spy → spies	dry → dries

4. For some words ending in -*o*, add -*es*. Some of them have a less common variant in -*s*:

noun plurals		noun plurals and verb -s forms	
archipelago → archipelagoes		echo → echoes	
buffalo → buffaloes		embargo → embargoes	
cargo → cargoes		go → goes	
hero → heroes		torpedo → torpedoes	
motto → mottoes		veto → vetoes	
potato → potatoes			
tomato → tomatoes			
tornado → tornadoes			
torpedo → torpedoes			
volcano → volcanoes			

5. For some nouns ending in -*f* or -*fe*, form the plural by changing the -*f* or -*fe* to -*ves*:

calf → calves	life → lives	thief → thieves
elf → elves	loaf → loaves	wife → wives
half → halves	self → selves	wolf → wolves

knife → knives   sheaf → sheaves
leaf → leaves   shelf → shelves

5.   verb forms: -*ing* participles

The rules for making the -*ing* participle apply to both regular and irregular verbs.

1. General rule: add -*ing*:

     play → playing   carry → carrying
     go   → going   wash → washing

2. If the word ends in -*e*, drop the *e* before the -*ing*:

     lose → losing   write → writing
     save → saving   judge → judging

     But if the word ends in -*ee*, -*ye*, or -*oe*, keep the *e*:

     see   → seeing   dye → dyeing
     agree → agreeing   hoe → hoeing

     Also, *singe* keeps the *e* in *singeing*, in contrast with *sing* – singing.
3. If the word ends in -*ie*, change *i* to *y* and drop the *e* before the -*ing*:

     die → dying   tie → tying   lie → lying

     Contrast *die* – *dying* with *dye* – *dyeing*.
4. The rules for doubling a single consonant before -*ing* are given in A. 4 (1):

     beg   → begging   boat → boating
     prefer → preferring enter → entering.

6.   verb forms: simple past and -*ed* participles

The simple past and -*ed* participle are the same in regular verbs. The following spelling rules, analogous to those in A.4(5), apply to regular verbs.

(a) General rule: add -*ed*:

     play → played   load → loaded
     mail → mailed   echo → echoed

(b) If the word ends in -*e*, add just -*d*:

        save → saved   note → noted
        agree → agreed   tie → tied

(c) If the word ends in a consonant plus *y*, change the *y* to *i* before the -*ed*:

        dry → dried   apply → applied
        cry → cried   imply → implied

There are three exceptions, where the *y* is changed to *i* after a vowel and just *d* is added:

        lay → laid   pay → paid   say → said

(d) The rules for doubling a single consonant before -*ed* are given in A.4(1):

        beg   → begged   boat → boated
        prefer → preferred   enter → entered

7.   -*ize* or -*ise*; -*ization* or -*isation*

Both variants are acceptable, though the spelling with -*s* is perhaps more common in British English:

        criticise   criticize
        colonisation colonization

The following words, and words formed from them, should be spelled with -*ise*:

advertise	comprise	enterprise	revise
advise	compromise	exercise	supervise
analyse	despise	franchise	surmise
arise	devise	improvise	surprise
chastise	disguise	merchandise	televise

8.   addition of -*ally* to adjectives ending in -*ic* to form adverbs

Add -*ally* to adjectives ending in –*ic* to form the corresponding adverbs. In normal conversation, the -*al* of -*ally* is not sounded:

basic	basically	realistic	realistically
emphatic	emphatically	specific	specifically

Exception: *publicly*.

9.   *-ful*

The suffix is *-ful*:

beautiful	successful	useful
hopeful	teaspoonful	wonderful

Notice also the usual spellings of *fulfil* and *fulfilment*.

A. 5   Prefixes

Do not add or subtract letters when you add a prefix:

un	+ easy	→ uneasy
un	+ necessary	→ unnecessary
dis	+ obey	→ disobey
dis	+ satisfied	→ dissatisfied
mis	+ inform	→ misinform
mis	+ spell	→ misspell
over	+ eat	→ overeat
over	+ rule	→ overrule
under	+ take	→ undertake
in	+ expensive	→ inexpensive
in	+ numerable	→ innumerable

The prefix *in-* is regularly changed to *il-*, *im-* or *ir-* according to the first letter of the word that it is added to. The prefix often means 'not', as in the examples that follow:

il- before *l*	*ir-* before *r*	*im-* before *m* or *p*
illegal	irrational	immoral
illegible	irregular	immortal
illegitimate	irrefutable	impartial
illiterate	irrelevant	impossible
illogical	irresponsible	impure

A.6   Other aids to spelling

1.   words run together

A common type of spelling error is to run words together by writing two words as one. Always write these phrases as separate words:

a lot	even if	in fact	no one
all right	even though	just as	of course

In some cases the spelling depends on the meaning. For example, write *nobody* as one word when it is a synonym of *no person*, but write *no body* as two words in other meanings (for example, 'no corpse'). Write *anyway* when it is a synonym of *anyhow*, but *any way* when it means 'any direction' or 'any manner'; *awhile* is an adverb meaning 'for a brief period' (e.g. *You can stay awhile*), but *a while* is a noun phrase, (always so when preceded by a preposition) meaning 'a period of time' (e.g *We'll be there in a (little) while* and *We haven't seen them for a (long) while*).

Here are some pairs that you write either as one or as two words, depending on the meaning you intend:

one word	two words
already	all ready
altogether	all together
always	all ways
anybody	any body
anyway	any way
awhile	a while
everyone	every one
everybody	every body
however	how ever
into	in to
maybe	may be
nobody	no body
someone	some one
somebody	some body
whatever	what ever
whoever	who ever

2.   ie or ei

When the sound of the vowel is as in *brief*, spell it *ie*; but after *c*, spell it *ei*:

ie		ei after c	
brief	thief	ceiling	deceit
belief	achieve	conceive	perceive
believe	field	conceit	receive
diesel	niece	deceive	receipt
relief	priest		
relieve	siege		

Exceptions for spelling *ei*:

either, neither, seize, weird

Exceptions for spelling *ie*:

1. *financier, species*
2. Words in which *y* has changed to *i* (cf. A.4 (3)) end in *ies* even after *c*: *prophecies, democracies*.

In most words that do not have the pronunciations as in *brief*, the usual order is *e* before *i*: *neighbour, weigh, reign, leisure*. The most common exception is *friend*.

3.   could, should, would

Notice the silent *l* in these three auxiliaries.

4.   -cede, -ceed, -sede

The most common spelling is *-cede*:

antecede, concede, precede, recede, secede

We find *-ceed* in three words:

exceed, proceed, succeed

We find *-sede* in one word:

supersede

A.7   Words pronounced similarly

You will find here a list of common **homophones** (words that are pronounced in the same way but have different meanings) that are spelled differently. The list includes some words that are pronounced not identically but similarly.

We begin with a group of very common homophones. The other homophones or near-homophones are listed alphabetically; they include several sets of three homophones.

1. **he's/his, it's/its, you're/your, they're/their/there, who's/whose**

Some contractions of *is*, *has*, and *are* result in words that can be confused with homophones.

1. *he's = he is* or *he has*

   > He'll tell you when *he's* back home. (= *he is*)
   > I know that *he's* sent the cheque. (= *he has*)

   Distinguish between *he's* and possessive *his*:

   > Do you know *his* name?

2. *it's = it is* or *it has*

   > *It's* in the kitchen. (= *It is*)
   > I believe *it's* stopped raining. (= *it has*)

   Distinguish between *it's* and possessive *its*:

   > The dog is wagging *its* tail.

3. *you're = you are*

   > Did you say that *you're* willing to volunteer? (= *you are*)

   Distinguish between *you're* and possessive *your*:

   > They enjoyed *your* jokes.

4. *they're = they are*

   > I wonder where *they're* staying. (= they are)

   Distinguish *they're* from possessive *their* and the adverb *there*:

   > We met *their* parents.

All my friends were *there*.

For the adverb *there*, compare the spellings of the related words *here* and *where*.

5. *who's* = *who is* or *who has*

>Can you see *who's* ringing the bell? (= who is)
>*Who's* found the reference? (= Who has)

Distinguish between *who's* and possessive *whose*:

>*Whose* book is that?
>There is no charge for patients *whose* income is below a specified level.

2. List of words pronounced similarly

accept	except
access	excess
advice	advise
affect	effect
aid	aide
aisle	isle
altar	alter
assistance	assistants
ate	eight
bare	bear
beach	beech
beer	bier
berry	bury
berth	birth
board	bored
born	borne
brake	break
bread	bred
breadth	breath
business	busyness
buy	by
canvas	canvass
capital	capitol

cell	sell	
censor	censure	
cereal	serial	
climactic	climatic	
coarse	course	
complement	compliment	
conscience	conscious	
council	counsel	
dairy	diary	
decent	descent	dissent
desert	dessert	
device	devise	
dew	due	do
discreet	discrete	
dual	duel	
dyeing	dying	
elicit	illicit	
emigrate	immigrate	
eminent	imminent	
envelop	envelope	
fair	fare	
father	farther	
flour	flower	
for	four	
formally	formerly	
forth	fourth	
gorilla	guerrilla	
grate	great	
hair	hare	
hear	here	
heard	herd	
higher	hire	
hostel	hostile	
idle	idol	
in	inn	
ingenious	ingenuous	
instance	instants	

irrelevant	irreverent	
knew	new	
know	no	
lead	led	
lessen	lesson	
loan	lone	
loose	lose	
made	maid	
main	mane	
maize	maze	
meat	meet	
medal	meddle	
miner	minor	
oar	ore	or
of	off	
one	won	
pain	pane	
passed	past	
patience	patients	
peace	piece	
peak	peek	pique
pear	pair	pare
personal	personnel	
pier	peer	
plane	plain	
poor	pour	pore
precede	proceed	
presence	presents	
principal	principle	
profit	prophet	
prophecy	prophesy	
quiet	quite	
rain	reign	rein
raise	rays	
read	red	
right	write	

role	roll	
sail	sale	
scent	sent	cent
seed	cede	
seem	seam	
shone	shown	
sight	site	cite
sole	soul	
son	sun	
stake	steak	
stationary	stationery	
steal	steel	
straight	strait	
taught	taut	
team	teem	
than	then	
threw	through	
tide	tied	
to	too	two
vain	vein	vane
wander	wonder	
waste	waist	
wave	waive	
way	weigh	
weak	week	
weather	whether	wether
were	where	wear
which	witch	
wood	would	
wrote	rote	

A.8   Words often misspelled

You will find here an alphabetical list of words that might cause spelling difficulties. Memorize those that look strange to you. If you are not sure of the meanings of some of the words, look them up in a dictionary. The list has been broken up into groups of ten so that you can review them conveniently:

(1) accident
     accommodate
     accurate
     achieve
     acknowledge
     acquaintance
     acquire
     across
     address
     adventure

(2) allege
     amateur
     analysis
     anniversary
     annual
     answer
     anxious
     apparent
     appearance
     appreciate

(3) approach
     appropriate
     argument
     assign
     athlete
     attempt
     attendance
     average
     bargain
     beauty

(4) because
     beginning
     believe
     benefit
     budget
     build
     bureaucracy
     business
     calendar
     cemetery

(5) ceremony
     certain
     climate
     college
     column
     committee
     condemn
     confusion
     conscious
     conscience

(6) conscientious
     controversy
     convenient
     country
     courage
     creature
     criticism
     damage
     dangerous
     daughter

(7) definite
     description
     desperate
     dictionary
     difference
     dilemma
     disappoint
     disastrous
     discipline
     educate

(8) efficient
     embarrass
     enough
     environment
     equation
     especially
     estimate
     every
     exaggerate
     exceed

(9) excellent
     exercise
     existence
     experience
     extension
     failure
     famous
     fashion
     fatigue
     February

(10) fiction
     foreign
     fortunate
     forty
     friend
     genius
     government

(11) handkerchief
     height
     hierarchy
     hygiene
     hypocrite
     imagine
     immediately

(12) initiate
     interest
     irrelevant
     irresistible
     jeopardy
     journey
     knowledge

guarantee   incidentally   laboratory
guess   inconvenient   language
guilty   independent   leisure

(13) library   (14) mission   (15) occasion
lightning   mortgage   occurred
listen   nation   omission
literature   naturally   opportunity
machine   necessary   opposite
marriage   neighbour   ordinary
mathematics   neither   original
medicine   nervous   parallel
message   nuisance   parliament
minute   obstinate   people

(16) permanent   (17) privilege   (18) psychology
personal   probable   purchase
persuade   probably   purpose
police   procedure   pursue
politician   proceed   question
possession   profession   questionnaire
possible   professor   ratio
practically   pronunciation   receipt
preferred   propaganda   receive
prejudice   psychiatry   recommend

(19) reference   (20) satellite   (21) soldier
referred   schedule   solemn
relevant   science   speak
religious   secretary   special
restaurant   sense   speech
rhetorical   sentence   subtle
rhyme   separate   succeed
rhythm   serious   sufficient
ridiculous   siege   suggest
sandwich   similar   surprise

(22) suspicious   (23) tragedy   (24) vague
technique   translate   valuable
temperature   tries   variety

temporary	trouble	various
tendency	truly	vengeance
therefore	unanimous	village
though	unnecessary	villain
thought	until	Wednesday
till	usual	width
tongue	usury	writing

Glossary

Absolute clause   An absolute clause is an adverbial clause that either has a non-finite verb (as in 1 below) or no verb at all (as in 2 below) but has its own subject:

1. *The work having been finished,* the gardener came to ask for payment.
2. The prisoners marched past, *their hands above their heads.*

Active   Sentences and verb phrases with transitive verbs are either active or passive. The active is more commonly used. The passive involves differences in the structure of the verb phrase: the passive verb phrase has the addition of a form of the verb *be*, which is followed by an *-ed* **participle**:

Active		Passive	
	loves		*is loved*
	will proclaim		*will be proclaimed*
	is investigating		*is being investigated*

The passive sentence differs from the corresponding active sentence in that the active subject corresponds to the passive object:

Active	*The police* (S) are investigating *the crime* (O).
Passive	*The crime* (S) is being investigated.

If the active subject (here *The police*) is retained in the passive sentence it is put into a *by*-phrase:

The crime is being investigated *by the police.*

Adjective   An adjective is a word that typically can modify a noun and usually can itself be modified by *very*; for example, (*very*) *wise,* (*very*) *careful.* Adjectives are called 'attributive' when they are used as pre-

210

modifier in a noun phrase (*a conscientious student*). They are called 'predicative' when they are used as **subject complement** (*She is conscientious*) or **object complement** (*I considered her conscientious*). Adjectives that can be used both attributively and predicatively are 'central adjectives'.

Adjective phrase   The main word in an adjective phrase is an **adjective**. Other constituents that often appear in the phrase are **premodifiers** (which come before the adjective) and **postmodifiers** (which come after the adjective):

>   quite (prem.) *hungry* (adj.)
>   extremely (prem.) *happy* (adj.) to see *you* (postm.)

Adverb   The class of words that are called adverbs is a miscellany, since not all adverbs can have the same range of functions. An adverb is a word that is used chiefly as a modifier of an adjective (*extremely* in *extremely pale*), or a modifier of another adverb (*very* in *very suddenly*), or as an **adverbial** (*frequently* in *I visit my family frequently*).

Adverb phrase   The main word in an adverb phrase is an **adverb**. Other constituents that often appear in the phrase are pre-modifiers (which come before the adverb) and postmodifiers (which come after the adverb):

>   very (prem.) *neatly* (adv.)
>   very (prem.) *luckily* (adv.) for me (postm.)

Adverbial   An adverbial is an optional element that is chiefly used to convey information about the circumstances of the situation depicted in the basic structure of the sentence. There may be more than one adverbial in a sentence:

>   *Every year* (A1) they rented a car *for two weeks* (A2) *to tour some European country* (A3).

In the above sentence, the adverbials convey information on frequency in time (A1), duration of time (A2), and purpose (A3).

We should distinguish the adverbial from the **adverb**. Like a noun, an adverb is a member of a word class.

An adverbial complement is an element that conveys the same information as some adverbials but is required by the verb:

> I am now living *in Manhattan.*

The verb that most commonly requires an adverbial complement to complete the sentence is the verb *be*, as in 'She is *on the way to New Zealand'*. An adverbial complement is also required by some transitive verbs to follow a direct object. See **Object**:

> I put *my car* (dO) *in the garage* (Ac).

Adverbial clause   An adverbial clause is a clause that functions as **adverbial** in sentence structure.

Adverbial complement   An adverbial complement is an obligatory element in sentence structure. See **Adverbial**.

Alternative question   An alternative question is a question that presents two or more choices and asks the hearer to choose one of them:

> Do you want a biscuit or (do you want) a piece of cake?

Antecedent   The antecedent of a pronoun is the unit that the pronoun refers to. The antecedent usually comes before the pronoun:

> *The brakes* were defective when I examined *them.*

Anticipatory *it*   The pronoun *it* is called 'anticipatory it' when the sentence is so structured that the pronoun takes the position of the subject and the subject is moved to the end:

> *It* is a pity *that Sue is not here.* (Cf. 'That Sue is not here is a pity.')
> *It*'s good *to see you.* (Cf. 'To see you is good.')

Apposition   Apposition is a type of relation between two or more units:

> *Peter, your youngest brother,* has just arrived.

Typically, the two units are identical in the kind of unit (here two noun phrases), in what they refer to (*Peter* and *your youngest brother* refer to the same person), and in having the same potential function (so that either can be here omitted (*Peter has just arrived* and *Your youngest brother has just arrived* are both acceptable). See also **Appositive clause.**

Appositive clause   An appositive clause is a type of clause that functions as a post-modifier in a noun phrase:

> the reason *that I am here today*

The conjunction *that* does not function in the clause (cf. **Relative clause**). Since the clause is in apposition to the noun phrase, the two units correspond to a sentence structure in which they are linked by a form of the verb *be*:

> The reason *is* that I am here today.

Aspect   Aspect is the grammatical category in the verb phrase that refers to the way that the time of the situation is viewed by the speaker. There are two aspects: perfect and progressive. The perfect combines a form of auxiliary *have* with the *-ed* **participle**: *has shouted, had worked, may have said*. The progressive combines a form of auxiliary *be* with the *-ing* **participle**: *is shouting, was working, may be saying*.

Auxiliary   Auxiliary ('helping') verbs typically come before the **main verb** (*see* in the following examples) in a verb phrase: *can see, has been seeing, should have been seen*. The auxiliaries are:

1. **modals:** e.g. *can, should*
2. **perfect** auxiliary: *have*
3. **progressive** auxiliary: *be*
4. **passive** auxiliary: *be*
5. **dummy operator:** *do*

Base form   The base form of the verb is the form without any **inflection**. It is the entry word for a verb in dictionaries.

Basic sentence structure   The seven basic sentence or clause structures are:

> SV: subject + verb
> SVA: subject + verb + adverbial (complement)
> SVC: subject + verb + (subject) complement

SVO: subject + verb + (direct) object
SVOO: subject + verb + (indirect) object + (direct) object
SVOA: subject + verb + (direct) object + adverbial
        (complement)
SVOC: subject + verb + (direct) object + (object) complement

See 3.13. One or more optional **adverbials** may be added to the basic
structures.

Case   Case is a distinction in nouns and pronouns that is related to their
grammatical functions. Nouns have two cases: the common case (*child,
children*) and the genitive case (*child's, children's*). The genitive noun
phrase is generally equivalent to an *of*-phrase:

> *the child's* parents
> the parents *of the child*

In *the child's parents*, the genitive phrase is a dependent genitive: it functions like a **determiner**. When the phrase is not dependent on a following
noun, it is an independent genitive:

> The party is at *Susan's*.

Personal pronouns and the pronoun *who* have three cases: subjective
(e.g. *I, we, who*), objective (e.g. *me, us, whom*), and genitive (e.g. *my, mine;
our, ours; whose*). The two genitive forms of the personal pronouns have
different functions: *My* is a possessive determiner in *my parents*, and *mine*
is a possessive pronoun in *Those are mine*.

The distinctions in case are neutralized in some personal pronouns.
For example, *you* may be either subjective or objective. See **Subjective
case**.

Chiasmus   See **Parallelism**.

Clause   A clause is a sentence or sentence-like construction that is
contained within another sentence. Constructions that are sentence-like
are **non-finite** clauses or **verbless clauses**. Non-finite clauses have a
non-finite verb phrase as their verb, whereas verbless clauses do not
have a verb at all. They are like sentences because they have sentence
elements such as **subject** and **direct object**.

We can parallel the non-finite clause in [1] with the finite clause in [1a]:

[1]   *Being just a student,* I'd . . .
[1a]   *Since I'm just a student,* I'd . . .

We can show similar parallels between the verbless clause in [2] and the finite clause in [2a]:

[2]   *Though fearful of road conditions,* they . . .
[2a]   *Though they were fearful of road conditions,* they . . .

In a wider sense, a clause may coincide with a sentence, since a **simple sentence** consists of just one clause.

Cleft sentence   A cleft sentence is a sentence divided into three parts. The first has the subject *it* and a form of the verb *be*; the emphasized part comes next; and the final part is what would be the rest of the sentence in a regular pattern.

> It was *Betty* that I wanted. (Cf. 'I wanted Betty.')
> It was *after lunch* that I phoned John. (Cf. 'I phoned John after lunch.')

Collective noun   A collective noun refers to a group, e.g. *class, family, herd, jury.*

Comma splice   See **Run-on sentence.**

Comparative clause   Comparative clauses are introduced by *than* or *as* and involve a comparison.

> Maurice is happier *than he used to be.*
> Terence is as good a student *as you are.*

Complement   A complement is the unit that may or must be introduced to complete the meaning of a word. For example, a preposition (e.g. *for*) is normally followed by a noun phrase (e.g. *my best friend*) as its complement, as in *for my best friend.* See **Object, Object complement, Subject complement.**

Complex sentence   A complex sentence is a sentence that contains one or more subordinate clauses. The subordinate clause may function as a sentence element [1] or as a post-modifier in a phrase [2] and [3]:

[1]   Jean told me *that she would be late.*
[2]   This is the man *who was asking for you.*
[3]   We are glad *that you could be here.*

Compound   A compound is a word formed from the combination of two words: *handmade, user-friendly.*

Compound sentence   A compound sentence is a sentence that consists of two or more clauses linked by a coordinator. The coordinators are *and, or,* and *but; but* can link only two clauses:

She is a superb administrator, *and* everybody knows that.

See 6.6.

Conditional clause   A conditional clause is a clause that expresses a condition on which something else is dependent:

If they hurry, they can catch the earlier flight.

The sentence conveys the proposition that their ability to catch the earlier flight is dependent on their hurrying.

Conjunction   The two classes of conjunctions are **coordinators** (or coordinating conjunctions) and **subordinators** (or subordinating conjunctions). The coordinators are *and, or,* and *but.* They link units of equal status (those having a similar function), e.g. clauses, phrases, pre-modifiers. Subordinators (e.g. *because, if*) introduce **subordinate clauses**:

The baby is crying *because* she is hungry.

Conversion   Conversion is the process by which a word is changed from one class to a new class without any change in its form. For example, the verb *bottle* ('put into a bottle') is derived by conversion from the noun *bottle.*

Coordination   Coordination is the linking of two or more units with the same function. The coordinators (or coordinating conjunctions) are *and, or, but*:

> There is a heavy duty on *cigarettes, cigars,* **and** *pipe tobacco.*
> They pierced their *ears* **or** *noses.*
> *We waited,* **but** *nobody came.*

Coordinator   See **Conjunction.**

Count   Count nouns refer to things that can be counted, and they therefore have a singular and a plural: *college, colleges.* Non-count nouns have only the singular form: *information.*

Dangling modifier   A dangling modifier is an adverbial clause that has no subject, but its implied subject is not intended to be identified with the subject of the sentence:

> *Being blind,* a dog guided her across the street.

The implied subject of *being blind* is not intended to be *a dog.*

Declarative   A declarative sentence is a type of sentence structure used chiefly for making statements. In declaratives, the **subject** generally comes before the **verb.**

> Sandra is on the radio.
> I'm not joking.
> The sea lashed out harshly, jabbing the shoreline.
> Much more work will be required to analyse the data before we can announce our conclusions.

Declarative question   A declarative question has the form of a declarative sentence but the force of a question:

> She agrees with us?

Definite   Noun phrases are definite when they are intended to convey enough information, in themselves or through the context, to identify uniquely what they refer to:

You'll find *the beer* in *the refrigerator*.

A likely context for using the definite article here is that this beer has been mentioned previously and that it is obvious which refrigerator is being referred to. Noun phrases are indefinite when they are not intended to be so identifiable:

You'll find *a beer* in the refrigerator.

Definite article   The definite article is *the*. Contrast **Indefinite article**.

Demonstrative   The demonstrative pronouns are *this, these, that, those*. The same forms are demonstrative determiners.

Dependent genitive   See **Case**.

Descriptive rules   See **Grammar**.

Determiner   Determiners introduce noun phrases. They fall into several classes: the **definite** and **indefinite articles, demonstratives, possessives, interrogatives, relatives, indefinites**.

Directive   The major use of **imperative** sentences is to issue directives, that is, requests for action. Directives include a simple request [1], a command [2], a prohibition [3], a warning [4], and an offer [5]:

[1]   Please send me another copy.
[2]   Put your hands up!
[3]   Don't move!
[4]   Look out!
[5]   Have another piece of cake.

You can convey a directive through sentence types other than imperatives:

I want you to send me another copy, please.
Would you please send me another copy?
I need another copy.

Direct object   See **Object**.

Direct speech   Direct speech quotes the actual words that somebody has said. Indirect speech reports what has been said but not in the actual words used by the speaker:

[1]   Mavis asked me, 'Have you any friends?' (direct speech)
[2]   Mavis asked me whether I had any friends. (indirect speech)

In both [1] and [2], *Mavis asked me* is the reporting clause.

Dummy operator   The dummy operator is the verb *do*. It is used to perform the functions of an **operator** when an operator is otherwise absent:

>   *Does* (op) Polly know?

The three verb forms are *do* and *does* for the present **tense** and *did* for the past tense.

Dynamic   See **Stative**.

Element   A sentence or clause element is a constituent of sentence or clause structure. Seven elements combine to form the **basic sentence structure**:

subject	S			
verb	V			
object	O	–	direct object	dO
		–	indirect object	iO
complement	C	–	subject complement	sC
		–	object complement	oC
		–	adverbial complement	Ac

In addition, the adverbial (A) is an optional element.

End-focus   The principle of end-focus requires that the most important information come at the end.

End-weight   The principle of end-weight requires that a longer unit come after a shorter unit whenever there is a choice of relative positions.

Exclamative An exclamative sentence is a type of sentence structure used chiefly to express strong feeling. Exclamatives begin with *what* or *how*. *What* is used with a **noun phrase** and *how* elsewhere:

> *What a good time* we had! ('We had a very good time.')
> *How well* she plays! ('She plays very well.')

Finite Finite is a term used in contrast with non-finite in the classification of verbs, verb phrases, and clauses. A finite verb allows contrasts in **tense** and **mood**. All verb forms are finite except **infinitives** and **participles**. A verb phrase is finite if the first or only verb is finite; all the other verbs are non-finite. A finite clause is a clause whose verb is a finite verb phrase:

[1]   Marian *has been working* hard.

A finite clause can constitute an independent sentence, as in [1]. Contrast the non-finite clause in *to work hard* in [2]:

[2]   Daniel was reluctant *to work hard.*

Foregrounding Foregrounding refers to the features that stand out in the language of a literary work.

Formal definition A formal definition defines a grammatical term, such as adverb, by the form of members of the category. For example, most adverbs end in *-ly*. In a wider sense, form includes **structure**. The form or structure of a noun phrase may be described as consisting of a noun or pronoun as the main word plus other possible constituents, such as **determiners** and modifiers. See **Structure**. Formal definitions are contrasted with **notional definitions**.

Fragmentary sentence Fragmentary sentences are irregular sentences from which some part or parts are missing that are normally present in corresponding regular sentences. We can 'regularize' the fragmentary sentence *in the kitchen* in this exchange:

> A: Where are you?
> B: *In the kitchen.*

In the kitchen corresponds to the regular sentence *I am in the kitchen.*

Front-focus Front-focus is a device for fronting an expression from its normal position so that it will acquire greater prominence:

> *Ronald* I like, but *Doris* I respect.

Here the two direct objects have been fronted from their normal position after the verb.

Function The function of a unit refers to its use within another unit. For example, the function of *your sister* is **subject** in [1] and **object** in [2]:

[1]   *Your sister* is over there.
[2]   I have already met *your sister*.

Gender Gender is a grammatical distinction among words of the same word class that refers to contrasts such as masculine, feminine, neuter. In English this distinction is found mainly in certain pronouns and in the **possessive determiners**.

Generic Noun phrases are generic when they refer to a class as a whole:

> *Dogs* make good pets.

They are non-generic when they refer to individual members of a class:

> *My dogs* are good with children.

Genitive case See **case**.

Gradable Words are gradable when they can be viewed as being on a scale of degree of intensity. Adjectives and adverbs are typically gradable: they can be modified by intensifiers such as *very* (*extremely hot, very badly*), and they can take comparison (*happier, more relevant*).

Grammar The grammar is the set of rules for combining words into larger units. For example, the rules for the grammar of standard English allow:

Home computers are now much cheaper.

They disallow:

[1]   Home computers now *much* are cheaper.
[2]   Home computers *is* now much cheaper.

They disallow [1] because *much* is positioned wrongly. They disallow [2] because the subject and the verb must agree in number, and the subject *Home computers* is plural whereas the verb *is* is singular.

Such rules are **descriptive rules**: they describe what speakers of the language use. There are also **prescriptive rules**: They advise people what they should use. These are found in style manuals, handbooks, and other books that advise people how to use their language, telling people which usages to adopt or avoid. The prescriptive rules refer to usages that are common among speakers of standard English, perhaps mainly when they are speaking informally; for example:

Don't use *like* as a conjunction, as in *Speak like I do*.

Grammatical sentence   A grammatical sentence in English is a sentence that conforms to the rules of the grammar of **standard English**. In a wider sense, grammatical sentences are sentences that conform to the rules of any variety, so that it is possible to distinguish between grammatical and non-grammatical sentences in different varieties of non-standard English.

Homograph   See **Homonym**.

Homonym   Homonyms are two or more words that are identical in sound or spelling but different in meaning: the verb *peep* refers either to making a kind of sound or to taking a kind of look. Homophones share the same sound but not necessarily the same spelling: *weigh* and *way*. Homographs share the same spelling but not necessarily the same sound: *row* ('line of objects' when it rhymes with *no* or 'quarrel' when it rhymes with *now*).

Homophone   See **Homonym**.

Imperative   An imperative sentence is a type of sentence structure used chiefly for issuing a **directive**. The imperative verb has the **base form**. The subject is generally absent, and in that case the missing subject is understood to be *you*:

> Take off your hat.
> Make yourself at home.

There are also first and third person imperative sentences with *let* and a subject:

> Let's go now.
> Let no one move.

Indefinite article   The indefinite article is *a* or (before a vowel sound) *an*. Constrast **Definite article**.

Indefinite pronoun   Indefinite pronouns are pronouns that refer to the quantity of persons or things. They include sets of words ending in *-one* and *-body* (*someone, nobody, everybody*), *many, few, both, either, neither, some, any*. Some of these pronouns have the same form as indefinite **determiners**.

Independent genitive   See **Case**.

Indicative   See **Mood**.

Indirect object   See **Object**.

Indirect speech   See **Direct speech**.

Infinitive   The infinitive has the base form of the verb. It is often preceded by *to* (*to stay, to knock*), but the infinitive without *to* is used after the central **modals** (*may stay, will knock*) and after **dummy operator** *do (did say)*.

Inflection   See **Suffix**.

Interrogative   An interrogative sentence is a type of sentence structure used chiefly for asking questions. In interrogatives the **operator** comes before the **subject** or the sentence begins with an interrogative word (e.g.

who, how, why) or with an interrogative expression (e.g. *on which day, for how long*):

> Did you hear that noise?
> Why is Pat so annoyed?
> At which point should I stop?

Interrogative pronoun   The interrogative pronouns are *who, whom, which* and *what*.

Intransitive verb   An intransitive verb does not require another element to complete the sentence:

> The baby is crying.
> It has been raining.

Intransitive verbs contrast with transitive verbs, which take an object; for example, the transitive verb *take* is followed by the object *my book* in this next sentence:

> Somebody has taken my book.

Many verbs may be either intransitive or transitive, for example *eat*:

> They have eaten.
> They have eaten breakfast.

Irregular sentence   See **Regular sentence.**

Linking verb   See **Subject complement.**

Main clause   A **simple sentence** [1] or a **complex sentence** [2] consists of one main clause:

[1]   You should be more careful.
[2]   You should be more careful when you cross the street.

A **compound sentence** [3] consists of two or more main clauses:

[3]   I know that you are in a hurry, *but* you should be more careful when you cross the street.

In [3], *but* joins the two main clauses.

Main verb   A main verb is the main word in a verb phrase. Regular main verbs have four forms: the base, *-s, -ing,* and *-ed* forms. The base form (e.g. *talk*) has no **inflection**; the other three forms are named after their inflections (*talks, talking, talked*). Some irregular verbs have five forms, two of them corresponding to the two uses of the regular *-ed* form: past (*spoke*) and *-ed* participle (*spoken*); others have four forms, but the *-ed* form is irregular (*spent*); others still have only three forms, since the base and the *-ed* forms are identical (*put*). The highly irregular verb *be* has eight different forms. See 4.12 and 5.11.

Medium   The medium is the channel in which the language is used. The main distinction is between speech and writing.

Modal   The central modals (or central modal auxiliaries) are *can, could, may, might, will, would, shall, should, must.*

Mood   Mood is the grammatical category that indicates the attitude of the speaker to what is said. Finite verb phrases have three moods: indicative, imperative, and subjunctive. The indicative is the usual mood in **declarative, interrogative,** and **exclamative** sentences. The imperative mood is used in **imperative** sentences. The subjunctive mood commonly conveys uncertainty or tentativeness. See 4.19.

Morphology   Morphology deals with the structure of words. Words may be combinations of smaller units. For example, *books* consists of the **stem** *book* and the **inflection** -s. *Sometimes* is a compound formed from the two stems *some* and *times. Review* consists of the **prefix** *re-* and the stem *view,* and *national* consists of the stem *nation* and the **suffix** *-al.*

Multiple sentence   See **Simple sentence.**

Multi-word verb   Multi-word verbs are combinations of a verb and one or more other words. The major types are phrasal verbs (*give in*), prepositional verbs (*look at*), and phrasal-prepositional verbs (*put up with*).

Neutralization   Neutralization involves reducing distinctions to one form. For example, *you* represents both the subjective form (**You** *saw them*) and the objective form (*They saw* **you**).

Nominal clause Nominal clauses are subordinate clauses that have a range of functions similar to that of noun phrases. For example, they can function as subject [1] or direct object [2]:

[1]   *That it's too difficult for him* should be obvious to everyone.
[2]   I think *that you should take a rest now.*

Nominal relative clauses are introduced by a nominal relative pronoun. The pronoun functions like a combination of **antecedent** and **relative pronoun**:

You can take *whatever you want* .('anything you want')

Nominal relative clause   See **Nominal clause.**

Nominal relative pronoun Nominal relative pronouns introduce nominal relative clauses. The pronouns are *who, whom* (formal), *which; whoever, whomever* (formal), *whichever, what,* and *whatever.* Several of these have the same form as nominal relative determiners.

Non-count   See **Count.**

Non-finite   See **Finite.**

Non-generic   See **Generic.**

Non-restrictive apposition   See **Restrictive apposition.**

Non-restrictive relative clause.   See **Restrictive relative clause.**

Non-sentences   Non-sentences may be perfectly normal even though they cannot be analysed as sentences. For example, the greeting *Hello!* is a non-sentence grammatically, and so is the written sign *Exit.*

Non-specific   See **Specific.**

Non-standard English   See **Standard English.**

Notional definition   A notional definition defines a grammatical term, such as a noun, by the meaning that members of the category are said to convey. For example, a traditional notional definition of a noun is 'the name of a person, thing, or place'. Notional definitions can help to identify a category such as a noun by indicating typical members of the category, but the definitions are usually not comprehensive. Nouns include words such as *happiness, information,* and *action* that are not covered by the traditional notional definition. Notional definitions are contrasted with **formal definitions.**

Noun Proper nouns are names of people (*Mary*), places (*Chicago*), days of the week (*Monday*), holidays (*Christmas*), etc. The **noun phrases** in which common nouns function refer to people (*teachers*), places (*the city*), things (*your car*), qualities (*elegance*), states (*knowledge*), actions (*action*), etc. Most common nouns take a plural form: *car, cars.*

Noun phrase The main word in a noun phrase is a noun or a pronoun. If the main word is a noun, it is often introduced by a **determiner** and may have modifiers. Pre-modifiers are modifiers that come before the main word and post-modifiers are modifiers that come after it:

> an (det.) old (prem.) *quarrel* (noun) that has recently flared up again (postm.)

Number Number is a grammatical category that contrasts singular and plural. It applies to nouns (*student, students*), pronouns (*she, they*), and verbs (*he works, they work*).

Object Transitive verbs require a direct object to complete the sentence as in [1]:

[1]   Dennis introduced *the speaker* (dO).

Some transitive verbs allow or require a second element: indirect object, which comes before the direct object [2]; **object complement** [3]; **adverbial complement** [4].

[2]   Nancy showed *me* (iO) *her book* (dO).
[3]   Pauline made *him* (dO) *her understudy* (oC).
[4]   Norma put *the cat* (dO) *in the yard* (Ac).

The direct object typically refers to the person or thing affected by the action. The indirect object typically refers to the person who receives something or benefits from the action. The object in an **active** structure (whether the object is direct or indirect) usually corresponds to the subject in a passive structure:

> The sentry fired *two shots* (dO).
> *Two shots* (S) were fired.
> Ted promised *Mary* (iO) two tickets (dO).
> *Mary* (S) was promised two tickets.
> *Two tickets* (S) were promised to Mary.

Object complement   Some transitive verbs require or allow an object complement to follow the direct object:

> The heat has turned *the milk* (dO) *sour* (oC).

The relationship between the direct object and the object complement resembles that between the subject and **subject complement**:

> *The milk* (S) turned *sour* (sC).

See **Object**.

Objective case   See **Subjective case**.

Operator   The operator is the part of the predicate that (among other functions) interchanges with the subject when we form questions [1] and comes before *not* or contracted *n't* in negative sentences [2] and [3]:

[1]   *Have* (op) *you* (S) seen my pen?
[2]   I *have* (op) *not* replied to her letter.
[3]   I *haven't* replied to her letter.

The operator is usually the first auxiliary in the verb phrase, but the main verb *be* is the operator when it is the only verb in the verb phrase, as in [4], while the main verb *have* may serve as operator, as in [5], or take the **dummy operator**, as in [6]:

[4]   *Are* you ready?
[5]   *Have* you a car?
[6]   *Do* you have a car?

Orthographic sentence   An orthographic sentence is a sentence in the written language, signalled by an initial capital letter and a final full-stop.

Orthography   Orthography is the writing system in the language: the distinctive written symbols and their possible combinations.

Parallelism   Parallelism is an arrangement of similar grammatical structures. In parallel structures at least some of the words have similar or contrasting meanings:

> It was too hot to eat; it was too hot to swim; it was too hot to sleep.
> They tended the wounded and they comforted the dying.
> The more you talk, the madder I get.

Chiasmus is a form of parallelism in which the order of parts of the structures is reversed:

> I respect Susan, but Joan I admire.

Particle   A particle is a word that does not change its form (unlike verbs that have past forms or nouns that have plural forms) and, because of its specialized functions, does not fit into the traditional classes of words. Particles include *not, to* as used with the infinitive, and words like *up* and *out* that combine with verbs to form **multi-word verbs,** for example, *blow up* and *look out.*

Participle   There are two participles, the *-ing* participle (*playing*) and the *-ed* participle. The *-ing* participle always ends in *-ing*. In all regular verbs and in some irregular verbs, the *-ed* participle ends in *-ed*. In other irregular verbs the *-ed* participle may end in *-n* (*speak* – spoken), or may have a different vowel from the base form (*fight – fought*), or may have both characteristics (*wear – worn*), or may be identical with the base form (*put – put*).

The *-ing* participle is used to form the progressive (*was playing*). The *-ed* participle is used to form the perfect (*has played*) and the passive (*was played*). Both participles can function as the verb in **non-finite** clauses:

> *Knowing Carol,* I am sure you can trust her:
> *When captured,* he refused to give his name.

See **Aspect, Active, Finite.**

Passive See **Active.**

Perfect See **Aspect.**

Person Person is the grammatical category that indicates differences in the relationship to the speaker of those involved in the situation. There are three persons: the first person refers to the speaker, the second to those addressed, and the third to other people or things. Differences are signalled by the **possessive determiners** (*my, your* etc.), some pronouns (e.g. *I, you*), and by verb forms (e.g. *I know* versus *She knows*).

Personal pronoun The personal pronouns are:

1. subjective case: *I, we, you, he, she, it, they*
2. objective case: *me, us, you, him, her, it, them*

See **Subject case.**

Phonetics Phonetics deals with the physical characteristics of the sounds in the language, their production, and their perception.

Phonology Phonology is the sound system in the language: the distinctive sound units and the ways in which they may be combined.

Phrasal auxiliary Phrasal auxiliaries convey meanings that are similar to the auxiliaries but do not share all their grammatical characteristics. For example, only the first word of the phrasal auxiliary *have got to* functions as an **operator**:

   Have we *got to* go now?

Phrasal auxiliaries include *have to, had better, be about to, be going to, be able to.*

Phrasal-prepositional verb See **Multi-word verb.**

Phrasal verb. See **Multi-word verb.**

Phrase   A phrase is a unit below the **clause**. There are five types of phrases:

noun phrase	*our family*
verb phrase	*was talking*
adjective phrase	*quite right*
adverb phrase	*very loudly*
prepositional phrase	*for you*

The first four phrases above are named after their main word. The prepositional phrase is named after the word that introduces the phrase.

In this book, and in many other works on grammar, a phrase may consist of one word, so that both *talked* and *was talking* are verb phrases. See 4.1.

Possessive determiner   The possessive determiners are *my, our, your, his, her, its, their*. See **Case**.

Possessive pronoun   The possessive pronouns are *mine, ours, yours, his, hers, its, theirs*. See **Case**.

Pragmatics   Pragmatics deals with the use of utterances in particular situations. For example, *Will you join our group?* is a question that might be intended as either a request for information or a request for action.

Predicate   We can divide most **clauses** into two parts; the **subject** and the predicate. The main parts of the predicate are the verb and any of its objects or complements.

Prefix   A prefix is added before the stem of a word to form a new word, e.g. *un-* in *untidy*.

Preposition   Prepositions introduce **prepositional phrases**. The preposition links the complement in the phrase to some other expression. Here are some common prepositions with complements in parentheses: *after* (*lunch*), *by* (*telling me*), *for* (*us*), *in* (*my room*), *since* (*seeing them*), *to* (*Ruth*), *up* (*the road*).

Prepositional object   A prepositional object is a word or phrase that follows the preposition of a prepositional verb:

> Tom is looking after *my children*.
> Norma is making fun of *you*.

Prepositional phrase The prepositional phrase consists of a preposition and the complement of the preposition:

> for (prep.) your sake (comp.)
> on (prep.) entering the room (comp.)

Prepositional verb See **Multi-word verb.**

Prescriptive rules See **Grammar.**

Progressive See **Aspect.**

Pronoun A pronoun is a closed class of words that are used as substitutes for a noun phrase or (less commonly) for a noun. They fall into a number of classes, such as personal pronouns and demonstrative pronouns. See 5.17.

Reciprocal pronoun The reciprocal pronouns are *each other* and *one another*.

Reflexive pronoun The reflexive pronouns are *myself, ourselves, yourself, yourselves, himself, herself, itself, themselves.*

Regular sentence A regular sentence conforms to the major patterns of sentences in the language. Those that do not conform are irregular sentences. See **Basic sentence structure.**

Relative clause A relative clause functions as a post-modifier in a noun phrase:

> the persons *who advised me*

The relative word or expression (here *who*) functions as an element in the clause (here as subject; cf. *They advised me*).

Relative pronoun Relative pronouns introduce **relative clauses.** The relative pronouns are *who, whom* (formal), *which,* and *that.* The relative pronoun is omitted in certain circumstances: *the apartment* (*that*) *I live in;* the omitted pronoun is known as a zero relative pronoun. *Which* and *whose* are relative determiners.

Reporting clause   See **Direct speech.**

Restrictive apposition   Apposition may be restrictive or non-restrictive. A restrictive appositive identifies:

> the fact *that they have two cars*
> my sister *Clarissa*

A non-restrictive appositive adds further information:

> the latest news, *that negotiations are to begin next Monday,*
> my eldest sister, *Clarissa,*

See **Restrictive relative clause.**

Restrictive relative clause   Relative clauses may be either restrictive or non-restrictive. A restrictive relative clause identifies more closely the noun it modifies:

> the sister *who was in your class*

A non-restrictive relative clause does not identify. It adds further information:

> your youngest sister, *who was in your class,*

Rhetorical question   A rhetorical question has the form of a question but the force of a strong assertion.

> How many times have I told you to wipe your feet? ('I have told you very many times to wipe your feet.')

Run-on sentence   A run-on sentence is an error in punctuation arising from the failure to use any punctuation mark between sentences. If a comma is used instead of a major mark, the error is a comma splice. See 7.3.

Semantics   Semantics is the system of meanings in the language: the meanings of words and the combinatory meanings of larger units.

Sentence fragment   A sentence fragment is a series of words that is punctuated as a sentence even though it is not grammatically an independent sentence:

>   You're late again. As usual.

Simple sentence   A simple sentence is a sentence that consists of just one **clause**:

>   I'm just a student.

A multiple sentence consists of more than one clause:

>   I'm just a student, and I've not had much work experience.
>   Since I'm just a student, I've not had much work experience.

See **Complex sentence** and **Compound sentence**.

Specific   Noun phrases are specific when they refer to specific persons, places, things, etc.:

>   I hired *a horse* and *a guide*.

They are non-specific when they do not have such reference:

>   I have never met *a Russian.* (non-specific: 'any Russian')

Standard English   Standard English is the variety of English that normally appears in print. Its relative uniformity is confined to grammar, vocabulary, spelling, and punctuation. There is no standard English pronunciation. There are some differences in the standard English used in English-speaking countries, so that we can distinguish, for example, between standard English in Britain, in the USA, and in Canada. Varieties other than the standard variety are called **non-standard**.

Stative   Stative verbs introduce a quality attributed to the subject (*Tom seems bored*) or a state of affairs (*We know the way*). Dynamic verbs are used in descriptions of events (*The kettle is boiling; Cathy listened intently*). Dynamic verbs can occur with the *-ing* form, as in *is boiling, has been listening*.

Structure   The structure of a unit refers to the parts that make up the unit. For example, a sentence may have the structure **subject, verb, object,** as in:

> Dinah (S) has written (V) a good paper (O).

Or a noun phrase may have the structure **determiner, pre-modifier, noun,** as in:

> a (D) good (P) paper (N)

Subject   The subject is an **element** that usually comes before the verb in a **declarative** sentence [1] and after the **operator** in an **interrogative** sentence [2]:

[1]   *We* (S) *should consider* (V) the rights of every class.
[2]   *Should* (op) *we* (S) consider the rights of every class?

Except in **imperative** sentences, the subject is an obligatory element. In **active** structures, the subject typically refers to the performer of the action.

Subject complement   Linking verbs require a subject complement to complete the sentence. The most common linking verb is *be*. Subject complements are usually **noun phrases** [1] or **adjective phrases** [2]:

[1]   Leonard is *Mary's brother*
[2]   Robert looks *very happy*.

The subject complement typically identifies or characterizes the subject.

Subjective case   The **personal pronouns** and the pronouns *who* and *whoever* distinguish between subjective case and objective case. The subjective case is used when a pronoun is the subject (*I* in *I know*). The objective case is used when a pronoun is a direct object (*me* in *He pushed me*) or indirect object (*me* in *She told me the truth*) or complement of a preposition (*for me*). The subject complement takes the subjective case in formal style (*This is she*), but otherwise the objective case (*This is her*) is usual.

Subject–operator inversion   In subject–operator inversion, the usual order is inverted: the **operator** comes before the **subject**:

[1]   *Are* (op) *you* (S) staying?

Subject–operator inversion occurs chiefly in questions, as in [1]. It also occurs when a negative element is fronted, as in [2]:

[2]   *Not a word* did we hear.

Compare [2a] and [2b]:

[2a]   We did *not* hear *a word*.
[2b]   We heard *not a word*.

Subject–verb agreement   The general rule is that a verb agrees with its subject in number and person whenever the verb displays distinctions in number and person:

The dog *barks*.   I *am* thirsty.
The dogs *bark*.   She *is* thirsty.

Subjunctive   The present subjunctive is the base form of the verb:

I demanded that Norman *leave* the meeting.
It is essential that you *be* on time.

The past subjunctive is *were*.

If Tess *were* here, she would help me.

See 4.19.

Subordinate clause   See **Complex sentence.**

Subordinator   See **Conjunction.**

Suffix   A suffix is added after the stem of a word to form a new word, e.g. *-ness* in *goodness*. A suffix that expresses a grammatical relationship is an inflection, e.g. plural *-s* in *crowds* or past *-ed* in *cooked*.

Superordinate clause   A superordinate clause is a clause that has a subordinate clause as one of its elements:

> I hear (A) *that you know* (B) *where Ken lives.*

The (A) clause *that you . . . lives* is superordinate to the (B) clause *where Ken lives*. The subordinate (B) clause is the direct object in the (A) clause.

Syntax.   This is another term for **Grammar**, as that term is used in this book.

Tag question   A tag question is attached to a sentence that is not interrogative. It invites agreement:

> You remember me, *don't you?*
> Please don't tell them, *will you?*

Tense   Tense is the grammatical category that refers to time and is signalled by the form of the verb. There are two tenses: present (*laugh, laughs*) and past (*laughed*).

There-structure   In a *there*-structure, *there* is put in the subject position and the subject is moved to a later position:

> There is somebody here to see you. (Cf. 'Somebody is here to see you.')

Transitive Verb   See **Object**.

Verb   A verb is either (like a noun) a member of a word class or (like a subject) an element in sentence or clause structure. As a verb, it functions in a **verb phrase**. The verb phrase *may be playing* is the verb of the sentence in [1]:

[1]   She *may be playing* tennis this afternoon.

It is the verb of the *that*-clause in [2]:

[2]   She says that she *may be playing* tennis this afternoon.

See **Main verb.**

Verbless clause   A verbless clause is a reduced clause that does not have a verb:

> Send me another one *if possible.* ('if it is possible')
> *Though in pain,* Joan came with us. ('Though she was in pain')

Verb phrase   A· verb phrase consists of a **main** verb preceded optionally by a maximum of four **auxiliaries.**

Voice   Voice is a grammatical category that applies to the structure of the sentence and to the structure of the verb phrase. There are two voices: the active voice and the passive voice. See **Active.**

Wh-**question**   A *wh*-question is a question beginning with an interrogative word or with a phrase containing an interrogative word. All interrogative words except *how* begin with the spelling *wh-*: *who, whom, whose, which, what, where, when, why.*

Yes–no **question**   A *yes–no* question is a question that expects the answer *yes* or *no. Yes-no* questions require **subject–operator inversion:**

> *Can* (op) *I* (S) have a word with you?

Zero relative pronoun   See **Relative pronoun.**

Exercises

Exercises marked with an asterisk are more advanced.

Chapter 1

*Exercise 1.1 (cf.1.1)

Which of the combinations of words below seem to you to be possible English sentences? If you are not sure, say so. Where there is a problem with a sentence, try to pinpoint it and then change the sentence to avoid the problem.

1. Whether these momentous changes will do what he wants them to do is another matter.
2. We think that it is hot to sit in the sun.
3. He could not understand why he lost the job, and I had to explain to him that it was since he was lazy.
4. Fortunately, my deputy can well attend the committee meeting in my place.
5. The large hall was containing over 500 people.
6. Surprisingly, mushrooms are unusual to find at this time of the year.
7. A good time was had by all of us.
8. All the children watched television until too tired to do so any more.
9. Robert allowed himself to be persuaded to undertake the unpleasant task.
10. We weren't sure if or not we were invited.
11. There is currently a tendency that I do not know how strong it is towards discounting the effects of pollution from factories.
12. Until he came out of his corner to face a man who many believed to

be the most awesome figure in the modern history of the heavy-weight division, it was not difficult to understand why the contest was of so little interest to prospective punters.

Exercise 1.2 (cf. 1.1)

Informally describe how the (a) sentences differ from the (b) sentences.

1a. Britain's worst terrorist incident is being investigated by its smallest police force.
 b. Is Britain's worst terrorist incident being investigated by its smallest police force?
2a. The president may be unable either to fulfil expectations or to contain expectations.
 b. The president may be unable either to fulfil expectations or to contain them.
3a. The party lost the will to uphold its rule at any cost.
 b. The party did not lose the will to uphold its rule at any cost.
4a. You are the one that everybody respects and admires.
 b. Be the one that everybody respects and admires.
5a. The child was bound to get excited from time to time.
 b. The children were bound to get excited from time to time.
6a. Sleepwalkers can never remember the sleepwalking episode when they wake up in the morning.
 b. Sleepwalkers can never remember the sleepwalking episode when waking up in the morning.
7a. We have never encountered so much resistance.
 b. Never have we encountered so much resistance.
8a. A professor of civil engineering has written a history of the pencil.
 b. A history of the pencil has been written by a professor of civil engineering.
9a. What she means is easy to see.
 b. It is easy to see what she means.
10a. Army privates are trained to obey orders, police constables are trained to exercise judgement under pressure.
 b. Army privates are trained to obey orders, police constables to exercise judgement under pressure.

*Exercise 1.3 (cf. 1.3)

Look up *one* of the following topics in *A Comprehensive Grammar of the English Language* by R. Quirk, S. Greenbaum, G. Leech, and J. Svartvik (Longman, 1985). Use the index to find places in the grammar where the topic is discussed, and follow up cross-references if necessary. Give a brief oral report on the topic in class.

1.	cataphoric pronoun	11.	style disjunct
2.	transferred negation	12.	echo question
3.	absolute clause	13.	downtoner
4.	double genitive	14.	mandative subjunctive
5.	resultant object	15.	deixis
6.	subjective genitive	16.	focus of negation
7.	attitudinal past	17.	distributive
8.	prop *it* subject	18.	performative
9.	historic present	19.	rhetorical condition
10.	hypothetical condition	20.	vocative

*Exercise 1.4 (cf. 1.6)

The following is an extract from a response given by somebody during an interview. The full stops mark short pauses and the dashes longer pauses, and the vertical lines mark the ends of rhythmic units in intonation. Ignoring these indications and the absence of normal punctuation, find features in the extract that show that the passage has been transcribed from conversation? Then rewrite the passage as ordinary prose.

> well that wasn't the view | that wasn't what he'd said to me you
> see | and I've er it isn't it wasn't the view I took | – – er I think
> he did want of course | – to be in very close – – er touch with the
> Transport Office | . and indeed when I became Chief Officer | I
> found this was the great . one of the problems | . the Transport
> Secretary must have his own line | . but he must work absolutely
> | – er like a partner | like a brother | with the Chief Officer | .
> that's why it's so important that it should be just across the street
> | – – I mean even the distance would be I opposed strongly | the
> Transport Office moving to Forest Grove Terrace | – just the

difference between getting into a car and making an appointment | . it's quite different | Transport Secretary to me | when I was Chief Officer | used to almost every day to walk in just before lunch | . a telegram to be answered | a new point that has arisen | . you could settle it | in a few moments | – but it must be like that |

---

*Exercise 1.5 (cf. 1.6)

The following passage comes from a book on British politics. Rewrite the passage (a) in a more informal written style, and (b) as if you were speaking in informal conversation.

> The situation thus described – of an electorate that is driven by selfish motives – may well appear grim and morally uncomfortable. It is none the less founded upon empirical evidence and it is also grounded in realism. Democracy consists in providing a government that gives voters what they want, rather than what politicians think they ought to have. By pursuing frankly populist policies the Conservative party has, under Mrs Thatcher's leadership, ingratiated itself with sufficient sections of an increasingly fragmented and sectionalised electorate to secure the lion's share of the votes, even if these amount neither to a majority of the voters nor to a majority of the electors. But this support is not evenly spread across the whole of Great Britain (while in Northern Ireland, of course, wholly different circumstances apply).
>
> [Geoffrey Alderman, *Britain: A One-Party State*, p. 22 London: Christopher Helm, 1989]

Exercise 1.6 (cf. 1.7)

Indicate whether the rules given below are descriptive rules or prescriptive rules.

1. In English, only nouns and pronouns display distinctions in case.
2. The superlative adjective is required for more than two items or sets of items: *the best of the* (*three*) *groups*, not *the better of the three groups*.
3. Where there is a choice between *if* and *whether*, prefer *whether* in

formal English, as in *I am not sure whether she is at home.*

4. Definite and indefinite articles come before their nouns in English, as in *the library* and *a restaurant.*
5. Words are frequently converted from one part of speech to another; for example, the noun *walk* from the verb *walk.*
6. Conditional clauses sometimes begin with an auxiliary and have no conjunction, as in *Had I known, I would have telephoned you.*
7. The preposition *but* should be followed by an objective pronoun, as in *nobody but me.*
8. The most common way of expressing future meaning is with *will.*
9. Adverbs such as *very* modify adjectives (e.g. *very good*) and other adverbs (e.g. *very carefully*).
10. When you are writing formally, use the subjective pronoun after the verb *be,* as in *It is he who communicated the news.*

Chapter 2

Exercise 2.1 (cf. 2.4)

Identify whether each sentence below is declarative, interrogative, imperative, or exclamative.

1. Move right to the front of the bus.
2. What have you got to say for yourself?
3. What a good time we had!
4. How will they find their way to the station?
5. How much weight you've lost!
6. How much does it cost?
7. It's been nice meeting you.
8. Will your parents be coming with you?
9. If it doesn't rain, I'll see you tonight.
10. Pass the bottle, please.
11. Take it!
12. How can I help?

Exercise 2.2 (cf. 2.5)

Make the positive sentences below negative and the negative sentences positive.

1. We accept credit cards.
2. I'm taking my car to work today.
3. The army is different from the police force.
4. The elders of the ruling party were not shocked at the election results.
5. Nobody can tell the difference.
6. The country has changed drastically.
7. Diet and longevity don't seem to be linked.
8. Do not hold your breath.
9. Africa will not find it as easy as America to apply a successful programme.
10. He does not fully understand their objections.

Exercise 2.3 (cf. 2.6)

Identify whether each sentence below is active or passive.

1. The Prime Minister postponed a press briefing last night.
2. Five demonstrators were shot before the meeting.
3. The confession was obtained in breach of the police codes of practice.
4. Most of the tests on the Roman treasure have been carried out at the Institute of Archaeology by one of its honorary research associates.
5. The astronomers expect to discover life on another planet.
6. The dispute changed the whole of world history.
7. A sharp fall in profits is being predicted.
8. Their hopes have been dashed once again.
9. A developer has recently obtained permission to turn some 160 acres of farmland into a golf course.
10. The motion was defeated by a large majority.

Chapter 3

---

*Exercise 3.1 (cf. 3.1)

From each sentence below, form as many other English sentences as you can by moving phrases or words within the phrases. The only changes you should make to each sentence are changes in the position of phrases or words. Some changes will have a major effect on meaning.

1. It is a peculiar effect of history that, in retrospect, the pioneer can look as though he or she did little more than follow the path of least resistance.
2. It has been pointed out that the legal status of an embryo, whether it is the subject of research or not, is obscure: is it a person or is it a chattel?
3. More and more people live on their own – as pensioners at one end of the age spectrum; as young mothers, on their own with babies; or as angry deserted wives, in the middle.
4. The public generally became aware of additives and their possible effects on children's behaviour in the mid-1980s, when, in compliance with EC regulations, the majority of food additives had to be specified by name or code or labels.

Exercise 3.2 (cf. 3.2)

In each sentence below, underline the subject and circle the verb constituent.

1. Genghis Khan was a thoughtful husband and a good father.
2. He was married at 15.
3. The marriage was an arranged union.
4. His wife's name was Burte.
5. Burte was kidnapped shortly after their marriage.
6. She had a child by another man.
7. Mongolia apparently had a kidnapping problem at that time.
8. Genghis was reunited with his wife.
9. He also accepted the child, a boy, into his family.
10. Everyone approved of Genghis's domestic life.
11. His wife must have loved him, despite his reputation for cruelty.
12. Genghis is known as a ruthless warrior.
13. He terrified the continent of Asia.
14. Europe too was threatened by him.
15. The Mongolian People's Republic is seeking his exoneration.
16. His patriotism is viewed as an example to all Mongolians.
17. The newest hotel in Ulan Bator has been named after him.

18. Genghis's empire disintegrated after his death.
19. His grandson, Kublai Khan, preferred the comforts of Xanadu to campaigns around Asia.
20. Kublai Khan apparently decreed a stately pleasure dome in Xanadu.

Exercise 3.3 (cf. 3.3, 3.4)

Use the contracted form *n't* to make each sentence below negative.

1. Protesters were in the streets.
2. The party was at war with itself.
3. The tide of revolution toppled one European government after another.
4. The changes had been foreseen.
5. The party could be humbled soon.
6. It will be forced to share power.
7. The party leader's aim is constant.
8. He wants to build a stronger party.
9. He proposes to end the party's guaranteed right to rule.
10. His reforms mean the end of the old guard.
11. The party apparatus has been the chief brake on the restructuring of the country.
12. His critics are right.
13. The party can hold on to power.
14. In their view, it should reimpose order.
15. Last week, however, the party leader moved closer to the radicals.

Exercise 3.4 (cf. 3.3, 3.4)

Turn each sentence below into a question that can be answered by *yes* or *no*, and underline the operator in the question.

1. Brain bulk is related to brain ability.
2. This correlation applies across species.
3. Within the human species, brain bulk is unimportant.
4. The largest human brains are those of idiots.

5. Humans are able to lose substantial portions of the brain without undue suffering.
6. The main part of the human brain is divided into two hemispheres.
7. Messages from one hemisphere can reach the other.
8. But the brain avoids the need for constant cross-references.
9. One hemisphere dominates the other.
10. Usually the left hemisphere is dominant.
11. It also contains the speech centre.
12. And it controls the right half of the body.
13. A psychiatrist discovered that human brains have fluctuating patterns of electric waves.
14. An electroencephalogram, or EEG, can record the constant electrical flickering of a living brain.
15. Many countries consider the absence of EEG fluctuations over a period of time to be evidence of death.

Exercise 3.5 (cf. 3.5)

Identify the subject in each of the questions or exclamations below and underline it. Circle the operator and (if relevant) the rest of the verb phrase.

1. How should I know?
2. How much does all this matter?
3. How we long to be home again!
4. Have you found any advantages in the present arrangements?
5. Can the roots of decline in the playing standards of English be traced back a long way?
6. What a fuss they made!
7. Did Britain recognize the Argentine at that time?
8. When is St Valentine's Day?
9. Is the economic strength of Japan and West Germany symbolized by their huge trade surpluses?
10. What has brought about the Government's change of heart?
11. Who can tell the difference?
12. Must they make so much noise?
13. How badly has tourism been hit this year?
14. Who have you chosen as your partner?

15.   How tight a rein was the Government keeping on public spending?

---

*Exercise 3.6 (cf. 3.5)

In each sentence below, underline the subject or subjects and circle the verb or verbs.

If a sentence contains more than one clause (cf. 2.3), it may have more than one verb. For example in the following sentence there are three subjects and four verbs:

> If *you* hold a strong man down for a long time, *his first instinct* may be to clobber you when *he* climbs to his feet.

Notice that the subject may itself be a clause or contain a clause, as in the following example:

> *What I earn* is no concern of yours.

1.   The 12 governments of the European Community are committed to economic and monetary union.
2.   Most agree that they must eventually create a single currency and a new Central Bank of Europe.
3.   The row about how this bank should be run has only just started.
4.   West Germany says it will not accept union unless the new Bank of Europe is as free from political influence as its own Bundesbank, but many Europeans disagree.
5.   The French stress the need for accountability, and the British argue that a Bank of Europe cannot be made properly accountable without full political union.
6.   However, citizens need protection from their own government, and a truly independent bank will protect citizens' rights.
7.   In principle, the Bundesbank is a good model for Europe's central bank but, in practice, it is likely that politicians will insist on a compromise.

---

*Exercise 3.7 (cf. 3.6)

In the sentence below, *there* has some of the characteristics of a subject. Discuss.

There were no deaths in the recent riots.

---

*Exercise 3.8 (cf. 3.6)

What evidence do you find in the sentence below to show that the implied subject of a subjectless imperative sentence is *you*?

Help yourself to another piece of cake.

Can you think of any other evidence that points in the same direction?

Exercise 3.9 (cf. 3.7)

The direct object is underlined in each declarative sentence below. Turn the sentence into a question introduced by *who* or *what*, as indicated in brackets. Use one of these interrogative words to replace the direct object. Position the operator and the subject after *who* or *what*, as in the following example:

> She introduced the school head to her parents.
> *Who* did she introduce to her parents?

1. Norma's parents met her English and Biology teachers on the Open Day. (*Who*)
2. Caroline submitted a poem about her dog to the school magazine. (*What*)
3. All the members of staff considered Janet the best student in the Upper Sixth. (*Who*)
4. The school head recommended a careers advice test. (*What*)
5. Marilyn chose Sussex as her first preference on her application form for university entrance. (*What*)
6. Her parents preferred York or Lancaster. (*What*)
7. Doris likes the Chaucer course best. (*What*)
8. She regards the Chaucer teachers as the most interesting lecturers. (*Who*)
9. She finds modern English grammar quite easy. (*What*)
10. She has learned by heart most of the Old English declensions and conjugations. (*What*)

*Exercise 3.10 (cf. 3.7)

In each sentence below, underline the direct objects.

If a sentence contains more than one clause, it may have more than one direct object. For example, in the following sentence there are two direct objects:

> The president has offered *substantial concessions,* but he should not expect *much gratitude.*

1. The president promised the end of racial domination, but he rejected the black demand for one man, one vote.
2. That sort of democracy would mean rule by a black majority, which might feel an understandable urge for retribution for past oppressions.
3. Whites, equally understandably, want safeguards for white rights, but you cannot ensure safeguards once you surrender your power.
4. Having made his gamble, the president will find himself under pressure from two directions.
5. Among blacks he has created an upward surge of expectations which he may be unable to fulfil.
6. He has frightened white defenders of apartheid, who might attempt a final, desperate and perhaps violent defence of their racist faith.

*Exercise 3.11 (cf. 3.7)

A small set of verbs have been called 'middle verbs'. They are illustrated in the following sentences:

> All the first-year students *have* the flu.
> Your clothes don't *fit* you.
> He *lacks* courage.

How do these verbs resemble transitive verbs and how do they differ from them?

Exercise 3.12 (3.8)

Underline the subject complement in each sentence below.

1. Outside, the company sign seems modest.
2. Inside, the atmosphere is one of rush and ferment.
3. The company is a genetic engineering firm.
4. It has become a leader of a brand-new industry.
5. The focus of the project is DNA recombination.
6. DNA recombination is the transfer of pieces of DNA from one type of organism to another.
7. The leaders of the company are research scientists.
8. They are also shareholders of the company.
9. All the shareholders seem happy with the progress of the company.
10. They do not feel afraid of competition.

Exercise 3.13 (cf. 3.9)

Underline the adverbials in the sentences below. Some sentences may have more than one adverbial.

1. Opossums frequently appear to be dead.
2. Sometimes they merely pretend to be dead.
3. In that way they avoid attacks by predators.
4. Often they simply are dead.
5. Few opossums remain alive far into the second year.
6. According to one biologist, two-year-old opossums show the systems of advanced old age.
7. Over many centuries, opossums have died at early ages because of accidents and predators.
8. As a result, natural selection ends especially early in opossums' lives.
9. Bad mutations accumulate in older opossums.
10. The natural-selection theory apparently explains their short lives.

---

*Exercise 3.14 (cf. 3.10)

Complete these sentences by adding an adverbial complement.

1. My parents live
2. Unfortunately, nobody is
3. Everybody behaved

4.   You can get
5.   The soldiers are keeping
6.   The fortress stands
7.   The food will last
8.   The motorway stretches
9.   The next lecture will be
10. I haven't been

Exercise 3.15 (cf. 3.11)

Underline the indirect objects in the sentences below. Some sentences do not have an indirect object.

1.   Can you tell me the time, please?
2.   Who taught you how to do that?
3.   Paul's parents promised him a bicycle for his twelfth birthday.
4.   You can save yourself the bother.
5.   The college provides accommodation for all first-year students.
6.   I owe my parents several hundred pounds.
7.   Show me your latest videos.
8.   Our local council gives a maintenance grant to all students in higher education.
9.   They can cause us a lot of trouble.
10. What can I offer you now?
11. The restaurant does not serve vegetarian meals.
12. What a meal they ordered for us!

---

*Exercise 3.16 (cf. 3.11)

Use each verb below to make up a sentence containing both direct and indirect objects.

1.	pay	6.	make
2.	bring	7.	cook
3.	leave	8.	spare
4.	read	9.	ask
5.	find	10.	charge

Exercise 3.17 (cf. 3.12)

State whether the underlined phrases are object complements (OC) or adverbial complements (AC).

1. Jack has put his coat and hat <u>in my bedroom</u>.
2. The noise is driving me <u>mad</u>.
3. They keep their house <u>too warm</u>.
4. I can see you <u>home</u>.
5. She made me <u>her assistant</u>.
6. My friend wants her coffee <u>black</u>.
7. Make yourself <u>comfortable</u>.
8. I want you <u>outside</u>.
9. We found everybody here <u>very helpful</u>.
10. Show me <u>to my seat</u>.

*Exercise 3.18 (cf. 3.12)

Use each verb below to make up a sentence containing both a direct object and an object complement.

1. like	3. find	5. appoint
2. consider	4. call	6. declare

*Exercise 3.19 (cf. 3.12)

Use each verb below to make up a sentence containing both a direct object and an adverbial complement.

1. place	3. wish
2. keep	4. get

Exercise 3.20 (cf. 3.13)

Identify each sentence element by writing the appropriate abbreviation in the brackets after it:

S   (subject)   SC   (subject complement)
V   (verb)   OC   (object complement)
dO   (direct object)   AC   (adverbial complement)
iO   (indirect object) A   (adverbial)

If the verb is split, put 'v' for the auxiliary.

1.   Salt ( ) was ( ) the first food seasoning ( ).
2.   Many people ( ) consider ( ) the accidental spilling of salt ( ) bad luck ( ).
3.   The Romans ( ) gave ( ) their soldiers ( ) special allowances for salt ( ).
4.   They ( ) called ( ) the allowance ( ) salarium ( ).
5.   That ( ) is ( ) the original of our word 'salary' ( ).
6.   By 6500 BC ( ), Europeans ( ) were ( ) actively ( ) mining ( ) salt ( ).
7.   The first salt mines ( ) were located ( ) in Austria ( ).
8.   Today ( ) these caves ( ) are ( ) tourist attractions ( ).
9.   Salt preserved ( ) meat and fish ( ).
10. Ancient peoples ( ) used ( ) salt ( ) in all their major sacrifices ( ).

---

*Exercise 3.21 (cf. 3.13)

The sentences below are ambiguous. For each meaning, state the structure (the set of sentence elements) and give a paraphrase. For example:

> They are baking potatoes.
> S + V + SC   They are potatoes for baking.
> S + V + dO   They have put potatoes in the oven.

1.   You will make a good model.
2.   I'll call you my secretary.
3.   Your men are revolting.
4.   They left him a wreck.
5.   You should find me an honest worker.
6.   She has appointed her assistant personnel manager.
7.   She teaches the best.
8.   He was subdued to some extent.
9.   My solicitor gives the poorest free advice.

10. His hobby is making friends.

Exercise 3.22 (cf. 3.14)

Identify the type of meaning that the underlined sentence element in each sentence conveys.

1. The lecturer explained the functions of subjects.
2. That man is my father.
3. Tell me the result of the match.
4. I'm baking a cake.
5. The Department has offered me a post.
6. Joan is good at mathematics.
7. Don't take offence.
8. You can put your clothes in the washing machine now.
9. I'm working for my father during the spring break.
10. Pay attention.
11. It is much colder today.
12. Norman speaks Russian fluently.
13. I thought the interviewer rather intimidating.
14. My sister has recovered from her operation.
15. Nobody was in, to my surprise.
16. Most of the contestants were immature.
17. You can switch on the television.
18. She gave me good advice.
19. I'm writing an essay on Milton.
20. The local authority closed the school.

---

*Exercise 3.23 (cf. 3.14)

Make up a sentence for each of the sequences listed below.

1. Agentive subject + dynamic verb + affected object + degree adverbial
2. Identified subject + stative verb + attribute subject complement + time adverbial
3. Agentive subject + dynamic verb + recipient indirect object + affected direct object + space adverbial
4. Agentive subject + dynamic verb + recipient indirect object + resultant direct object + time adverbial

5. Evaluation adverbial + agentive subject + dynamic verb + affected direct object + attribute object complement
6. Truth-value adverbial + affected subject + stative verb + attribute subject complement + cause adverbial

Chapter 4

Exercise 4.1 (cf. 4.2–5)

Indicate whether each underlined noun phrase contains a pre-modifier, a post-modifier, or both.

1. The umbrella originated in Mesopotamia over 3000 years ago.
2. It was an emblem of rank and distinction.
3. It protected Mesopotamians from the harsh sun.
4. For centuries, umbrellas served primarily as a protection from the sun.
5. The Greeks and Romans regarded the umbrella as effeminate and ridiculed men who carried umbrellas.
6. On the other hand, Greek women of high rank favoured umbrellas.
7. Roman women began to oil their paper umbrellas to waterproof them.
8. In the mid-eighteenth century a British gentleman made umbrellas respectable for men.
9. Coach drivers were afraid that the umbrella would threaten their livelihood if it became a respectable means of shelter from the rain.
10. Eventually, men realized that it was cheaper to carry an umbrella than to take a coach every time it rained.

*Exercise 4.2 (cf. 4.2–5)

Underline the noun phrases in each sentence below. Some sentences may have more than one noun phrase. If a noun phrase contains a noun phrase within it, underline the embedded noun phrase a further time. For example:

> Microwave cooking is an absolutely new method for the preparation of food.

1. Fire is not used in microwave cooking.
2. Electromagnetic energy agitates the water molecules in the food.
3. The agitation produces sufficient heat for cooking.
4. The electronic tube that produces microwave energy is called a magnetron.
5. The magnetron was in use a decade before the birth of the microwave oven.
6. Two scientists invented it during World War II.
7. The magnetron was essential to Britain's radar defences.
8. The application of microwaves to the heating of food resulted from an accident.
9. An engineer was testing a magnetron tube.
10. He reached into his pocket for a chocolate bar.
11. The chocolate had melted.
12. He had not felt any heat.
13. The chocolate had been near radiation from the tube.
14. Later experiments showed that heat from microwaves could cook food.
15. The food was cooked from the inside.

---

*Exercise 4.3 (cf. 4.5)

Combine the (a) and (b) sentences in each set below by turning one of the sentences into a relative clause.

1a. The drugs inevitably damage a patient's healthy cells as well.
 b. The drugs are used for chemotherapy.
2a. Human infants pass through a critical period.
 b. The period lasts a few years.
3a. It was a mystery.
 b. They could not solve the mystery.
4a. The fundraising campaign has recruited a core of graduates.
 b. They in turn contact more graduates.
5a. Most of the bannings of books were overturned.
 b. The bannings have recently been sent to the Appeal Board.
6a. I saw a young Canadian.
 b. The Canadian was being treated for burns.
7a. He consulted with the leaders.
 b. The leaders were released from prison last year.

8a.   Those cannot be regarded as democrats.
  b.   They prefer intolerance and violence.

Exercise 4.4 (cf. 4.6)

Indicate whether each underlined clause is a relative clause or an appositive clause.

1.   The manager lacked the experience that would have helped him over-
     come the crisis.
2.   You have undermined my conviction that a nuclear war is inevitable.
3.   She has heard the news that all the passengers and crew escaped
     unhurt.
4.   I cannot dispute the fact that you have won the support of most
     members.
5.   The car hit a bus that was full of children on a school outing.
6.   I have read the report that I received last week.
7.   They have accepted the recommendation that my daughter be pro-
     moted to the next grade.
8.   Here is the report that the accusations should be referred to the
     police.

Exercise 4.5 (cf. 4.7)

Underline the appositives in the sentences below.

1.   The accelerator hurled ions of carbon and neon at a foil target of
     bismuth, a metal related to lead.
2.   They removed genes from the cells of one strain of mice, genes which
     make them resistant to a toxic drug.
3.   Berkeley scientists have finally realized the mediaeval alchemist's
     dream: transmuting a base metal into gold.
4.   Wood can supply 5 per cent of our energy needs, leaving 95 per cent
     that must come from other sources – solar, wind, coal, nuclear,
     biomass.
5.   In 1969 two University of Nevada psychologists claimed to have
     taught Washoe, a chimpanzee, to communicate in a human language.
6.   Most cells contain many mitochondria, semi-independent structures
     that supply the cell with readily usable energy.

7. Scientists have discovered two sets of hydrothermal vents (ocean hot springs).

Exercise 4.6 (cf. 4.8)

The coordinated noun phrases below are ambiguous. Rewrite the phrases unambiguously to show the different meanings.

1. my friends and good neighbours
2. aged cheese and wine
3. their properties and other businesses
4. deceitful and vicious youths
5. those books and assorted notes
6. some bread and butter

---

*Exercise 4.7 (cf. 4.2, 4.9)

Describe the structure of the three underlined noun phrases in examples [3]–[5] of Section 4.9 in terms of the structure of the noun phrase outlined in 4.2:

(determiners) (pre-modifiers) noun (post-modifier)

Set out your response for each noun phrase by writing down the elements and the words that correspond to each of them.

Exercise 4.8 (cf. 4.10)

Identify the function of each underlined noun phrase by writing the appropriate abbreviation in the brackets after it:

S	(subject)	OC	(object complement)
dO	(direct object)	cP	(complement of preposition)
iO	(indirect object)	pM	(pre-modifier of a noun
SC	(subject complement)		or noun phrase)
		A	(adverbial)

1. A survey of social trends in Britain (   ) was published last year (   ).

2. More and more Britons ( ) are living alone, despite the Government's emphasis on family ( ) values.
3. In 1987 Britain, with Portugal ( ), had the highest marriage rate ( ) within the European Community ( ).
4. But, with Denmark, it ( ) also had the highest divorce rate ( ).
5. Women ( ) are drinking more alcohol ( ) than men.
6. More people ( ) are taking more holidays ( ).
7. In 1988, Blackpool Pleasure Beach ( ) was the most popular free tourist ( ) attraction while Madame Tussaud's was the most popular paid-for attraction ( ).
8. In 1988, 62 per cent of girls ( ) left school ( ) with at least one GCSE grade A–C ( ), compared to 54 per cent of boys ( ).
9. In 1988, 16 of the 47 High Court and circuit judges ( ) were women ( ).
10. Despite the growing economic importance of women ( ), both sexes still consider some jobs ( ) a male preserve ( ).
11. The survey will give social scientists ( ) ideas for further research ( ).

Exercise 4.9 (cf. 4.12)

Identify whether the underlined verb in each sentence is the base form, -*s* form, past form, -*ing* participle, or -*ed* participle.

1. Cats were held in high esteem among the ancient Egyptians.
2. Egyptian law protected cats from injury and death.
3. The Egyptians used to embalm the corpses of their cats.
4. They put them in mummy cases made of precious materials.
5. Entire cat cemeteries have been unearthed by archaeologists.
6. The Egyptians were impressed by the way a cat could survive numerous high falls.
7. They originated the belief that the cat possesses nine lives.
8. Dread of cats first arose in Europe in the Middle Ages.
9. Alley cats were often fed by poor, lonely old women.
10. When witch hysteria spread through Europe, such women were accused of witchcraft.
11. Their cats, especially black ones, were also considered guilty.
12. Many innocent women and their cats were burnt at the stake.

13.   Some superstitious people think that if a black cat <u>crosses</u> their path they will have bad luck.
14.   I have been <u>thinking</u> of buying a black cat.

Exercise 4.10 (4.12)

Specify the tense (present or past) of the underlined verbs in the sentences below. Where necessary, distinguish also the person and number of the verbs.

1.   The price of oil <u>has</u> dropped considerably in the past few years.
2.   Prices <u>dropped</u> a few years ago because there was an oil glut.
3.   Prices <u>continue</u> to drop because oil-producing nations are refining too much crude oil.
4.   OPEC <u>wants</u> prices to rise.
5.   However, its members <u>disagree</u> about how to raise prices.
6.   'I <u>am</u> in favour of higher prices,' an OPEC member was recently quoted as saying.
7.   'However, we <u>are</u> not in favour of lowering our production because of the many debts we have.'
8.   Unless OPEC nations <u>lower</u> their production quotas, prices will remain low.

Exercise 4.11 (cf. 4.14)

Identify the italicized verbs as present perfect, past perfect, present progressive, past progressive, present perfect progressive, or past perfect progressive.

1.   People *are realizing* that trying to keep fit can be dangerous.
2.   Ted *was celebrating* his 40th birthday last week.
3.   She implied that he *had become* stale.
4.   She believes that she *has been enjoying* good health by taking large daily doses of Vitamin C.
5.   They *had been making* regular visits to an osteopath.
6.   Doreen *has been looking* much younger lately.
7.   They *have given* evidence of the health advantages of a sedentary life.

8.   We *have been jogging* several times a week.
9.   She *has* never *taken* time off to relax.
10. Some tycoons *are* regularly *eating* heavy four-course business lunches.

---

*Exercise 4.12 (cf. 4.14)

Make up a sentence using each verb below in the specified tense and aspect (or aspects).

1. *enjoy* – present perfect
2. *find* – past perfect
3. *refuse* – present progressive
4. *convince* – past progressive
5. *go* – present perfect progressive
6. *win* – past perfect progressive

Exercise 4.13 (cf. 4.15)

Identify whether the sentences below are active or passive.

1. Sotheby's is auctioning a highly important collection of antiquities.
2. In the late 1970s a huge copper cauldron was discovered in a cellar.
3. Inside the cauldron were hidden a number of very beautiful objects.
4. They included silver plates two feet across.
5. The plates were decorated with scenes from hunting and mythology.
6. Apparently the treasure was made for Seuso, perhaps a high-ranking officer in the Roman empire.
7. Possibly the family was based in Hungary.
8. It was then moved to Lebanon for military manoeuvres.
9. The Lebanese authorities issued export documents for the treasure in 1981.
10. Nothing has been revealed about the discoverers.
11. The discovery site has never been located.
12. Nobody doubts the importance of the collection.
13. Because of its strange history several museums have rejected the collection.

14.   With an expected price of over 40 million pounds, who can afford the collection?

Exercise 4.14 (cf. 4.15)

Identify whether the underlined words are passive participles or adjectives.

1.   Her book has just been <u>published</u> in New York.
2.   I was <u>amazed</u> at Patrick's indifference.
3.   Their arrival was certainly <u>unexpected</u>.
4.   His face was <u>distorted</u> with rage.
5.   Many of these projects should not have been <u>built</u> at all.
6.   I was chiefly <u>interested</u> in modern novels.
7.   I cannot understand why you are so <u>depressed</u>.
8.   None of these products are <u>manufactured</u> in our country.
9.   Daniel's series of tennis victories is still <u>unbroken</u>.
10.   Tony was <u>disgusted</u> with all of us.

---

*Exercise 4.15 (cf. 4.15)

Discuss the problems of deciding whether the underlined words are passive participles or adjectives.

1.   Norman felt <u>appreciated</u> by his parents.
2.   Jane was very <u>offended</u> by your remarks.

---

*Exercise 4.16 (cf. 4.14, 4.15)

We may raise questions about *-ing* forms that are similar to those for *-ed* forms (see Exercises 4.14 and 4.15). Discuss whether the underlined words below are participles, adjectives, or ambiguous between the two.

1.   A few of the lectures were <u>interesting</u>.
2.   Some teenagers have been <u>terrifying</u> the neighbourhood.
3.   Your offer is certainly <u>tempting</u>.

4. Timothy is always <u>calculating</u>.
5. Why are you <u>embarrassing</u> me?
6. I was <u>relieved</u>.

Exercise 4.17 (cf. 4.17)

Identify whether the underlined auxiliary is a modal, perfect *have*, progressive *be*, or passive *be*.

1. The employment agency <u>should</u> be contacting you soon about the job.
2. My insurance company has <u>been</u> informed about the damage to my roof.
3. Jeremy <u>has</u> been researching into the optical industry.
4. I <u>can</u> be reached at my office number.
5. The committee <u>is</u> holding its next meeting later this month.
6. The remains <u>were</u> accidentally discovered by a team of palaeontologists.
7. Who has <u>been</u> disturbing my papers?
8. The junk-bond market <u>has</u> collapsed.

---

*Exercise 4.18 (cf. 4.17)

Construct sentences containing the combinations of auxiliaries specified below.

1. modal + progressive *be*
2. dummy operator *do*
3. phrasal auxiliary
4. modal + passive *be*
5. perfect *have* + progressive *be*
6. perfect *have* + passive *be*
7. modal + perfect *have*
8. modal + perfect *have* + passive *be*

---

*Exercise 4.19 (cf. 4.17)

Construct verb phrases as specified below.

1. present perfect passive of *eat*
2. present modal passive of *capture*
3. past perfect progressive of *destroy*
4. past progressive passive of *see*
5. past perfect passive of *tell*
6. past modal perfect progressive of *hope*
7. present modal progressive passive of *discuss*
8. past perfect progressive passive of *blow*

Exercise 4.20 (cf. 4.18)

Specify whether the underlined verbs are finite or non-finite.

1. We must <u>make</u> the telephone a socially tolerable instrument.
2. I thought that after being <u>woken</u> up once again by an overseas call.
3. I am more <u>phoned</u> against than phoning.
4. I <u>have</u> been following the controversy in America about a new telephone device.
5. A small screen on your telephone shows the number of the person trying to <u>call</u> you.
6. If you don't <u>want</u> to talk to the caller, you don't.
7. There <u>is</u> a great deal of argument about the legality and ethics of the new device.
8. Some people are <u>insisting</u> that callers should be allowed to preserve their anonymity.
9. The argument is that callers <u>have</u> the right to privacy.
10. But it <u>could</u> be argued that they are invading someone else's privacy.
11. We should <u>welcome</u> the new device as a return to civilized behaviour.
12. No longer <u>will</u> any voice be able to gatecrash your home.

Exercise 4.21 (cf. 4.19)

Specify whether the underlined verb is indicative, imperative, present subjunctive, or past subjunctive.

1. If I <u>were</u> you, I would keep quiet.
2. After that there <u>were</u> no more disturbances.

3. Heaven <u>forbid</u> that we should interfere in the dispute.
4. If it's not raining, <u>take</u> the dog for a walk.
5. I asked that references <u>be</u> sent to the manager.
6. No warships <u>were</u> in the vicinity at that time.
7. If you happen to meet them, <u>be</u> more discreet than you were last time.
8. It is essential that she <u>return</u> immediately.

Exercise 4.22 (cf. 4.19)

Each sentence contains an expression of requesting or recommending followed by a subordinate clause. Fill the blank in each subordinate clause with an appropriate verb in the present subjunctive (the base form of the verb).

1. I demand that he _____ at once.
2. She is insistent that they _____ dismissed.
3. It is essential that she _____ every day.
4. We suggested that your brother _____ our home this evening.
5. I move that the motion _____ accepted.
6. They rejected our recommendation that the student grant _____ raised.
7. They proposed that David _____ on our behalf.
8. I suggest that she _____ the offer.

Exercise 4.23 (cf. 4.20)

Specify whether the verbs in each sentence are phrasal verbs, prepositional verbs, or phrasal-prepositional verbs.

1. I will not *put up with* your insolence any longer.
2. Michael *opened up* the shop before his employees arrived.
3. You must *concentrate on* your studies if you want a good result.
4. Mary *came down with* the flu last week.
5. My lawyer has *drawn up* the contract.
6. Tom is *looking after* his younger brother and sister.
7. All the students *handed in* their essays on time.
8. I don't *approve of* your behaviour in this matter.

9. Their car *broke down* on the way to the airport.
10. Can I *put away* the dishes now?

Exercise 4.24 (cf. 4.20)

Specify whether the prepositional verbs in the sentences below contain a prepositional object, a direct object and a prepositional object, or an indirect object and a prepositional object.

1. Has she *told* you *about* her experiences in Romania?
2. They are *taking* advantage *of* an inexperienced teacher.
3. Don't *listen to* what he says.
4. The waiter *thanked* us *for* the generous tip.
5. I *congratulate* you *on* your promotion.
6. He cannot *cope with* the jibes of his colleagues.
7. I *forgive* you *for* your rude behaviour.
8. We have *received* many donations *from* listeners to this programme.

Exercise 4.25 (cf. 4.21)

Underline each adjective phrase.

1. Fragrant homemade bread is becoming common in many American homes.
2. In a recent sample, 30 per cent of the subscribers to a woman's magazine said that they baked bread.
3. The first bread was patted by hand.
4. The early Egyptians added yeast and made conical, triangular, or spiral loaves as well as large, flat, open-centred disks.
5. Bakers later devised tools to produce more highly refined flour.
6. White bread was mixed with milk, oil, and salt.
7. People used to eat black bread because they were poor.
8. Bread lovers now buy black bread by choice.

Exercise 4.26 (cf. 4.21)

Complete the sentences below by adding a post-modifier to the adjectives at the ends of the sentences.

1. No doubt you are aware
2. My children are always happy
3. It is sometimes possible
4. They are sure
5. I am sorry
6. We are conscious
7. She is fond
8. He was not averse

Exercise 4.27 (cf. 4.22)

Identify the function of each underlined adjective phrase by writing the appropriate abbreviation in the brackets after it:

> Pre (pre-modifier in noun phrase)
> Post (post-modifier in noun phrase)
> SC (subject complement)
> OC (object complement)

1. The former (   ) champion is now very ill (   ).
2. He has a rare (   ) viral (   ) infection.
3. The drugs he takes make him sick (   ).
4. His body looks no different than it looked before (   ).
5. His doctor has arranged preliminary (   ) tests for heart surgery.
6. His general (   ) health is good (   ), but surgery is always somewhat risky (   ).

Exercise 4.28 (cf. 4.23)

Underline each adverb phrase.

1. Disposing of nuclear waste is a problem that has recently gained much attention.
2. Authorities are having difficulties finding locations where nuclear waste can be disposed of safely.
3. There is always the danger of the waste leaking very gradually from the containers in which it is stored.
4. Because of this danger, many people have protested quite vehemently against the dumping of any waste in their communities.

5. In the past, authorities have not responded quickly enough to problems at nuclear waste sites.
6. As a result, people react somewhat suspiciously to claims that nuclear waste sites are safe.
7. The problem of nuclear waste has caused many new nuclear power plants to remain closed indefinitely.
8. Authorities fear that this situation will very soon result in a power shortage.

Exercise 4.29 (cf. 4.24)

Identify the function of each underlined adverb phrase by writing the appropriate abbreviation in the brackets after it:

> A (adverbial)
> M Adj (modifier of adjective)
> M Adv (modifier of adverb)

1. Small forks <u>first</u> (   ) appeared in eleventh-century Tuscany.
2. They were <u>widely</u> (   ) condemned at the time.
3. It was in late eighteenth-century France that forks <u>suddenly</u> (   ) became fashionable.
4. Spoons are thousands of years older than forks and began as thin, <u>slightly</u> (   ) concave pieces of wood.
5. Knives were used <u>far</u> (   ) earlier than spoons.
6. They have changed <u>little</u> (   ) over the years.
7. When meals were <u>generally</u> (   ) eaten with the fingers, towel-size napkins were essential.
8. When forks were adopted to handle food, napkins were retained in a <u>much</u> (   ) smaller size to wipe the mouth.
9. A saucer was <u>originally</u> (   ) a small dish for holding sauces.
10. Mass production made the saucer inexpensive <u>enough</u> (   ) to be <u>merely</u> (   ) an adjunct to a cup.

---

*Exercise 4.30 (cf. 4.24)

In the following sentences the underlined adverbs are modifiers, but they are not modifiers of adjectives or adverbs. Circle the expression they are modifying and identify the class of that expression.

1. His hand went <u>right</u> through the glass door.
2. We stayed there <u>almost</u> three weeks.
3. I was <u>dead</u> against his promotion.
4. <u>Virtually</u> all my friends were at the party.
5. <u>Nearly</u> everybody agreed with me.
6. She finished <u>well</u> before the deadline.
7. They left <u>quite</u> a mess.
8. Who <u>else</u> told you about my accident?

*Exercise 4.31 (cf. 4.24)

What is the function of the underlined adverb in the following phrases?

1. for <u>ever</u>
2. that man <u>there</u>
3. until <u>recently</u>
4. the <u>then</u> president
5. (He is) <u>rather</u> a fool
6. the <u>above</u> photograph

Exercise 4.32 (cf. 4.25)

Underline each prepositional phrase and circle each preposition. If a prepositional phrase is embedded within another prepositional phrase, underline it twice.

1. It may come as a surprise to you that massage is mentioned in ancient Hindu Chinese writings.
2. It is a natural therapy for aches and pains in the muscles.
3. The Swedish technique of massage emphasizes improving circulation by manipulation.
4. Its value is recognized by many doctors.
5. Some doctors refer to massage as manipulative medicine.
6. Non-professionals can learn to give a massage, but they should be careful about applying massage to severe muscle spasms.
7. The general rule is that what feels good to you will feel good to others.
8. A warm room, a comfortable table, and a bottle of oil are the main requirements.

9. The amount of pressure you can apply depends on the pain threshold of the person on the table.
10. You can become addicted to massages.

---

*Exercise 4.33 (cf. 4.25)

Rewrite the sentences below, moving prepositions to alternative positions that they can occur in. You may need to make some consequent changes.

1. The secretary is the person who you should send your application to.
2. Relativity is a theory on which many modern theories in physics are based.
3. Who are you writing to?
4. This article is one that researchers in economics often make reference to.
5. For whom does John plan to do the work?
6. Both of the workers are people I have a lot of trust in.
7. What platform are we supposed to be on?
8. The women are authors whose books we have obtained much valuable information from.

Exercise 4.34 (cf. 4.26)

Identify the function of each underlined prepositional phrase by writing the appropriate abbreviation in the brackets after it:

pN (post-modifier of noun)
pAdj (post-modifier of adjective)
A (adverbial)

1. Politicians in the United States must raise large sums of money ( ) if they want to get elected.
2. A candidate can no longer win with little campaign money ( ).
3. Candidates are keenly aware of the need for huge financial contributions ( ).
4. They need the money to employ staff and for the frequent advertisements they run on television ( ).

5. In recent campaigns ( ), television advertisements have been quite belligerent.
6. They frequently distort the policies of opposing candidates ( ).
7. They often resemble extravagant Hollywood films in their lavish production ( ).
8. The advertisements are making many Americans cynical of politicians ( ).
9. To them ( ), a politician is simply a person who will say anything to get elected.
10. Many people want elections to be conducted in a more dignified and honest manner ( ).

Exercise 4.35 (Ch. 4)

Identify each underlined phrase by writing the appropriate abbreviation in the brackets after it:

Np (noun phrase)
AdjP (adjective phrase)
VP (verb phrase)
AdvP (adverb phrase)
PP (prepositional phrase)

1. The release of Mr Mandela ( ) was an event of vast political significance ( ).
2. The Savoy theatre was opened ( ) in 1881 by Richard D'Oyly Carte ( ) for the purpose of showing Gilbert and Sullivan operas ( ).
3. The top prize at Crufts Dog Show ( ) went to a little West Highland ( ) terrier.
4. We stopped ( ) in front of the sentry box beside a barrier over the road ( ).
5. They stayed true to their old belief in the Buddhist religion ( ).
6. Life is much less ( ) prosperous than in our own country.
7. I consider this refusal to accept that we can behave badly ( ) nauseating ( ).
8. He ( ) posed as a world-weary and cultured ( ) aristocrat.

*Exercise 4.36 (Ch. 4)

Construct sentences containing the sequences of phrases given below.

1. prepositional phrase + noun phrase + verb phrase + adverb phrase
2. adverb phrase + noun phrase + verb phrase + adjective phrase
3. noun phrase + verb phrase + noun phrase + prepositional phrase + prepositional phrase
4. prepositional phrase + noun phrase + verb phrase + prepositional phrase.
5. noun phrase + verb phrase + adverb phrase
6. adverb phrase + prepositional phrase + noun phrase + verb phrase + adjective phrase + adverb phrase

Chapter 5

Exercise 5.1 (cf. 5.3)

Convert the following words into nouns by adding noun suffixes and making any other consequent changes. Some words may take more than one noun suffix.

1.	perform	6.	press
2.	able	7.	satisfy
3.	conceive	8.	govern
4.	speak	9.	repeat
5.	construct	10.	real

*Exercise 5.2 (cf. 5.4)

Construct two sentences for each of the following nouns. Use the noun in the (a) sentence as a count noun and the noun in the (b) sentence as a non-count noun.

1.	beer	6.	salt
2.	beauty	7.	experience
3.	sound	8.	cake
4.	sugar	9.	work
5.	paper	10.	power

Exercise 5.3 (cf. 5.5)

Supply the plural form for each of the singular nouns listed below.

1.	analysis	6.	ovum
2.	thief	7.	phenomenon
3.	criterion	8.	hypothesis
4.	deer	9.	basis
5.	stimulus	10.	criterion

Exercise 5.4 (cf. 5.8)

Specify whether the underlined genitives are dependent or independent by putting 'D' or 'I' in the brackets that follow each genetive.

1. In a recent poll 48 per cent of Americans thought that Japan's ( ) economy is bigger than America's ( ).
2. The British government's ( ) £50 billion sale of state-owned housing is going at a snail's ( ) pace.
3. For Lloyd's ( ) of London, the frauds of the early 1980s seem a thing of the past.
4. New Zealand plans to deregulate the country's ( ) industry.

---

*Exercise 5.5 (cf. 5.8)

Construct two sentences for each of the following genitives. Use the genitive in the (a) sentence as a dependent genitive and in the (b) sentence as an independent genitive.

1.	the neighbours'	3.	my sister's
2.	Russia's	4.	the dentist's

Exercise 5.6 (cf. 5.9)

Convert the following words into verbs by adding verb suffixes and making any consequent changes. Some words may take more than one verb suffix.

1. real   4. random
2. hyphen   5. ample
3. ripe   6. example

Exercise 5.7 (cf. 5.11)

Give the three principal parts for each of these irregular verbs.

1. grow   6. do
2. put   7. go
3. drive   8. read
4. send   9. fall
5. break   10. throw

Exercise 5.8 (cf. 5.12)

Convert the following words into adjectives by adding adjective suffixes and making any consequent changes. Some words may have more than one adjective suffix.

1. style   6. monster
2. cycle   7. hair
3. wish   8. use
4. allergy 9. sex
5. care   10. confide

---

*Exercise 5.9 (cf. 5.13)

Construct three sentences for each of the following central adjectives. Use the adjective in the (a) sentence as a pre-modifier of a noun, in the (b) sentence as a subject complement, and in the (c) sentence as an object complement.

1. useful   4. nervous
2. foolish   5. necessary
3. difficult 6. unusual

Exercise 5.10 (cf. 5.14)

Give the inflected comparative and superlative of each of these adjectives.

1.	pure	6.	simple
2.	cruel	7.	clean
3.	easy	8.	common
4.	narrow	9.	quiet
5.	happy	10.	handsome

*Exercise 5.11 (cf. 5.14)

Discuss the meanings of these three sentences in relation to their forms.

1. She was a most kind teacher.
2. She was the most kind teacher.
3. She was most kind.
4. She was kindest.

*Exercise 5.12 (cf. 5.14)

Discuss the use of *more* in the sentences below.

1. They were more than happy to hear the news.
2. He is more shrewd than clever.

Exercise 5.13 (cf. 5.17)

Circle the antecedents of the underlined pronouns and possessive determiners.

1. Scientists have discovered that pets have a therapeutic effect on their owners.
2. A dog, for instance, can improve the health of the people it comes in contact with.
3. In a recent study, the blood pressure of subjects was measured while they were petting their pets.

4. In general, an individual's blood pressure decreased while <u>he</u> was in the act of petting his pet.
5. Since many of the elderly have experienced the loss of a spouse, it is particularly important that <u>they</u> be allowed to have a pet.
6. This is a problem, since the elderly often live in flats whose landlords will not allow <u>their</u> tenants to own pets.
7. Recently, however, a local landlord allowed <u>her</u> tenants to own pets on an experimental basis.
8. This landlord found that when <u>they</u> were allowed to have pets, the elderly proved to very responsible pet owners.

Exercise 5.14 (cf. 5.18)

Specify the person (first, second, or third), number (singular or plural), and case (subjective or objective) of the underlined pronouns. If the pronoun has a form that neutralizes the distinction in number or case, state the alternatives, and if only one of the alternatives fits the context underline that alternative.

1. Most of <u>us</u> don't have the time to exercise for an hour each day.
2. <u>We</u> have our hearts in the right place, though.
3. <u>I</u> think 'diet' is a sinister word.
4. <u>It</u> sounds like deprivation.
5. But people who need to lose weight find that <u>they</u> need to lose only half the weight if they exercise regularly.
6. The reason is that exercises help <u>you</u> to replace fat with muscle.
7. My exercise class has helped <u>me</u> to change my attitude to body shape.
8. The instructor says that <u>she</u> objects to bony thinness.
9. To quote <u>her</u>, 'Who wants to be all skin and bones?'
10. My husband approves of her view, and <u>he</u> is thinking of joining the class.

Exercise 5.15 (cf. 5.19)

Indicate whether the underlined words are possessive determiners or possessive pronouns.

1. Can you tell me <u>your</u> address?

2. You've made a mistake. The phone number is not <u>his</u>.
3. This is Doris and this is <u>her</u> husband David.
4. Justin borrowed one of my videos, but I can't remember <u>its</u> title.
5. This book is <u>yours</u>, Robert.
6. Benjamin has already read one of <u>his</u> books.
7. She claimed that the bicycle was <u>hers</u>.
8. They are concerned about the fall in <u>their</u> standard of living.

Exercise 5.16 (cf. 5.20)

Fill in each blank with the appropriate reflexive pronoun.

1. We congratulated _____ on completing the job in good time.
2. I _____ have arranged the meeting.
3. I wonder, Tom, whether you wouldn't mind helping _____ .
4. I hope that you all enjoy _____ .
5. She did the entire job by _____ .
6. The surgeon needs to a allow _____ more time.
7. They can't help _____ .
8. The dog hurt _____ when it jumped over the barbed wire fence.

Exercise 5.17 (cf. 5.21)

Specify whether the underlined word is a demonstrative pronoun or a demonstrative determiner.

1. <u>This</u> happens to be the best meal I've eaten in quite a long time.
2. Put away <u>those</u> papers.
3. <u>That</u> is not the way to do it.
4. You'll have to manage with <u>these</u> for the time being.
5. We can't trace <u>that</u> letter of yours.
6. Who told you <u>that</u> ?
7. Where can I buy another one of <u>those?</u>
8. <u>These</u> ones are the best for you.

Exercise 5.18 (cf. 5.24)

Indicate whether the underlined clause is a relative clause or a nominal relative clause.

1. We could see <u>whoever we wanted</u>.
2. They spoke to the official <u>who was working on their case</u>.
3. This is the bank <u>I'm hoping to borrow some money from</u>.
4. You can pay <u>what you think is appropriate</u>.
5. <u>What is most urgent</u> is that we reduce the rate of inflation as soon as possible.
6. The police have found the person <u>that they were looking for</u>.
7. Tell me <u>what I should do</u>.
8. I know <u>who made that noise</u>.

Exercise 5.19 (cf. 5.25)

Indicate whether the underlined pronouns are personal, possessive, reflexive, demonstrative, reciprocal, interrogative, relative, or indefinite.

1. <u>Nobody</u> has ever seen a unicorn.
2. <u>I</u> intend to collect beetles.
3. <u>What</u> do you want me to do?
4. He can resist <u>everything</u> except temptation.
5. She did it all by <u>herself</u>.
6. There are some pressure groups <u>that</u> support only one party.
7. <u>One</u> cannot be too careful in the choice of one's friends.
8. We are commanded to love <u>one another</u>.
9. The next turn is <u>yours</u>.
10. Is <u>this</u> war?
11. <u>Who</u> is it now?
12. I heard the story from somebody on <u>whom</u> I can rely.

Exercise 5.20 (cf. 5.25)

Indicate whether the underlined determiners are definite articles, indefinite articles, demonstratives, possessives, interrogatives, relatives, or indefinites.

1. <u>His</u> parents would not let him see the video.
2. <u>Many</u> applicants were given an interview.
3. <u>Whose</u> shoes are those?
4. <u>What</u> plans have you made for the weekend?
5. There are some children <u>whose</u> parents don't speak English.

6.   This generation has never had it so good.
7.   The community policeman warned the children not to talk to strangers.
8.   No dogs are allowed in here.
9.   That collection forms the core of the new library.
10. China is the last nation on earth to make such trains.

Exercise 5.21 (cf. 5.28)

Indicate whether the underlined phrases are generic or non-generic.

1.   There is no such beast as a unicorn.
2.   The train is late again.
3.   The dinosaur has long been extinct.
4.   Teachers are poorly paid in this country.
5.   He came on a small market where women were selling dried beans.
6.   Beans are a highly efficient form of nutrition.
7.   We rebuilt the kitchen in just four weeks.
8.   People who throw stones shouldn't live in greenhouses.
9.   History graduates have a hard time finding jobs.
10. A standard bed may not be right for everyone.

Exercise 5.22 (cf. 5.28)

Indicate whether the underlined phrases are specific or non-specific.

1.   Can you find me a book on English grammar?
2.   Here is a book on English grammar.
3.   I'd like a strawberry ice cream.
4.   He says he hasn't any stamps.
5.   Who is the woman you were talking to at lunch?
6.   I'm looking for a hat that will go with my dress.
7.   I'm looking for the hat that will suit me best.
8.   You can borrow either tie.
9.   We bought some furniture this morning.
10. Can someone tell me the time?

Exercise 5.23 (cf. 5.32)

Paraphrase the meanings of the underlined modals in the sentences below.

1. Canary Wharf, on London's Isle of Dogs, <u>must</u> be the biggest building site in Europe.
2. It <u>may</u> be the largest single current business development in the world.
3. It <u>will</u> have the highest tower in the British Isles.
4. Nobody <u>can</u> deny that it will provide the most astonishing working environment to be found anywhere in London.
5. It <u>should</u> provide plenty of jobs for the local population.
6. The youngsters are guaranteed jobs, but first they <u>must</u> acquire advanced technical skills.
7. Existing travel facilities are poor and they <u>should</u> be improved.
8. Despite pessimistic forecasts, it <u>could</u> be argued that too much money has been invested in Canary Wharf for the project to fail.
9. The owners <u>must</u> ensure that the cost of space will be competitive.
10. Those who built the outlying suburbs of London in the last century <u>must</u> have asked themselves whether their projects would be successful.

---

*Exercise 5.24 (cf. 5.32)

Explain the ambiguity of the underlined modals in the following sentences by paraphrasing the different meanings.

1. They <u>may</u> not smoke during the meal.
2. <u>Could</u> you explain these figures to the tax inspector?
3. They <u>must</u> pass this way.
4. We <u>should</u> be at the office before nine o'clock.

---

*Exercise 5.25 (cf. 5.33)

Examine the sentences below. Then explain the differences in the uses of the coordinators (*and* and *or*) and the subordinator *when*.

1. The election was held last month, *and* the government was decisively defeated.
2. The election will be held in June *or* in July.
3. I intend to travel where I like *and when* I like.
4. I phoned her, I wrote to her, *and* I saw her in person.
5. The government was decisively defeated *when* the election was held last month.
6. *When* the selection was held last month, the government was decisively defeated.

Exercise 5.26 (cf. 5.34)

Indicate whether the underlined words are subordinators or prepositions by putting 'S' or 'P' in the brackets that follow each word.

> <u>While</u> (   ) he developed the theory of special relatively <u>in</u> (   ) about 1905, Albert Einstein lived <u>with</u> (   ) a fellow student of physics who became his first wife. Some researchers believe <u>that</u> (   ) his wife Mileva should get at least some of the credit <u>for</u> (   ) the theory, <u>since</u> (   ) there are letters <u>from</u> (   ) Einstein to her that refer to 'our work' and 'our theory'. Furthermore, a Russian physicist who is now dead claimed to have seen both names <u>on</u> (   ) the original manuscripts of four papers, but some scholars discount his evidence <u>because</u> (   ) the original manuscripts have disappeared. <u>Although</u> (   ) Mileva was certainly capable of understanding Einstein's work and perhaps of collaborating <u>with</u> (   ) him, the present evidence is too meagre to upset the traditional view of Albert Einstein's contribution <u>to</u> (   ) the theory of special relativity, a view held <u>since</u> (   ) the publication of the theory.

Exercise 5.27 (Chapter 5)

At the end of each sentence you will find a label for a part of speech. Underline any words in the sentence that belong to that part of speech.

1. It is remarkably difficult to define what literature is. – *main verbs*
2. Some definitions of literature say that it is language used for making fiction. – *nouns*

3. Other definitions say that it is language used for the purpose of pleasing aesthetically. – *prepositions*
4. However, some critics have shown convincingly that the two definitions are necessarily connected. – *adverbs*
5. Certainly, the fiction definition alone is not sufficient, since some literature is not fiction (e.g. biography) and some fiction is not literature (e.g. the story told in an advertisement). – *determiners*
6. Attempts to identify literary language through its abundance of rhetorical or figurative devices have also failed. – *adjectives*
7. Some have argued that it is a mistake to set up a dichotomy between literary and non-literary language, since literature is defined simply by what we as readers or literary critics regard as literature. – *pronouns*

Chapter 6

Exercise 6.1 (cf. 6.2)

Indicate whether the sentences below are *yes-no* questions, *wh*-questions, declarative questions, or alternative questions.

1. When will working conditions be improved?
2. Will there be a large increase in car ownership in this country by the end of the decade?
3. How many people do you think will attend our meeting, twenty or thirty?
4. How often should I take the medicine?
5. You say that she took your car without your permission?
6. Hasn't the book been published yet?
7. Do bears suffer from toothache?
8. Do you want me to buy tickets for your sisters as well or just for us?

*Exercise 6.2 (cf. 6.2)

Discuss the differences in meaning between the following pairs of sentences.

1a. Do you trust them?

   b. Don't you trust them?

2a. Has anyone told you what to say?
  b. Has someone told you what to say?

3a. She is quite clever.
  b. She is quite clever, isn't she?

4a. Why do you complain?
  b. Why don't you complain?

Exercise 6.3 (cf. 6.3)

Comment on the difference in meaning between the following two sentences.

1. Tell me what you think.
2. Do tell me what you think.

Exercise 6.4 (cf. 6.4)

Rewrite each sentence, turning it into an exclamation. Use *what* or *how* in combination with the underlined words.

1. Those paintings look <u>peculiar</u>.
2. He's been behaving <u>foolishly</u> today.
3. It's been <u>a long time</u> since I've enjoyed myself so much.
4. She seems <u>young</u>.
5. That was <u>a party</u>!

Exercise 6.5 (cf. 6.5)

Suggest a plausible speech act that might be performed by the utterance of each of the following sentences.

1. I can't find my pen.
2. Do you have a match?

3. It's too hot in here.
4. Do you know the time?
5. The front of the oven is extremely hot.
6. I'll be at your lecture tomorrow.
7. Have a good time.
8. Why don't you have a rest now?

Exercise 6.6 (cf. 6.6)

Combine each of the following pairs of sentences into one sentence by using the coordinator given in the brackets. Wherever possible, avoid repetition by omitting words or using pronouns.

1. Guinea-worms are born in ponds and open wells. Guinea-worms are ingested as larvae by tiny water-fleas. (*and*)
2. Managers have no right to analyse. They have no right to make decisions. (*and*)
3. Driving should be a pleasant experience. At the very least, driving should be an uneventful experience. (*or*)
4. I needed violence in the play. I didn't want the violence to be gratuitous. (*but*)

Exercise 6.7 (cf. 6.8)

Indicate whether the underlined clauses are *-ing* clauses, *-ed* clauses, infinitive clauses, or verbless clauses.

1. England's initial target was <u>to scrape together 22 runs from their last two wickets</u>.
2. The Finnish boat capsized after <u>losing its keel 120 miles off the Argentine coast</u>.
3. If the Rugby Football Union had wanted to engineer the triumph of the western region it could not have done better than <u>keep Bath and Gloucester apart in the Cup semi-final draw</u>.
4. It was from a cross by Simon Morgan that Wright had the first shot, <u>although pulled wide</u>.
5. Blackpool, <u>lying second from bottom</u>, must now concentrate on avoiding relegation.

6.   Down 6–0 in the third set, he delivered a toucher, a short which for once resisted his opponent's efforts to remove.
7.   The season begins in earnest on Sunday with the Worth tournament, won by Sevenoaks last year.
8.   With his final bowl to come, he leapt in, picked up the jack and claimed his precious shot.
9.   There may be as many as 400 players in the game of street football, with the goals being separated by up to three or four miles of open countryside.
10. The two weightlifters stripped of their medals following positive drug tests at the Commonwealth Games will learn of their punishment today.

Exercise 6.8 (cf. 6.8)

In each of the following sentences a non-finite or verbless clause is italicized. Identify the italicized element in the clause by writing the appropriate abbreviation in the brackets after it:

S	(subject)	SC	(subject complement)
V	(verb)	OC	(object complement)
dO	(direct object)	AC	(adverbial complement)
iO	(indirect object)	A	(adverbial)

1.   Treating *sufferers from anorexia and bulimia* (   ) is difficult.
2.   Researchers have discovered that antidepressants control some symptoms of bulimia, *reducing the number of eating binges* (   ).
3.   She fell ill soon after she arrived and was found to be suffering *from malaria.* (   ).
4.   Many malaria cases could be prevented if people bothered to take anti-malarial drugs *regularly* (   ).
5.   His doctors realized that the hypoglycaemic spells might be caused by *additional insulin* flooding his body (   ).
6.   Beyond the early weeks, light to moderate drinking doesn't seem to *cause pregnant women any problems* (   ).
7.   Large-scale studies in progress are intended to *give researchers reliable data on heavy drinking in particular* (   ).
8.   Immediately she sees the envelope from her dentist she starts *to feel sweaty* (   ).

*Exercise 6.9 (cf. 6.8)

Combine the sentences in each pair by making one of the sentences a non-finite clause or a verbless clause.

1. He was accused once of a lack of gravity. He replied that this was his natural bent.
2. The play is a talking piece. Its action consists exclusively of monologues and duologues.
3. He was ill but still irrepressible. He related former triumphs and famous anecdotes.
4. The actor impersonates the playwright. The playwright is giving a lecture in Paris.
5. He gave a promise to his friend. The promise was that he would drink no more than a pint of wine a day.
6. His wife died. She left him with five children.
7. He believed himself to be a failure. He had made no career for himself either in politics or the law.
8. He wrote to his young son. He was repaid with an inspiring reply listing all his achievements.
9. He was predictably conservative. He even opposed the abolition of slavery.
10. In religion he was eclectic. He tried several churches.

Exercise 6.10 (cf. 6.9)

Identify the function of each of the underlined clauses by putting the appropriate abbreviation in the brackets that follow the clause.

nominal clause (N)	reduced relative clause (RR)
nominal relative clause (NR)	comparative clause (C)
relative clause (R)	adverbial clause (A)

1. The ancient discipline of rhetoric was intended to prepare the beginner for tasks <u>that involved speaking in public</u> (   ).
2. The classical view of <u>how to present a case in argument</u> (   ) involved a structure of sequent elements.
3. Stylistic propriety was formalized by the Roman rhetoricians, <u>who</u>

distinguished the three levels of the Grand, the Middle, and the Plain style ( ).

4. The Grand style was most appropriate to the task of <u>stirring the profounder emotions of one's audience</u> ( ).

5. From these ideas on style originated the notion of 'decorum', <u>continually discussed by English Renaissance writers</u> ( ).

6. The study of rhetoric is complex <u>because new conventions of performance for particular purposes are being generated all the time</u> ( ).

7. It is not surprising <u>that myth should be a prominent element in the rhetoric of persuasion</u> ( ).

8. In myths and parables <u>what we are asked to take literally</u> ( ) is accompanied by one or more possible levels of interpretation.

9. A view expressed by some modern critics is that creative writers are no more the complete masters of what they do <u>than are any other writers</u> ( ).

10. Creative writers are frequently blind to their own intentions and to the nature of <u>what they are doing</u> ( ).

11. <u>To assign to any metaphor a merely decorative value</u> ( ) is <u>to undervalue the linguistic and literary power of this device</u> ( ).

12. You cannot, as a reader, wholly appreciate the rhetorical sport of a convention or a style <u>if you have a poor knowledge of literary language and conventions</u> ( ).

---

* Exercise 6.11 (cf. 6.9)

Construct sentences consisting of clauses introduced by each pair of the following correlatives :

more . . . than	*the . . . the*
as . . . so	*scarcely . . . when*
no sooner . . . than	*if . . . then*

---

*Exercise 6.12 (cf.6.10)

Describe the relationship of clauses in the following sentences, and explain the functions of the subordinate clauses.

1. Savage gales caused another wave of destruction today after yester-

day's storms left 14 dead and thousands homeless.

2. The London Weather Centre warned that fierce winds would build up in the South East and they might gust up to 70 mph.
3. In Folkestone the sea defence wall gave way, causing flooding of up to five feet, and police were considering evacuation.
4. In one town in North Wales 1000 people were made homeless and the local council asked the Government to declare the town a disaster area because the emergency services said that they could not prevent more damage.

Exercise 6.13 (cf. 6.11)

Turn the sentences below into *there*-structures.

1. Nobody is at home.
2. We can do nothing more to help him.
3. A number of universities in this country are worried about their financial situation.
4. Too many people don't work hard enough.

Exercise 6.14 (cf. 6.12)

Turn the sentences below into pseudo-cleft sentences.

1. I need a strong drink.
2. He intends to be at least as outspoken as his predecessors.
3. A Cabinet committee will look at a plan to open up disused hospital wards to the homeless.
4. The gossip columnist made very serious allegations against a prominent politician.

Exercise 6.15 (cf. 6.13)

Turn the sentences below into sentences with anticipatory *it*.

1. Whether you finish the painting or not is irrelevant.
2. How house prices rise and fall is entirely arbitrary.
3. That responsibility for the decline in living standards must be laid at

the door of the Prime Minister is obvious to everybody.
4.   To make mistakes is human nature.

Exercise 6.16 (Ch. 6)

Identify the function of each underlined subordinate clause by writing the appropriate abbreviation in the brackets after the clause.

S	(subject)
dO	(direct object)
iO	(indirect object)
SC	(subject complement)
OC	(object complement)
AC	(adverbial complement)
A	(adverbial)
cP	(complement of a preposition)
mN	(modifier of a noun phrase)
mA	(modifier of an adjective phrase)
mAdv	(modifier of an adverb phrase)

1.   The computer system allows employees to change files if they wish ( ).
2.   The next decade should be pleasanter than the one we have just lived through ( ).
3.   She accused him of wasting his talents ( ).
4.   His first job had been selling insurance ( ).
5.   Metal-particle tapes accept and hold high-frequency magnetic pulses much more readily than do metal-oxide tapes ( ).
6.   One theory of climate that has gained wide acceptance ( ) is used to predict the duration of periodic changes in climate ( ).
7.   When food is withdrawn from their stomach after a meal is finished ( ), rats will compensate by eating the same amount of food ( ).
8.   You can tell whoever is interested ( ) that I am cancelling my subscription ( ).
9.   He showed us what he had written ( ).
10.   She made him what he is ( ).
11.   The food is better than average, although prices are somewhat higher ( ).

12. He would certainly have won the mayoral election comfortably <u>had he run</u> (   ).
13. Until now the government's approach was <u>to appease demonstrators</u> (   ).
14. <u>Giving evidence to the committee during its six-month investigation</u> (   ), he was unrepentent.
15. The Chancellor of the Exchequer faces intense pressure <u>to halt inflation</u> (   ).

Chapter 7

Exercise 7.1 (cf. 7.1)

Read the following passage and mark where you pause. How many of the places where you have paused have punctuation marks and how many do not? You will find it convenient to use a tape recorder for this exercise.

> We expect our children's childhood to pass as slowly as we remember our own to have done. And so it does - to them. To them a week or a month or a year can appear ocean-like in its expanses of sameness or changeableness. To us, however, to the parents we have become, the childhood of our children passes as swiftly as everything else in adult years. From moment to moment, we feel, we are left vainly grasping after people who are no longer there. They have vanished even while we were looking at them. How can we recall the six-week-old infant when he has been shouldered out of his own life and out of our minds by someone of the same name and with something of the same features who is now six months old; and how can we recall the six-month-old infant when another infant aged two years or three years or five years has taken his place? And the fifteen-year-old who replaces that five-year-old will in turn be swiftly replaced by an adult with whom our relationship is bound to be quite different from the other, provisional relationships we had before with all his or her other, provisional selves.

> [*Time and Time Again* by Dan Jacobson, p. 136. London: Andre Deutsch, 1985]

Exercise 7.2 (cf. 7.2)

This passage contains several sentence fragments. Re-punctuate the passage to remove the sentence fragments.

> Northrop Frye once remarked that there are only two kinds of readers. Those who skip lists and those who relish them. One of the chief stumbling-blocks for readers of the Bible is no doubt the lengthy genealogical lists which appear so often in the Pentateuch and Chronicles. And also occasionally crop up elsewhere. We are now, however, in a position to understand their function.
>
> The genealogical lists in the Bible do not seek to trace a line back from a present emperor or leader to a god. As happens in other ancient Near Eastern cultures and in ancient Greece and Rome. They are there simply to keep alive the memory of the family. That memory is traced back to Abraham. Who was adopted by God. He did not particularly deserve to be adopted, yet once the covenant had been made between himself and God the relationship was sealed. With heavy obligations on both sides. The genealogies, like the narratives, keep alive the memory of these wondrous facts. That Abraham was called. That he left Haran. That Sarah bore a child though she was long past the age for doing so. That Jacob stole the blessing. That Tamar conceived and bore a child to Judah. That God brought the people out of Egypt. Such amazing things cannot be repeated often enough. But they can be repeated as a continuous and continuing story. Because Jacob is Isaac's son and Judah Jacob's.
>
> [Adapted from *The Book of God: A Response to the Bible* by Gabriel Josipovici, page 140. New York: Yale University Press]

Exercise 7.3 (cf. 7.3)

Correct errors in run-on sentences and comma splices.

1. One of the more popular methods of reducing waste is by incineration, this method is used where land is scarce for burial.
2. Ask the first people you see if they can help you I'm sure they will.
3. He is not the world's leading authority on coins, however, he is often consulted by foreign buyers.

4. Universities now have problems filling some science courses, the applications are not there.
5. The peace talks collapsed, we therefore expect an immediate renewal of fighting.
6. The agency relaxed its security procedures it did so against a background of warnings of an imminent terrorist threat.

Exercise 7.4 (cf. 7.4)

Insert commas to separate main clauses linked by central or marginal coordinators.

1. The woman was anxious about the interview she was to have the next week and she spent many hours worrying about it.
2. She had always wanted to be a stockbroker but she was still nervous about changing jobs.
3. She knew she had to find another type of job because as a legal secretary she was not exercising her talents to the full yet she was afraid that the interviewers might reject her because of her lack of experience.
4. She had lost her fears by the time she was interviewed nor did she seem anxious at the interview.
5. There were over ten candidates for the job but she won the job.

Exercise 7.5 (cf. 7.5)

Insert quotation marks where necessary.

1. Do you like it here? asked Bob Portman.
2. I have lived here all my life, said Sally Mason with pride.
3. You have lived here all your life! he said.
4. I was born here, and my father before me, and my grandfather, and my great-grandfathers. She turned to her brother. Isn't that so?
5. Yes, it's a family habit to be born here! the young man said with a laugh.
6. Your house must be very old, then, said Bob.
7. How old is it, brother? asked Sally.

8. It was built in 1783, the young man replied. That's old or new, according to your point of view.
9. Your house has a curious style of architecture, said Bob.
10. Are you interested in architecture? asked the young man.
11. Well, I took the trouble this year, said Bob, to visit about fifty churches.Do you call that interested?
12. Perhaps you are interested in theology, said the young man ironically.
13. Not particularly, said Bob.
14. The young man laughed and stood up. Good, he exclaimed. I'll show you the house.
15. Sally grasped Bob's arm. Don't let him take you, she said; you won't finding it interesting. Wouldn't you prefer to stay with me?
16. Certainly! said Bob. I'll see the house some other time.

Exercise 7.6 (cf. 7.6)

Insert underlining and quotation marks where necessary.

1. She was in Cambodia as a reporter for the Sunday Times.
2. Henry Green's first novel, Blindness, is divided into three parts: Caterpillar, Chrysalis, and Butterfly.
3. Words like doctor and lawyer can be used for both sexes.
4. Monsoon comes from the Arabic mansim, meaning season.
5. You can find the story in this week's Radio Times.
6. Your article Were the Vikings the First to Arrive? contains several factual errors.
7. Some people avoid using die, preferring a euphemism like pass away.
8. Before his execution, St Valentine sent a farewell message to the jailer's daughter with whom he had fallen in love, signing it From your Valentine.

Exercise 7.7 (cf. 7.7)

Eliminate incorrect or unnecessary question marks in the sentences below.

1. Would you please send your payment with the subscription form?
2. It's time to leave, isn't it?

3. She asked whether we had finished our essays yet?
4. Is there a doctor in the house?
5. Can a man and a woman be friends, or does sex always get in the way?
6. Do you know whether she wants to be prime minister?
7. I asked, 'Is it right for a teacher to set such a difficult task?'
8. I asked the tax inspector how the penalty was calculated?

Exercise 7.8 (cf. 7.8)

Leave the restrictive clauses below unpunctuated. Punctuate the non-restrictive clauses with commas. If you think that a clause may be either restrictive or non-restrictive, insert the commas in the appropriate positions and discuss the two interpretations.

1. I hate attending meetings which last longer than an hour.
2. She gives the impression of an umpire judging a game in which the players have no idea of the rules.
3. Look out for grey or brown fungi which may or may not be edible.
4. Sporting bodies can punish those who break their rules by fines, suspensions, or permanent bans withdrawing the right to participate in the sport altogether.
5. The 'cab-rank' rule requires advocates to represent any client in an area of law in which they practise.
6. Some 2000 fans who began queuing at six that morning barely slept the night before.
7. They seem gloomy about the prospects for the domestic film industry which has experienced all the problems British film-makers have agonised over for 20 years.
8. The concert is the first in the twelfth annual music festival which is devoted to electroacoustic music.
9. Teenagers who drive carelessly should be banned from driving until they are 21.
10. This engine completely redesigned since the last model is much quieter.

Exercise 7.9 (cf. 7.9)

Leave the restrictive appositives below unpunctuated. Punctuate the non-restrictive appositives with commas.

1. An old friend of mine Bill Harris has invited us both for dinner at his home on Friday week.
2. Most doctors disapprove of the saying 'An apple a day drives the doctor away'.
3. We spent last winter in Arizona one of the best places to visit when it is cold and plenty of snow is on the ground.
4. The panel discussed the allegation that there was sexual discrimination in the selection of parliamentary candidates.
5. The latest device to give a suntan to thoroughbred horses a high-performance solar-therapy unit was unveiled at a stable near Lambourn yesterday.
6. They admired Shakespeare the poet more than Shakespeare the dramatist.

Exercise 7.10 (cf. 7.10)

Punctuate the adverbials that require punctuation. If you think that the punctuation is optional, insert the punctuation and indicate that it is optional.

1. The law on the relationship between sporting bodies and players has reluctantly followed the changes in sports trying to adapt.
2. Nowadays most sporting discipline bodies have procedures to ensure fair hearings with lawyers present.
3. Most sportsmen accept their punishment often before their club or team pressures them to do so.
4. Even though courts are more prepared than they used to be to look at the way sporting bodies' decisions are reached they will still be reluctant to interfere with them.
5. People who have a contractual relationship with their sporting body can always go to court to claim a breach of contract if the circumstances fit.
6. Most sports people however do not have that sort of direct contract with the body that regulates their sport.
7. In football for instance the legal relationship is between player and club.
8. So far the regulatory bodies have managed to keep control of their decisions without too much interference from the courts.

Exercise 7.11 (cf. 7.11)

Punctuate the vocatives and interjections in the sentences below.

1. Dave you don't know what you're doing.
2. Oh I wasn't aware that the end of the line was further back.
3. Yes Mr Patton I'm ready.
4. Is that you Shirley?
5. Well make sure that you replace any pieces of glass that you break.
6. Navigation officers report to your positions immediately.
7. It may be sir that we are running out of fuel.
8. Yes you may leave the class when you finish the exam.
9. What's the verdict Dr. Ronson?
10. Give the package to Dorothy Gloria.

Exercise 7.12 (cf. 7.12)

Insert commas where they help to make the meaning clear. If you think that the commas may appear in two positions, insert them in both and enclose them in brackets.

1. As the new year opens stores are putting on their annual sales.
2. Although 92 per cent Catholic Mexico lacks formal diplomatic ties with the Vatican.
3. News of the demonstrations spread quickly embarrassing government officials.
4. As things stand now the government has no way to block the visit.
5. Often as not the women work in the fields.
6. Still though most union branches are publicly backing the national leaders they will make what seem the best deals for their members.
7. To obtain the same amount of energy through wind power assuming a windy enough location would require a large capital investment.
8. With quantities low prices will continue to rise.

Exercise 7.13 (cf. 7.13)

Change the *of*-phrase into a genitive construction.

1. the eldest son of my brother
2. the leaders of our country
3. the best team of the women
4. the conviction of the prisoners
5. the influence of the President
6. the first papers of the students
7. the torn coat of somebody
8. the last play of Shakespeare
9. the many novels of Dickens
10. the strike of the air pilots
11. the catch of the fishermen
12. the friends of my sisters
13. the accusation of the leader of the opposition
14. the toys of our children
15. the security of our nation.
16. the flight of the American astronauts
17. the advice of his father-in-law
18. the support of the alumni
19. the desperate plight of the poor
20. the rights of women

Exercise 7.14 (cf. 7.13, 7.14)

Insert apostrophes where necessary. Some sentences may not require an apostrophe.

1. Eds friends will arrive later.
2. The womans coat was destroyed at the cleaners.
3. The childrens toys were lost in the fire.
4. Everybodys tickets arrived in the post yesterday.
5. The dog entangled its leash while it was tied outside.
6. The Burns house was put up for sale last week.
7. For heavens sake don't park your car on the grass.
8. The computer is ours, not theirs.
9. Somebodys bike was stolen last night.
10. We should proofread each others papers before we turn them in.

Exercise 7.15 (Ch. 7)

You may often choose to write a pair of sentences as one sentence. Write each pair of sentences as one sentence with two main clauses. Change the punctuation accordingly, using commas between the clauses wherever they are permitted. Do not change words or insert words.

1. He has cut two record albums of his own songs. Furthermore, he has made three full-length films.
2. They cannot face the shameful facts. And consequently they try to shift the responsibility onto others.
3. A number of technical reforms have been suggested. However, there is no consensus on any of them.
4. The reality was harsh. Yet they faced it steadfastly.
5. You must have been out of the country at the time. Or else I would have asked for your advice.
6. They have recently bought a car. So you can ask them for a lift, if you wish.
7. Hardly anyone gave New York's canine litter law a chance of succeeding. Nevertheless the cynics were wrong.
8. The windmills resemble oil rigs. But still their overall effect is somehow comforting.
9. Her back has not been troubling her for the last couple of years. So she has stopped doing the exercises that her doctor prescribed.
10. We fought like tigers over the box. Unfortunately, however, he was a stronger tiger than I was.
11. I can't help him. Nor can you.
12. No better appointment could have been made. For her talents and enthusiasm created a balanced, integrated, happy research unit that was quickly recognized internationally.

Exercise 7.16 (Ch. 7)

Each item has one punctuation error. The error may be wrong punctuation or the absence of a punctuation mark. Correct the error in each item.

1. Amnesty estimates that there are half a million political prisoners in the world it is investigating about one per cent of these cases.
2. Researchers on the Amnesty staff are generally graduates and can speak several languages, each of them keeps watch on hundreds of political prisoners in a particular country.
3. Torture techniques have become so refined that they rarely leave marks doctors often collaborate in the deception.

4. Amnesty reseachers do not feel that human beings are inherently cruel, they should know.

5. One South American officer sent a letter to Amnesty describing the tortures that he had witnessed, he included photographic proof.

6. No one was safe from torture, some cases were more brutal than others, but all prisoners were beaten and tortured.

7. The letters to political prisoners never bear the Amnesty letterhead; and often chat about innocuous matters.

Chapter 8

Exercise 8.1 (cf. 8.1)

Select the appropriate verb form given in brackets at the end of each sentence, and write it down in the blank space.

1. He _____ his neighbour jogging. (see, sees)
2. He _____ know what kind of exercise to do. (don't, doesn't)
3. Exercise for the middle-aged _____ considered a prophylactic. (is, are)
4. Too many people _____ up with heart attacks. (end, ends)
5. To undertake an exercise test _____ prudent. (is, are)
6. The test _____ your level of fitness. (determine, determines)
7. Usually the test _____ after a physical examination. (come, comes)
8. Finding out what your heart can do _____ the goal of the test. (is, are)
9. Most tests _____ a treadmill. (use, uses)
10. Some clinics also _____ a bicycle. (use, uses)
11. Walking on an elevated fast-moving treadmill _____ hard work. (is, are)
12. The doctors constantly _____ your heart rate. (monitor, monitors)
13. On the basis of the tests, the doctor _____ likely to recommend an exercise programme. (is, are)
14. To take up a regular programme _____ discipline. (require, requires)
15. Exercise improves the heart, _____ it? (don't, doesn't)

16. That you shouldn't overexert yourself _____ without saying. (go, goes)

17. On the other hand, we _____ too little exercise. (do, does)

18. We _____ want heart trouble at our age. (don't, doesn't)

Exercise 8.2 (cf. 8.6)

Rewrite each sentence to avoid sexist bias.

1. Each student must fill out an application form if he wishes to be considered for a postgraduate studentship.

2. Everybody worked his hardest to ensure that the event was a success.

3. An astronaut runs the risk of serious injury, even death, if his spacecraft malfunctions while he is in orbit.

4. Each worker should show up promptly for work or run the risk of having an hour's pay deducted from his pay-packet.

5. An American politician must raise considerable sums of money if he wishes to be elected to office.

6. Every individual is responsible for his own welfare.

7. Any engineering graduate will find that he can easily get a job.

8. The shop steward has less influence than he had twenty years ago.

Exercise 8.3 (cf.8.1–12)

Select the appropriate verb form given in brackets at the end of each sentence, and write it down in the blank space.

1. Surgeons in the US successfully _____ clouded vision or outright blindness by transplanting about 10,000 corneas a year. (alleviate, alleviates)

2. The congregation _____ mainly of factory workers. (consist, consists)

3. Analysis with the aid of computers _____ those accounts that appear to be conduits for drug money. (select, selects)

4. What makes the situation serious _____ that no new antibiotics have been discovered in the past 15 years. (is, are)

5. To ride a bicycle in a city _____ courage and agility. (demands, demand)

6. Each _____ capable of the first 90 minutes of sustained high-altitude running. (is, are)

7. He was fascinated by the stories in the Old Testament that _____ history to be determined by chance meetings and by small, personal incidents. (show, shows)

8. The job of establishing sufficient controls and measurements so that you can tell what is actually happening to athletes _____ tediously complex. (is, are)

9. Both science and medicine _____ to preparing athletes for competition. (contribute, contributes)

10. The only equipment they work with _____ a blackboard and some chalk. (is, are)

11. Another area of current research that shows great promise _____ diabetes. (is, are)

12. Doris Lessing's *A Man and Two Women* _____ shortlisted for the Booker prize. (was, were)

13. The blind _____ not want pity. (does, do)

14. These are not the conclusions that she _____ from her survey of the current economic policies of countries in the European Community. (draw, draws)

15. Where he went wrong _____ in the arbitrary way he allowed dialect to pepper his narrative. (was, were)

16. The extraordinary _____ described as though it were ordinary. (is, are)

Exercise 8.4 (cf. 8.1–12)

These sentences form a connected passage. The base form of a verb is given in brackets at the end of each sentence. Write down the appropriate form of the verb in the blank space.

1. The young woman now sitting in the dermatologist's waiting room _____ an itchy rash. (have)

2. The rash on her elbows and legs _____ due to an allergic reaction. (be)

3. There are many allergies that _____ rashes. (cause)

4. The existence of allergies _____ known long before scientists had any understanding of their nature. (be)

5. The nature of allergy _____ still not fully understood. (be)

6. The victims of allergy seldom die and seldom _____. (recover)
7. There _____ nothing like an itchy rash for wearing a person down. (be)
8. Some allergies, such as asthma, _____ no external cause. (have)
9. Others _____ caused by contact with a foreign substance. (be)
10. The young woman's allergy _____ brought about by contact with copper. (be)

Exercise 8.5 (cf. 8.14)

Select the pronoun form given in brackets that would be appropriate in formal writing, and write it down in the blank.

1. Edward and _____ went for a walk after the talk. (I, me)
2. Our boss thinks that Mary and _____ talk too much when we work together. (I, me)
3. The police officer gave the driver and _____ a stern lecture on the condition of our car. (I, me)
4. _____ Australians are proud of our culture. (We, Us)
5. Between you and _____, this class is much harder than I thought it would be. (I, me)
6. Your parents expressed their appreciation of how well Fred and _____ had decorated the house. (I, me)
7. Either Rebecca or _____ will be in contact with you about the campaign. (I, me)
8. Everyone except John and _____ were present at the rally. (I, me)

Exercise 8.6 (cf. 8.18)

Select the pronoun form given in brackets that would be appropriate in formal writing, and write it in the blank.

1. She is the only person _____ I trust completely. (who, whom)
2. Go to the office and speak to _____ is working at the reception desk. (whoever, whomever)
3. Ted is the only person _____ I think is capable of filling the position. (who, whom).
4. People should vote for the candidate _____ they feel will best

represent their interests. (who, whom)

5. The manager has already decided _____ to promote. (who, whom)

6. _____ is selected to chair the committee must be prepared to devote several hours a week to the task. (Whoever, Whomever)

7. Naomi is the one _____ is to be transferred to Liverpool. (who, whom)

8. I will vote for _____ you suggest. (whoever, whomever)

9. We have supervisors _____ are themselves supervised. (who, whom)

10. The shop will press charges against _____ is caught shoplifting. (whoever, whomever)

Exercise 8.7 (cf. 8.13–18)

Select the appropriate word given in brackets at the end of each sentence, and write it down in the blank space. If more than one seems appropriate, give the more formal word.

1. We should help those _____ we know are helping themselves. (who, whom)

2. We do not know _____ to ask (who, whom)

3. They will pay the reward to _____ you nominate (whoever, whomever)

4. Grandmother had been one of six sisters, each of _____ had at least five daughters. (who, whom)

5. Speak to the person _____ is in charge. (who, whom)

6. Joan and _____ are about to leave. (I, me)

7. _____ do you want to see? (Who, Whom)

8. I am playing the record for _____ is interested. (whoever, whomever)

9. They called while you and _____ were at the party. (I, me)

10. Did you see _____ was there? (who, whom)

11. Let you and _____ take the initiative. (I, me)

12. He speaks English better than _____. (she, her)

13. It was _____ who seconded the motion. (I, me)

14. They recommended that I consult the lawyer _____ they employed. (who, whom)

15. Their advice is intended for Bruce and _____ . (I, me)

16. Noboby knows the way but _____. (I, me)
17. People were speculating about _____ was in charge. (who, whom)

Exercise 8.8 (cf. 8.19)

Select the appropriate word given in brackets at the end of each sentence, and write it down in the blank space. If more than one seems possible, give the more formal word.

1. I watched _____ playing football. (them, their)
2. They were angry at _____ refusing to join the strike. (him, his)
3. Are you surprised at _____ wanting the position? (me, my)
4. They can at least prevent _____ infecting others. (him, his)
5. I certainly do not object to _____ paying for the meal. (you, your)
6. _____ writing a recommendation for me persuaded the manager to give me the position. (You, Your)
7. They were annoyed at their _____ telephoning after eleven. (neighbour, neighbour's)
8. I cannot explain _____ not answering your letters. (them, their)
9. They appreciated _____ explaining the differences between the two policies. (me, my)
10. I was delighted to hear of _____ passing the examination. (you, your)

Exercise 8.9 (cf. 8.20–21)

Select the verb form given in parentheses that would be appropriate in formal writing, and write it in the blank.

1. You _____ completed the assignment before leaving the office. (should have, should of)
2. I wanted to _____ down before preparing dinner. (lie, lay)
3. I _____ played in the game but I had injured my ankle the previous day. (could have, could of)
4. Joan _____ down for a few hours because she wasn't feeling well. (laid, lay)
5. George has been _____ down during the entire football game. (lying, laying)

6. The children _____ play quietly or they will upset their mothers. (had better, better)

7. They must have _____ down for quite some time. (laid, lain)

Exercise 8.10 (cf. 8.22)

For each verb listed in its base form, give the -s form (third person singular present)

1.	think	9.	push	17.	camouflage
2.	taste	10.	die	18.	do
3.	say	11.	refuse	19.	go
4.	imply	12.	fly	20.	have
5.	type	13.	be	21.	bury
6.	cry	14.	shout	22.	crush
7.	make	15.	undertake	23.	disagree
8.	wrong	16.	recognize	24.	crouch

Exercise 8.11 (cf. 8.23)

For each irregular verb listed in its base form, give the past. For example, *live* has the past *lived* as in *I lived in Sydney last year.*

1.	choose	9.	lead	17.	shake
2.	have	10.	hide	18.	make
3.	bring	11.	write	19.	see
4.	cost	12.	put	20.	set
5.	teach	13.	lose	21.	keep
6.	hold	14.	catch	22.	throw
7.	go	15.	do	23.	begin
8.	draw	16.	take	24.	tear

Exercise 8.12 (cf. 8.23)

For each irregular verb listed in its base form, give the *-ed* participle. For example, *live* as in *I have lived here for a long time.*

1.	hear	9.	grow	17.	drive
2.	win	10.	tell	18.	think
3.	fall	11.	give	19.	see
4.	make	12.	have	20.	find
5.	spend	13.	forget	21.	show
6.	go	14.	do	22.	stand
7.	know	15.	take	23.	come
8.	meet	16.	read	24.	eat

Exercise 8.13 (cf. 8.23)

Select the form given in brackets that would be appropriate in formal writing, and write it down in the blank.

1. We _____ an accident on our way to work this morning. (saw, seen)
2. Her husband _____ home late after spending the night with his friends. (came, come)
3. The other workers and I _____ the job without even being asked to do so. (did, done)
4. He was _____ for the murder that he had committed. (hung, hanged)
5. I _____ out the washing so that it would dry. (hung, hanged)
6. You should have _____ to me before you came to a decision. (spoke, spoken)

Exercise 8.14 (cf. 8.24)

Select the verb form that would be appropriate in formal writing, and write it down in the blank.

1. If I _____ you, I would make an effort to come to work on time. (was, were)
2. We did not know if she _____ the right person to ask. (was, were)
3. If the United States were to become involved in a war in Central America, many US troops _____ have to be sent there. (will, would)

4. The commander acts as though he _____ ready for combat at any time. (was, were)
5. If he _____ to work a little harder, he would have no trouble getting into a very good university. (was, were)
6. Had the train arrived a few minutes earlier, we _____ have made the first act of the play. (will, would)
7. I believe strongly that if the committee _____ to pass the amendment our problems would be solved. (was, were)
8. If I _____ given a second interview, I am sure that I would be offered the position. (am, were)

Exercise 8.15 (cf. 8.25)

Rewrite the sentences containing non-standard double negatives. Some sentences may not need any revision.

1. I can't hardly hear with the radio turned up so loud.
2. We are not displeased with the jury's verdict.
3. Nobody has no alternative ideas.
4. You can't not become involved in such an emotional issue as saving baby seals from being murdered by hunters.
5. I am not unhappy.
6. Those two suspects didn't do nothing to nobody.
7. It is not unusual for there to be cold weather in Scotland even in April or May.
8. It is not police policy to say nothing about police corruption.

Exercise 8.16 (cf. 8.26)

Correct these sentences where necessary by substituting adjectives for adverbs or adverbs for adjectives. Some of the sentences do not need to be corrected.

1. The child is eating too fast.
2. Do your pants feel tightly?
3. They fought hard against the change.
4. I didn't sleep too good last night.
5. We left early because I was not feeling well.
6. The milk tasted sourly this morning.

7. I felt good about the way they treated you.
8. Your dog is barking loud.
9. They should think more positive about themselves.
10. He hurt his neck bad.

Exercise 8.17 (cf. 8.27)

Give the inflected comparative and superlative of each adjective or adverb.

1.	wise	6.	strong	11.	friendly
2.	hard	7.	heavy	12.	risky
3.	sad	8.	large	13.	fierce
4.	angry	9.	deep	14.	tall
5.	rare	10.	happy	15.	red

Exercise 8.18 (cf. 8.29)

Rewrite each sentence, avoiding dangling modifiers.

1. Having completed the balloon crossing, hundreds of French villagers welcomed the three balloonists.
2. Unwilling to lay down his gun, the police shot dead the escaped convict.
3. When delivered, they found the merchandise spoiled.
4. When approaching the building, no single feature has an impact on the viewer.
5. A weak student, his teacher gave him extra essays and went over them with him privately.
6. After completing the first four columns, each should be added separately.
7. Being in charge, the accusation was particularly annoying to me.
8. Having found the first stage of our work to be satisfactory, permission was given by the inspector for us to begin the second stage.

---

* Exercise 8.19 (Ch. 8)

Write an essay on a usage topic.

(1)   Select a usage topic. Some examples of usage topics are listed in (A) below.

(2)   Look up the topic in at least three books on usage. Some examples of usage books are listed in (B) below.

(3)   In your essay summarize what you have found in the usage books, showing the similarities and differences in their approaches. Draw conclusions from your reading on the topic.

(A) Usage topics

1. split infinitive
2. *like* as a conjunction
3. ending a sentence with a preposition
4. uses of *who* and *whom*
5. uses of *shall* and *will*
6. uses of subjunctives
7. apostrophe with names ending in -*s*
8. case of pronouns after *be*
9. case of pronouns after as and *than*
10. number of verbs with *either . . . or* and *neither . . . nor*
11. use of *they, them,* and *their* as gender-neutral singular words
12. case of pronouns and nouns with -*ing* clauses (see under 'gerund' and 'fused participle')

(B) Usage books

Crystal, D. (1984) *Who Cares About English Usage?* Penguin Books.

Fieldhouse, H. (1982) *Everyman's Good English Guide*. Dent.

Fowler, H.W. (1965) *Modern English usage*, 2nd edition revised by Sir Ernest Gowers. Clarendon Press.

Gowers, Sir Ernest (1987) *The Complete Plain Words*, 3rd edition revised by S. Greenbaum and J. Whitcut. Penguin Books.

Greenbaum, S. and J. Whitcut (1988) *Guide to English Usage*. Longman.

Partridge, E. (1973) *Usage and Abusage*. Penguin Books.

The Right Word at the Right Time (1985) Reader's Digest.

Weiner, E.S.C. (1985) *The Oxford Guide to English Usage*. Oxford University Press.

* Exercise 8.20 (Ch. 8)

Write an essay on a usage topic (see Exercise 8.19). For your evidence of actual usage, conduct a survey of opinions and report the results. Include relevant biographical data about your informants; for example, their age group, education level, and the areas in which they have lived.

* Exercise 8.21 (Ch. 8)

Write an essay on one of the following topics listed below.

1. Sexist language
2. What is Good English?
3. Characteristics of my dialect
4. Rhetorical devices in advertising *or* newspaper editorials *or* political pamphlets *or* religious pamphlets
5. Taboos in language
6. Slang
7. Jargon
8. Plain English
9. Consumer protection for language use
10. Doublespeak
11. Euphemism
12. Language play

Chapter 9

Exercise 9.1 (cf. 9.2)

Rewrite the following sentences so that the underlined part is placed in the emphatic end position.

1. <u>No other nation in the world</u> consumes more oil than the United States.
2. <u>That car</u> belongs to my sister.

3. It is <u>easy</u> to underestimate Peter.
4. Susan and <u>Martha</u> are similar in their temperaments.
5. <u>Serious malnutrition</u> affects more than a third of the people in the world.
6. <u>The whole class</u> was interested in the lecture on the origins of English words.
7. <u>Rats</u> were crawling all over the building.
8. <u>The government's tax policy</u> benefits the wealthy most of all.
9. <u>A drink of water</u> was all they wanted.

Exercise 9.2 (cf. 9.3)

Put the underlined part in front to give it strong emphasis.

1. The soil <u>no longer</u> has to be rested every three or four years to regain its natural fertility.
2. They must <u>sign</u>, or they will not be freed.
3. They <u>not only</u> consult doctors more frequently, but they do so about more minor problems.
4. He rejected the treatment <u>only after thorough investigation</u>.
5. Though they may be <u>reluctant</u>, they will accept the task.
6. The greatest difficulty we had was <u>raising sufficient funds to staff the shelter for the homeless</u>.
7. A great sanatorium will arise <u>out of the desert</u>.

---

* Exercise 9.3 (cf. 9.2–3)

Rewrite the following paragraph to achieve a better arrangement of information.

> Michael Ramsey was the 100th Archbishop of Canterbury. But his sole claim to distinction is by no means that. He will probably be the last genuine scholar who was Archbishop of Canterbury. The Church of England was also transformed by him. The Church of England had ceased to be an adjunct of the Establishment by the time he retired in 1974. The old taint of its being simply 'the Tory party at prayer' his initiatives effectively removed.

Exercise 9.4 (cf. 9.5)

An adverbial is given in brackets at the end of each sentence. Rewrite each sentence, inserting the adverbial in an appropriate place and punctuating it with commas. More than one place may be appropriate.

1. The committee was not as docile as the chairman expected. (as it happens)
2. Heart disease was the principal cause of death. (however)
3. That woman is not the person you should try to contact. (in fact)
4. You should make every effort to perform your duties to the best of your ability. (nevertheless)
5. The car is beyond repair and should be scrapped. (probably)
6. This version of the manuscript illustrates the originality of the author's ideas. (for instance)

Exercise 9.5 (cf. 9.6)

Rewrite the following sentences by making the predicate longer than the underlined subject.

1. An open letter beseeching the all-male College of Cardinals to incorporate women into the election of the Pope was issued.
2. A statue of the statesman holding a sword in one hand and a shield in the other stood at the entrance.
3. The provocative thought that the bureaucracy is a public service for the benefit of citizens is offered.
4. Public health officials, social workers, police, civil liberties lawyers, and even divorce lawyers distract teachers from their teaching.
5. To do whatever can be done to motivate students to improve their reading and writing skills is necessary.
6. Many waste products from the catalytic combustions of petrol are emitted.

Exercise 9.6 (cf. 9.7)

Rewrite each sentence to avoid the misplaced constructions that are underlined. If the sentence is ambiguous, give two versions – one for each interpretation.

1. Brian asked how she was getting on <u>quite routinely</u>.
2. Treating children <u>naturally</u> can be pleasant.
3. To spend a vacation <u>in many ways</u> is necessary for mental health.
4. The doctor advised her <u>on every occasion</u> to take sedatives.
5. They claimed <u>when they were young</u> they had very little money.
6. Drinking <u>normally</u> made him happy.
7. Exercises <u>frequently</u> prolong one's life.

---

* Exercise 9.7 (cf. 9.10)

Rewrite the following sentence to make it clearer.

> In the United States public confidence in airline safety has been undermined as a result of numerous plane crashes in recent years and due to the fact that inspections of planes have resulted in a substantial number of reports that have shown that the airlines have committed numerous safety violations, which officials in the Federal Aviation Administration think is the result of the de-regulation of airlines in the 1970s and which many other experts in the field of airline safety believe will continue to occur until new laws are passed by Congress.

Exercise 9.8 (cf. 9.11)

Correct the faulty parallelism in the sentences below.

1. At present we know enough neither about animals nor ourselves to make categorical statements on the nature of human communication.
2. You will find considerable difference between the paragraphs of deaf children compared to hearing children.
3. His shoulder bag contained a pipe, a tobacco pouch, address book, and a calculator.
4. He either smokes cigars or cigarettes, but I cannot remember which.
5. The optical effects in recent space films are more spectacular than past films.

Exercise 9.9 (cf. 9.12)

Rewrite the sentences to avoid unnecessary repetition of sounds or words with different meanings.

1. The audience was noisy at first, but later it became quite quiet.
2. The government has not yet decided on the form that the formal inquiry will take.
3. My intention is to give more attention in the future to my children.
4. I find that trying to find where a class is being held can be frustrating.

Exercise 9.10 (cf. 9.13)

Rewrite each sentence so that the reference to an antecedent is clear.

1. Experience shows that when abortion laws are liberalized, *they skyrocket*.
2. The old man told his son that *he* was not allowed to smoke.
3. The teachers made the students put *their* names on the top of each sheet.

Exercise 9.11 (cf. 9.14)

Rewrite each sentence to eliminate inconsistencies in pronouns.

1. If one is conscientious, they will do well in life.
2. If one can speak the language fluently, you can negotiate a better price.
3. I recommend that you buy a British pale ale. They're quite good.
4. We should strive to get the best education possible. You can then be sure that you will have a satisfying life.
5. Trying one's hardest to get in good shape can ruin your health if you're not careful.

Exercise 9.12 (cf. 9.15)

Rewrite each sentence to remove inconsistencies in tenses.

1. The spheres rotate and sent out streams of light in every direction.
2. Once she knows a better way to study, she would feel much better.
3. After I spoke to the contractor, but before I sign any contract, I would ask for references.
4. Even though I had done all the work, I still do poorly in examinations.

Chapter 10

---

* Exercise 10.1 (cf. 10.1)

Identify and explain the examples below of deviation from what is normal in language.

1.   Wild men who caught and sang the sun in flight,
        And learn, too late, they grieved it on its way,
        Do not go gentle into that good night.

        [Dylan Thomas, 'Do Not Go Gentle into That Good Night']

2.   he sang his didn't he danced his did

        [e.e. cummings, 'anyone lived in a pretty how town']

3.   The hour-glass whispers to the lion's roar

        [W.H. Auden, 'Our Bias']

4.   Slowly the poison the whole blood stream fills.

        [William Empson, 'Missing Dates']

5.   Starts again always in Henry's ears
        the little cough somewhere, an odor, a chime.

        [John Berryman, 'The Dream Songs: 29']

---

* Exercise 10.2 (cf. 10.2)

Identify instances of foregrounding in the poems below and explain their effects.

1.   This bread I break was once the oat,
This wine upon a foreign tree
Plunged in its fruit;
Man in the day or wind at night
Laid the crops low, broke the grape's joy.

Once in this wine the summer blood
Knocked in the flesh that decked the vine,
Once in this bread
The oat was merry in the wind;
Man broke the sun, pulled the wind down.

This flesh you break, this blood you let
Make desolation in the vein,
Were oat and grape
Born out of the sensual root and sap;
My wine you drink, my bread you snap.

[Dylan Thomas, 'This Bread I Break']

2.   A slumber did my spirit seal;
   I had no human fears:
She seemed a thing that could not feel
   The touch of earthly years.

No motion has she now, no force;
   She neither hears nor sees;
Rolled round in earth's diurnal course,
With rocks, and stones, and trees.

[William Wordsworth, 'A Slumber Did My Spirit Seal']

3.   Lord, Who createdst man in wealth and store,
   Though foolishly he lost the same,
     Decaying more and more,
       Till he became
       Most poore:

       With Thee
      O let me rise,
    As larks, harmoniously,
  And sing this day Thy victories:
Then shall the fall further the flight in me.

My tender age in sorrow did beginne;
And still with sicknesses and shame
Thou didst so punish sinne,
That I became
Most thinne.

With Thee
Let me combine,
And feel this day Thy victorie;
For, if I imp my wing on Thine,
Affliction shall advance the flight in me.

[George Herbert, 'Easter Wings']

4.   ygUDuh
          ydoan
          yunnuhstan

          ydoan o
          yunnuhstan dem
          yguduh ged

          yunnuhstan dem doidee
          yguduh ged riduh
          ydoan o nudn
LISN bud LISN

                dem
                gud
                am

                lidl yelluh bas
                tuds weer goin

duhSIVILEYEzum

[e.e. cummings, 'ygUDuh']

---

* Exercise 10.3 (cf. 10.3)

1.   In the stanza below, *leaned* may be a simple past or an -ed participle.
     Discuss the effects of the ambiguity.

Webster was much possessed by death
And saw the skull beneath the skin;
And breastless creatures under ground
Leaned backward with a lipless grin.

> [T.S. Eliot, 'Whispers of Immortality', cited in *Seven Types of*
> *Ambiguity* by William Empson (London: Chatto and Windus, 1953)]

2. Below are the first four lines of one of Shakespeare's sonnets. Consider the effects of the ambiguities in those lines. Line 1: (a) *So* may be a manner adverb ('in this way') or a resultative conjunctive adverb ('therefore'), *supposing* may be an *-ing* participle ('I suppose that you are true') or a conditional conjunction ('if'). The sentence may be declarative or interrogative. Line 2: *so* may be resultative ('therefore') or a purpose conjunction ('so that', 'in order that'). Line 3: *new* may be an adverb ('newly') or an adjective ('to something new'); *altered* may refer back to *love's face* or to *love*.

So shall I live, supposing thou art true,
Like a deceivèd husband – so love's face
May still seem love to me, though altered new:
Thy looks with me, thy heart in other place.

> [William Shakespeare, 'Sonnet 93', from *Shakespeare's Sonnets*, edited
> by Stephen Booth (New Haven: Yale University Press, 1977)]

3. In the stanza below, *Bitter* may be a direct object or a subject complement. Discuss the ambiguity and its effects.

I am gall, I am heartburn. God's most deep decree
Bitter would have me taste; my taste was me;
Bones built in me, flesh filled, blood brimmed the curse.

> [G.M. Hopkins, ' I Wake and Feel the Fell of Dark, not Day']

4. Discuss the effect of the punctuation of the stanza below on the meaning of the passage.

To dispense, with justice; or, to dispense
with justice. Thus the catholic god of France,
with honours all even, honours all, even
the damned in the brazen Invalides of Heaven.

[Geoffrey Hill, 'The Mystery of the Charity of Charles Peguy']

Appendix

Exercise A.1 (cf. A.1)

The first word in each set has a letter in italics. In each of the other words, underline the spelling that represents the same sound. You may need to underline two letters.

1. *z*oo, fizz, has, dessert
2. *s*ure, ship, ocean, passion, nation, machine
3. *s*un, scientific, pass, psychiatry, deceive
4. *f*ull, off, rough, telephone
5. n*o*, boat, show, sew, toe
6. *a*way, common, dozen, column, dungeon

Exercise A.2 (cf. A.1)

The spelling *ough* has a number of different pronunciations. Some common words with *ough* are listed below in alphabetical order. Rearrange the words in groups so that all the words with the same pronunciation of *ough* are in the same group.

bough	drought	thorough
bought	enough	though
brought	fought	thought
cough	ought	through
dough	rough	tough

Exercise A.3 (cf. A.1)

Underline the silent letters (letters that have no corresponding pronunciation) in the following words.

climb, weigh, honest, write, knee, condemn, pneumonia, island, listen, guest, two

Exercise A.4 (cf.A.2)

Look up the following words in two or more dictionaries. Do the dictionaries give spelling variants for each word? Do they indicate that one variant is more common or to be preferred?

1.	archaeology	7.	fiord	13.	mileage
2.	collectible	8.	guaranty	14.	millionaire
3.	despatch	9.	halal	15.	nosy
4.	disc	10.	judgment	16.	nought
5.	digitise	11.	kilogram	17.	phony
6.	employee	12.	likable	18.	vendor

Exercise A.5 (cf. A.2)

Say the following words (a) as you normally say them, and (b) very slowly. Have you kept a syllable in your slow pronunciation that you did not have in your normal pronunciation?

1.	average	4.	incidentally	7.	medicine
2.	dangerous	5.	interest	8.	ordinary
3.	definite	6.	library	9.	temporary

Exercise A.6 (cf. A.4 (1))

Form words by joining the parts.

1.	panel + ing	6.	snob + ish	11.	short + er
2.	loyal + ist	7.	sin + er	12.	similar + ity
3.	green + ish	8.	dark + en	13.	paint + er
4.	sad + en	9.	rag + ed	14.	confer + ence
5.	commit + ed	10.	differ + ence	15.	big + est

Exercise A.7 (cf. A.4 (2))

Form words by joining the parts.

1.	segregate + ion	9.	delete + ion
2.	care + ful	10.	base + less
3.	waste + age	11.	type + ing
4.	revive + al	12.	rare + ly
5.	style + ize	13.	true + ly
6.	advantage + ous	14.	courage + ous
7.	argue + ment	15.	rare + ity
8.	deplore + able		

Exercise A.8 (cf. A. 4(3))

Form words by joining the parts:

1.	dry + ing	9.	symmetry + cal
2.	necessary + ly	10.	identify + able
3.	pity + ful	11.	biography + cal
4.	momentary + ly	12.	shy + ness
5.	play + ful	13.	luxury + ous
6.	simplify + cation	14.	funny + ly
7.	lazy + ness	15.	happy + ness
8.	day + ly		

Exercise A.9 (cf. A.4(4))

Give the plurals of these nouns.

1.	day	6.	century	11.	thief
2.	beach	7.	race	12.	journey
3.	wife	8.	loaf	13.	hero
4.	historian	9.	stove	14.	coach
5.	potato	10.	speech	15.	belief

Exercise A.10 (cf. A.4(4))

Give the *-s* forms of these verbs.

1.	imply	6.	fly	11.	marry
2.	think	7.	die	12.	type
3.	refuse	8.	push	13.	bury
4.	agree	9.	taste	14.	try
5.	camouflage	10.	crouch	15.	reach

Exercise A.11 (cf. A.4(5))

Give the *-ing* participles of these verbs.

1.	apply	5.	lie	9.	die	13.	bring
2.	see	6.	begin	10.	win	14.	create
3.	continue	7.	make	11.	support	15.	spot
4.	occur	8.	get	12.	brag		

Exercise A.12 (cf. A.4(6))

Give the *-ed* form (simple past and *-ed* participle) of these verbs.

1.	study	6.	delay	11.	deliver
2.	persuade	7.	point	12.	surprise
3.	trick	8.	parallel	13.	pay
4.	dot	9.	occupy	14.	taste
5.	comfort	10.	distinguish	15.	reply

Exercise A.13 (cf. A.5)

Form words by joining the parts.

1.	dis + similar	9.	under + expose
2.	mis + apprehend	10.	out + talk
3.	ir + reverent	11.	mis + shapen
4.	un + informed	12.	over + rated
5.	im + mobile	13.	out + argue
6.	un + natural	14.	dis + solve
7.	dis + associate	15.	hyper + active
8.	il + licit		

Index